ETHICS OF SEX

Ethics of Sex is a remarkable book in that it not only contains moral analysis of standard subjects like contraception and marriage, but also it addresses cutting-edge issues such as transgenderism and disorders of sexual development. What is more impressive, however, is the focus of this book—*Ethics of Sex* is biblically faithful, theologically sound, and above all, Christ-centered. While the authors responsibly draw from fields such as science and psychology, they constantly return to the cross, emphasizing themes such as forgiveness, healing, and reconciliation. Christians across denomination lines will appreciate this book for its winsome style, pastoral tone, and Kingdom focus.

—*David W. Jones, PhD, Professor of Christian Ethics, Southeastern Baptist Theological Seminary*

Our freewheeling, libertine age has fallen abysmally short in its stewardship of one of God's most precious, delightful, and mysterious gifts, our sexuality. In profound concord, yet without redundancy, the authors of these essays provide informed, convicted comment and godly counsel on a variety of topics often avoided in discussions of sexual ethics. They remind us as well that in their conjugal relationship, faithful wedded couples confess the Christ, who is coming for His Body and Holy Bride, even as those chaste and celibate in Christ also share in His love that will never end. Highly recommended to all, it should be included in every pastor's and congregation's library.

—*Rev. Dr. Thomas V. Aadland, Dean of the Theological Faculty, Matongo Lutheran Theological College*

While teaching at a Christian university for fourteen years, I continue to be amazed at how student attitudes are impacted by public opinion. Abortion used to trigger the most heated discussions in my classrooms. Now it seems that any critique of LGBTQ lifestyles receives the strongest push-back. Contraception, however, continues to produce the most bewildered looks. I believe *Ethics of Sex* provides two important elements for moral decision-making: pertinent facts about each issue and biblical ethical standards that ought to guide our conduct. I strongly endorse this book for use in ethics courses at high schools, colleges, and seminaries.

—*Rev. Kevin E. Voss, DVM, PhD, FCA, Associate Professor of Philosophy; Director, Concordia Center for Bioethics, Concordia University Wisconsin*

Ethics of Sex is a necessary resource to the Church; something that will help open dialogue around topics that are far too often ignored.

—*Rev. Bart Day, Executive Director, The Office of National Mission, The Lutheran Church—Missouri Synod*

The collection of essays in *Ethics of Sex* addresses the questions that our young people simply can't help but ask, giving them the biblical and practical response that they both need and want, while not ignoring the science of the day. The world around us is certainly not shy to present its views. The Church must be at least equal to the task. What a complete joy this book will be for all who read and discuss its contents as we seek to proactively tackle together the issues that we face on topics related to marriage and sexuality in the years to come.

—*Rev. Marcus T. Zill, LCMS Director of Campus Ministry & LCMSU*

From Taboo to Delight

ETHICS OF SEX

Gifford A. Grobien, General Editor

CONCORDIA PUBLISHING HOUSE · SAINT LOUIS

3558 S. Jefferson Ave., St. Louis, MO 63118-3968
1-800-325-3040 • www.cph.org

Manufactured in the United States of America

Library of Congress Cataloging-in-Publication Data

Grobien, Gifford Andrew, editor.

Ethics of sex : from taboo to delight / Gifford A. Grobien, general editor.

St. Louis : Concordia Publishing House, 2016.

LCCN 2016041656 (print) | LCCN 2016044379 (ebook) | ISBN 9780758651655 | ISBN 9780758651662

LCSH: Sex—Religious aspects—Christianity. | Sex—Biblical teaching. | Sexual ethics—Biblical teaching.

LCC BT708.E83 2016 (print) | LCC BT708 (ebook) | DDC 261.8/357—dc23

LC record available at https://lccn.loc.gov/2016041656

---

1 2 3 4 5 6 7 8 9 10 26 25 24 23 22 21 20 19 18 17

CONTENTS

ABBREVIATIONS

AE	*Luther's Works*, American Edition
Ap	Apology of the Augsburg Confession
ESV	English Standard Version
KJV	King James Version
LC	Large Catechism
NKJV	New King James Version
NPNF[1]	*The Nicene and Post-Nicene Fathers*. Series 1. Edited by P. Schaff. 14 vols. Repr. Peabody, MA: Hendrickson, 1994
PL	*Patrologia Latina*. Edited by J. P. Migne. 217 vols. Paris, 1844–64
SA	Smalcald Articles
SC	Small Catechism
WA	Weimar Ausgabe ("edition") of Luther's Works. *Luthers Werke: Kritische Gesamtausgabe*. 65 vols. Weimer: Hermann Böhlau, 1883–1993
WA DB	Weimer Ausgabe Deutsche Bible ("German Bible"). *Luthers Werke: Kritische Gesamtausgabe. Deutsche Bibel*. 12 vols. Weimar: Hermann Böhlau, 1906–61

TABOO OR DELIGHT? SEXUAL PROHIBITION AND CHRISTIAN IDENTITY

"Ethics" in contemporary usage may have negative connotations. It is not that ethics are seen as unimportant or obsolete, but that they are something of a necessary evil. Ethics prohibit. Certain workplace behaviors are prohibited in order to maintain a pleasant, productive environment. Rules and laws exclude inappropriate, bad, or wicked behavior and sanction violations with punishments.

The ethics of sex today are viewed no differently. In fact, negative perspectives of ethics may be most intensified in the realm of sex. Michel Foucault observed that Western sexuality in general is defined by the restrictive coercion of prohibition. Such prohibition is purely negative, forbidding the exploration and expression of sexual desire that is outside of heterosexual monogamy. By consequence, a person is restricted so that he cannot express the sexual fullness that is his natural right. By restricting his sexuality, his very being and existence are restricted.[1]

Yet, Christians have always properly opposed such a restrictive way of thinking about ethics. To be sure, God forbids all kinds of thought, speech, and behavior in the Scriptures. However, these prohibitions are derivative from and supportive of what is true, good, proper, and fulfilling for human life. The Law of God is first of all His eternal good will, which includes His desire for human flourishing. This flourishing begins with salvation in Christ and always finds its vitality in it, while also including the life and activity of those who are saved in Christ.

Like all Christian ethics, then, sexual ethics are deeply and inherently positive in their expectation for human life. Prohibitions serve as a kind of limit that directs us back to the delight and richness of life lived in accordance with the will of God. It never goes without saying that, in this life, no person lives perfectly in accordance with the will of God. For times when we fall short, we are not left only with prohibitions, but with the mercy and salve of God's great compassion in Christ. Receiving this great compas-

1 Michel Foucault, *The History of Sexuality* (New York: Pantheon Books, 1978), 1:84.

sion, we are renewed again to live as the Spirit strengthens us in the pattern of the divine life, in accordance with the flourishing God has set before us. Although our flourishing this side of heaven is never perfect, it is presented to us as a way of life in which we can delight while we remain here.

The essays in this volume offer an account of sexual ethics that embraces the positive and flourishing nature of sex. Many of the essays are adapted from topics at the "Taboo" National LCMS Campus Ministry Conference held at St. Louis University January 5–7, 2015. Both the title of this conference and some of the limits set forth in these essays highlight the prohibitive character of ethics. However, the prohibitive character serves to direct us back to a way of life in harmony with the Lord's created order, an order that bears fruit in intimacy, compassion, love, and joy. Ultimately, these essays invite us to attend again to the way that Christ's love for His Church works forgiveness, healing, reconciliation, and new life, not only in the area of ethics, but in every way. Good sexual activity reflects Christ's love for His Church; Christ's love for His Church forgives sexual sin and restores us to the fellowship of the divine life reflected by sexual relations.

CHRIST'S LOVE FOR HIS CHURCH FORGIVES SEXUAL SIN.

In "Male and Female Sex Differences," Cynthia Lumley takes us not only through what it means to be created male and female but also through an overview of the physiological processes of sexual development. She recognizes that, in a fallen world, sexual development may not always manifest in a simply binary fashion, but that our sexual identity as male or female finds its healing and perfection in our baptismal identity in Christ.

Christopher Mitchell in "What Is Marriage?" presents a theology of marriage based on sexual difference in creation, but also in view of marriage as a type of Christ's love for His Church. The self-sacrificial love of Christ and the Church's faithful reception of this love exemplify and characterize human marriage, and also become the way of forgiveness and healing when and where marriages struggle or fail. In view of this theology of marriage, David Kind demonstrates the scriptural opposition to polygamy in view of contemporary practices, such as polyamory and spouse swapping.

In view of the procreative character of sexual relations, Donna Harrison and Richard Stuckwisch address the question of contraception, the former from a scientific perspective, the latter from a theological and pastoral perspective. Harrison explores especially the physiological effects of artificial contraception, raising concerns not only over the suppression of ovulation and restricting the possibility of conception but also over the hindering of the implantation of already conceived embryos in the uterus, leading to abortion. Stuckwisch presents the married life as one open to receiving children as gifts of God. Reminding us of the vocations of husband and wife, father and mother, he directs us to the joy we have in serving each other accordingly, and to trusting in the care and provision of our heavenly Father for the nurture of children.

Contemporary perspectives on sexual ethics have been shaped by sex education, and Matthew Rueger explains the way the Church's acceptance of secular standards for sex education has injured modesty and the intimacy of sex. He challenges the conventional wisdom that detailed knowledge of sexual relations is important at an early age and suggests as an alternative that children learn from parents or parental figures what is needed as they develop, and not in a classroom setting that desensitizes children's natural modesty.

Modern sex education has sometimes encouraged the view that masturbation is acceptable and can even be encouraged. Benjamin Mayes revisits the scriptural understanding of masturbation and offers pastoral suggestions for forgiveness, healing, and self-control.

Tom Eckstein and Robert Weise address the questions of homosexuality and transgenderism, respectively, giving a thorough account of the biblical teaching on these issues in view of sex as a reflection of Christ's love for His Church. At the same time, recognizing the strong temptations of many in these areas, they offer pastoral encouragement and reorientation to the Scriptures for addressing questions along these lines.

The final chapter explores the theology of sex and its close relationship to love, especially as exemplified by Christ in His love for the Church. Treating foundational texts in Genesis 1–2, Song of Songs, Matthew 19, Ephesians 5, and elsewhere, the essay emphasizes the positive view of sex presented in Scripture as a contrast to the debilitating practices of satisfying mere sexual desire. The essay also draws on recent research in psychology and neurochemistry that complements the scriptural understanding.

Gifford A. Grobien
Commemoration of St. Irenaeus, Bishop of Lyons
June 28, 2016

CHAPTER 1

MALE AND FEMALE SEX DIFFERENCES

Cynthia E. Lumley

> Then God said, "Let Us make man in Our image, after Our likeness. And let them have dominion over the fish of the sea and over the birds of the heavens and over the livestock and over all the earth and over every creeping thing that creeps on the earth." So God created man in His own image, in the image of God He created him; male and female He created them. (Genesis 1:26–27)

Social scientist Sarah Richardson writes, "Classification of the particulars of nature into 'kinds' is an integral part of scientific reasoning. However, what do we do with a kind that is at once one and two?"[1] Man was created as two distinct entities, male and female, which are now called "sexes" and "divided on the basis of their reproductive functions."[2] The sexes are not autonomous but are interdependent, a relationship established at creation when God said, "It is not good that the man should be alone. I will make him a helper fit for him" (Genesis 2:18). The Hebrew word עֵזֶר (*'ezer*), translated as *helper*, is most often used in relation to God in the Old Testament (e.g., Hosea 13:9 and particularly in the Psalms). The Holy Spirit is also called "the Helper" (e.g., John 14:26; 15:26). A helper is not inferior nor superior to the one being helped. Rather, the helper is required in order for the one being helped to achieve their goals.[3] Male and female were created as equals, both in the image of God, both required for procreation. However, equal does not mean interchangeable, and it is wrong to try to demonstrate that the sexes are indistinguishable in order to justify equality.[4]

---

1 Sarah S. Richardson, *Sex Itself: The Search for Male & Female in the Human Genome* (Chicago and London: University of Chicago Press, 2013), 197.

2 *Oxford Dictionaries*, s.v. "sex," accessed February 10, 2016, www.oxforddictionaries.com/definition/english/sex.

3 Commission on Theology and Church Relations, *Creator's Tapestry: Scriptural Perspectives on Man-Woman Relationships in Marriage and the Church* (St. Louis: The Lutheran Church—Missouri Synod, 2010), 13.

4 Steven Pinker, *The Blank Slate* (London: Penguin Books, 2002), 340.

This concept is important because, in contrast to the persistent message of popular media, there are many well documented, important differences between the sexes;[5] for example,[6] in psychological and emotional characteristics, spatial and language abilities, speech styles, physiology, response to epigenetic factors, gene expression, brain structure and chemistry and the prevalence and severity of a range of physical and psychiatric diseases, disorders, and conditions. Females and males have different gametes (egg and sperm), gonads, hormone-mediated physiologies, and secondary sex characteristics. Even individual organs and cells are sexually differentiated,[7] including the placenta.[8] Whether one is male or female is an important part of who we are. Historically, sex has had a large impact on conditions of life because of cultural conceptions and expectations for males and females. This has stimulated extensive and emotional debate about equality and interchangeability between the sexes. The importance of sex differences is such that their study has become a discipline in itself.

The pinnacle of God's creation is man, created as male and female. Understanding the differences between the sexes is fundamental to any discussion of sexual ethics. This chapter, therefore, begins with an overview of male and female biology,[9] followed by a description of some disorders of sexual development, and concludes with a discussion of the theology of male and female sex differences. Space limitations prevent more than a superficial overview; however, an extensive bibliography is provided for those who wish to examine this topic in more detail.

What Determines Who Is Male and Who Is Female?

For millennia, the sex of newborn infants was determined primarily by their external genitalia.[10] (See Box 1 for a description of "normal" gonads

5 Differences between the sexes are generally reported as averages for groups of males and females, recognizing that, "There are always women who do better than the average man in tasks where males excel, and there are always men who outscore the average woman in tasks where females excel." Olive Skene Johnson, "Sexing the Brain: Sex Differences in Cognitive Abilities," in *The Sexual Spectrum: Exploring Human Diversity* (Pacific Place Publishing Smashwords Edition, 2004).

6 See bibliography for references providing evidence of sex differences (marked *).

7 Geert J. de Vries and Nancy G. Forger, "Sex Differences in the Brain: A Whole Body Perspective," *Biology of Sex Differences* 6 (2015): 1, http://bsd.biomedcentral.com/articles/10.1186/s13293-015-0032-z; Nicole C. Berchtold et al., "Gene Expression Changes in the Course of Normal Brain Aging Are Sexually Dimorphic," *National Academy of Sciences* 105, no. 40 (2008): 15610.

8 Anne Gabory et al. "Placental Contribution to the Origins of Sexual Dimorphism in Health and Diseases: Sex Chromosomes and Epigenetics," *Biology of Sex Differences* 4 (2013): 4–14.

9 It should be noted that the science of genomics and human sex differences is advancing rapidly; the danger of describing current understanding is that it may be out of date even by the time this book is published.

10 See Appendix 1: Glossary of Terms.

and genitalia.) Following their discovery in 1890 and 1905, respectively,[11] the X and Y chromosomes became the determining factor of sex. However, it is now known that sex determination is much more complex than the simple presence or absence of a Y chromosome, involving a cascade of many steps and the combined function of multiple and complex paternal and maternal factors[12] including endocrinology, chromosomal karyotype, genes, gonads, genitals, and secondary sex characteristics.[13]

A simplistic overview of sex determination might be seen as a three-step biological process:[14]

1. chromosomal and genetic initiation of sex organ (gonad) determination (ovaries or testes),
2. followed by the production of the correct ratio of sex hormones (androgens and estrogens),
3. leading to the development and differentiation of the reproductive organs and secondary sexual characteristics.

Box 1 What Is "Normal"?

A "normal" boy may be born with a penis (defined as a phallus that has a urethral tube [through which urine flows] running lengthwise through its center and opening at the tip). The boy also has one X and one Y chromosome (XY), two testes descended into scrotal sacs, and a variety of tubing, which in the sexually mature male transports sperm and other components of the seminal fluid to the outside world.

In a "normal" girl the urethra opens near the vagina, a large canal surrounded at its opening by two sets of fleshy lips. The canal walls connect on the inside to the cervix, which in turn opens up into the uterus. Attached to the uterus are oviducts, which, after puberty, transport egg cells from the nearby pair of ovaries toward the uterus and beyond. If this child also has two X chromosomes (XX), we say she is female.

—From Anne Fausto-Sterling, *Sexing the Body: Gender Politics and the Construction of Sexuality* (New York: Basic Books, 2000), 48–49.

11 Richardson, *Sex Itself*, 23.

12 Devra Davis et al., "Declines in Sex Ratio at Birth and Fetal Deaths in Japan, and in US Whites but Not African Americans," *Environmental Health Perspectives* 115, no. 6 (June 2007): 941; Takashi Sato et al., "Brain Masculinization Requires Androgen Receptor Function," *Proceedings of the National Academy of Sciences of the United States of America* 101, no. 6 (February 10, 2004): 1678.

13 Elof Axel Carlson, "The Body as a Biological and Genetic Entity," *Social Research* 28, no. 2 (Summer 2011): 356; Richardson, *Sex Itself*, 8.

14 Richardson, *Sex Itself*, 6.

CHROMOSOMAL SEX DETERMINATION

It has been estimated that the average human body contains about 37.2 trillion cells[15] of many different types but with the same general structure. Most (but not all) human cells have a nucleus that contains DNA (the genetic information that determines growth and development), organized into genes that are packaged into chromosomes. All of the genes that make up an organism are referred to as its genome. Although the human genome is 99.9 percent identical across males and females,[16] the inherent differences in the genome are sufficient to lead to sex differences.[17]

With the exception of the gametes (egg and sperm), which have a single set of chromosomes, every healthy human cell with a nucleus is diploid (i.e., contains pairs of chromosomes). Generally, one chromosome in each pair is inherited from the mother and one from the father. The chromosomes are numbered roughly according to size. Pairs 1–22 are called "autosomes." Chromosomes in pair 23 are called the "sex chromosomes" because they differ between male and female and, until recently, were thought to be the sole determinant of sex. In females, pair 23 contains two X chromosomes; in males, pair 23 has one X chromosome (inherited from the mother) and one Y chromosome (inherited from the father). The Y chromosome is much smaller than the X chromosome[18] (as can be seen in Figure 1) and carries one-twentieth the coding genetic content of the X.[19] In females, who have two X chromosomes, one copy in each female cell is randomly inactivated (turned off) early in development and only one X chromosome is expressed, as in males who have only one X chromosome.[20] Random X inactivation is "perhaps the prime example of a sex difference that exists in order to make the sexes more similar."[21]

THE PRESENCE OR ABSENCE OF A Y CHROMOSOME IS IMPORTANT IN DETERMINING WHETHER SOMEONE IS MALE OR FEMALE.

15 Eva Bianconi et al., "An Estimation of the Number of Cells in the Human Body," *Annals of Human Biology* 40, no. 6 (November–December 2013): 463.

16 Richardson, *Sex Itself*, 1.

17 R. M. McCarthy and A. P. Arnold, "Reframing Sexual Differentiation of the Brain," *Nature Neuroscience* 14 (2011): 677, quoted in Richardson, *Sex Itself*, 214.

18 Susan Offner, "The Y Chromosome," *The American Biology Teacher* 72, no. 4 (April 2010): 237.

19 Richardson, *Sex Itself*, 206.

20 Richardson, *Sex Itself*, 179; Roseanne F. Zhao, "The Y Chromosome: Beyond Gender Determination," *NIH National Human Genome Research Institute*, accessed February 15, 2016, www.genome.gov/27557513/.

21 De Vries and Forger, "Sex Differences in the Brain," 2.

Although the genetics that determine sex differences are still being worked out,[22] the presence or absence of a Y chromosome is important in determining whether someone is male or female.[23] However, other genetic elements on other chromosomes are also required.[24] Until recently, it was thought that an embryo is female until the genetic pathway for male testes development was triggered. However, scientific evidence is accruing to show that separate genes are involved and that female sexual development is directed by hormones acting together with genes carried by many chromosomes.[25] More work is required to elucidate the genetic basis for sexual differences and in particular the biology of female sex determination, which has received less attention than that of the male. It is the complex differentiation into male and female that makes sexual reproduction possible.[26]

Humans reproduce through the combination of egg and sperm. The egg[27] carries one chromosome from each of the female's 22 pairs of chromosomes plus one of her X chromosomes; the sperm carries one chromosome from each of the male's 22 pairs of chromosomes, plus either an X or a Y. About equal numbers of sperm with X and with Y chromosomes are produced. When a sperm cell penetrates an egg cell, the 23 chromosomes of the sperm cell and the 23 chromosomes of the egg cell line up to result in 46 chromosomes. The correct balance of maternal and paternal genomes is important for normal growth of a human embryo.[28]

For the first six weeks of development, XX and XY human embryos are anatomically identical and sexually bipotential.[29] This means the embryo has the potential to develop into a male or a female and so the gonads are referred to as "indifferent" at this stage. However, sex is already determined at conception by the presence or absence of the Y chromosome. At around

---

22 Carlson, "The Body as a Biological and Genetic Entity," 356.

23 Richardson, *Sex Itself*, 9; Chanley M. Small, "Reinventing Sex: The Construction of Realistic Definitions of Sex and Gender," *The American Biology Teacher* 60, no. 8 (October 1998): 590.

24 Fiona Godlee, "Two More Genes Are Discovered. 1. The Sex Determining Gene," *BMJ* 301 (1990): 195.

25 Joan H. Fujimura, "Sex Genes: A Critical Sociomaterial Approach to the Politics and Molecular Genetics of Sex Determination," *Signs* 32, no. 1 (Autumn 2006): 59; D. C. Page and E. Vilain, "Expert Interview Transcript" in *Rediscovering Biology: Molecular to Global Perspectives*, electronic media, (Oregon Public Broadcasting Annenberg-Media.org, 2004), quoted in Richardson, *Sex Itself*, 145; Sarah S. Richardson, "How the X Became the 'Female Chromosome,'" *Signs* 37, no. 4 (Summer 2012): 909.

26 John Bancroft, "Biological Factors in Human Sexuality," *The Journal of Sex Research* 39, no. 1 (February 2002): 15.

27 Females are born with a lifetime supply of oocytes, cells that mature into eggs beginning at puberty. Each month following puberty, a hormonal trigger causes a number of eggs to begin the maturation process. One becomes dominant and is released. This monthly cycle ceases at the menopause, when a female's supply of eggs has been depleted. In contrast, sperm continue to be generated throughout the lifetime of males.

28 I. N. Lebedev, "Genomic Imprinting and Human Reproduction," in *Epigenetics and Epigenomics*, ed. Christopher Payne (Rijeka, Croatia: InTech, 2014), accessed January 25, 2016, www.intechopen.com/books/epigenetics-and-epigenomics/genomic-imprinting-and-human-reproduction.

29 Small, "Reinventing Sex," 591.

the tenth or eleventh week of gestation, a cascade of hormonal changes leads to the differentiation of XX and XY fetuses.[30] A working SRY gene must be present on the Y chromosome for the cascade resulting in differentiation of the gonads to become testes to be triggered.[31] Female sexual development is stimulated by hormones acting together with genes located on many different chromosomes.[32] Thus the genes play a crucial role in hormone regulation, which, in turn, influences primary and secondary sex characteristics. In fact, sex differentiation is principally caused by exposure to sex hormones at key time-points in development, mostly during prenatal stages.[33]

Box 2 Typical Male and Female Development

Typical male development begins with a 46,XY chromosomal complement. By the 6th week after conception, the embryo has developed two bipotential gonads. The *SRY* gene (located on the Y chromosome) causes production of the *SRY* transcription factor which, in conjunction with genes not located on the Y chromosome, induces the gonads to differentiate into testes. Although the embryo initially forms both the Wolffian (male) and Mullerian (female) ducts, the testes produce Mullerian-inhibiting substance (MIS), causing the Mullerian ducts to regress. By about the twelfth week, testosterone produced by the testes cause the Wolffian ducts to form the spermatic ducts. The external genitalia are sexually undifferentiated until the 7th week. Androgens produced by the testes cause the external genitalia to develop into the typical male; the proto-phallus becomes a penis, the labioscrotal folds fuse in the midline to form the scrotum, and the urethra migrates distally to a male-typical position. At puberty, testicular production of testosterone contributes to further sex differentiation. Sex differentiation in the brain appears to be the result of hormonal differentiation and social factors.

Typical female development begins with a 46,XX chromosomal complement. Unless the *SRY* and *TDF* genes are present, the bipotential gonads develop into ovaries, the Wolffian ducts atrophy, and the Mullerian ducts develop into the uterus, Fallopian tubes, cervix, and the upper portion of the vagina. Because ovaries do not produce androgens, the proto-phallus becomes a clitoris, the labioscrotal folds become the labia, and the urethra maintains a

30 Small, "Reinventing Sex," 592.

31 Richardson, "Female Chromosome," 909.

32 Richardson, "Female Chromosome," 909.

33 J. L. Rinn and M. Snyder, "Sexual Dimorphism in Mammalian Gene Expression," *Trends in Genetics* 21, no. 5 (2005): 300, quoted in Richardson, *Sex Itself*, 190.

female-typical position. At puberty, the ovaries produce estrogen and so contribute to further sex differentiation. Sex differentiation in the brain appears to be the result of hormonal differentiation and social factors.

—Reproduced from: Consortium on the Management of Disorders of Sex Development *Clinical Guidelines for the Management of Disorders of Sex Development in Childhood* March 25, 2006, p. 4 (web version available at: www.dsdguidelines.org/htdocs/clinical/dsds_defined.html)

HORMONAL SEX DETERMINATION

The hormones testosterone, estrogen, and progesterone are all important in the development of both sexes. All three occur in both men and women, but females produce more estrogen and progesterone while males produce more testosterone. The biggest hormonal difference between the sexes is seen in the level of testosterone,[34] which, in male vertebrates, is particularly important in the regulation of appearance, physiological characteristics, and behavior.[35]

The exposure *in utero* to sex hormones, particularly testosterone, is also thought to influence brain development, with the critical period being between weeks 12 and 19 of gestation.[36] Scientific evidence that prenatal exposure to testosterone creates "masculinized" brains with consequent male-typical behaviors in children and adults is accumulating.[37] Receptors for the sex hormones are found in many areas of the brain, some of which have been shown to "become sexually differentiated during development, giving rise to sex differences in sexual behavior, aggression and play behavior."[38] Johnson suggests that males and females "end up with brains wired to handle certain information differently, and to have different cognitive and emotional styles. Though their brains are also affected by learning and experience, those effects are believed to be limited by the biological con-

34 Jack Van Honk et al., "Testosterone Administration Impairs Cognitive Empathy in Women Depending on Second-to-Fourth Digit Ratio," *Proceedings of the National Academy of Sciences of the United States of America* 103, no. 8 (February 22, 2011): 3448.

35 See Marta Soares et al., "Hormonal Mechanisms of Cooperative Behaviour," *Philosophical Transactions: Biological Sciences* 365, no. 1553 (September 12, 2010): 2738.

36 Pinker, *The Blank Slate*, 347; Van Honk et al. "Testosterone Administration Impairs Cognitive Empathy," 3448; Melissa Hines, Mihaela Constantinescu, and Debra Spencer, "Early Androgen Exposure and Human Gender Development," *Biology of Sex Differences* 6, no. 3 (2015): 3, accessed February 1, 2016, www.bsd-journal.com/content/6/1/3.

37 Johnson, "Sexing the Brain: Brains Are Not Sexually Neutral"; Sato et al., "Brain Masculinization," 1673–78; Hines, Constantinescu, and Spencer, "Early Androgen Exposure," 4.

38 Kerrie Lewis Graham and Gordon M. Burghardt, "Current Perspectives on the Biological Study of Play: Signs of Progress," *The Quarterly Review of Biology* 85, no. 4 (December 2010): 407.

straints laid down in early brain development."[39] Several authors emphasize the importance of the interaction between biological (and genetic) processes and the environment (or culture), pointing out that human social interactions and long development times provide opportunities to influence the biological predisposition.[40] The ability of the brain to undergo physical change in response to experience is referred to as "plasticity."[41] As explained by Eagleman, everything a human being experiences alters the physical structure of the brain.[42] However, even the ways in which "nature" and "nurture" work together to shape each individual human being have been shown to differ between individuals with XX and XY chromosomes (i.e., are sexually dimorphic).[43]

THE BIGGEST HORMONAL DIFFERENCE BETWEEN THE SEXES IS SEEN IN THE LEVEL OF TESTOSTERONE.

Feminists in the 1970s and 1980s, in their attempts to demonstrate a lack of difference between the sexes, tried to split biology from behavioral differences by using the term *gender* as distinct from *sex*.[44]

Sex vs. Gender

According to the Oxford Dictionary, "The word *gender* has been used since the 14th century as a grammatical term, referring to classes of noun designated as *masculine*, *feminine*, or *neuter* in some languages."[45] The psychologist John Money is thought to be the first to make a distinction between sex and gender, using the term *gender* to signify "the overall degree of masculinity and/or femininity that is privately experienced and publicly manifested in infancy, childhood, and adulthood, and that usually though not invariably correlates with the anatomy of the organs of procreation."[46] Many medical texts and scientific publications still use the terms *sex* and

39 Johnson, "Sexing the Brain: Brains Are Not Sexually Neutral."

40 For example: Daphne Joel and Anne Fausto-Sterling, "Beyond Sex Differences: New Approaches for Thinking about Variation in Brain Structure and Function," *Philosophical Transactions of the Royal Society B* 371, no. 0451 (2015): 1. http://rstb.royalsocietypublishing.org; de Vries and Forger, "Sex Differences," 11.

41 Lise Eliot, *Pink Brain, Blue Brain* (Oxford: OneWorld Publications, 2010), 6.

42 David Eagleman, *The Brain: The Story of You* (Edinburgh and London: Canongate, 2015), 19.

43 Gabory, "Placental Contribution," 4–14.

44 Fujimura, "Sex Genes," 52.

45 *Oxford Dictionaries*, s.v. "Gender: Usage," accessed February 2, 2016, www.oxforddictionaries.com/definition/english/gender.

46 John Money, *Gendermaps: Social Constructionism, Feminism, and Sexosophical History* (New York: Continuum, 1995), 18–19, quoted in David A. Rubin, "'An Unnamed Blank That Craved a Name': A Genealogy of Intersex as Gender," *Signs* 37, no. 4 (Summer 2012): 893.

gender interchangeably.[47] Neuroscientist Eliot expresses the view that the term *sex* is "more scientifically correct even if it's less politically so. *Sex* is a biological attribute, defined by chromosomes and anatomic characteristics. It is a binary, either/or trait. *Gender*, by contrast, is a social construct, the sum of all the attributes typically associated with one sex. It is not fixed and binary but a fluid spectrum between masculinity and femininity."[48]

Disorders of Sexual Development

One of the drivers for the distinction between *sex* and *gender* in use today was recognition of the prevalence of individuals who do not fit into the standard medical description of male or female, often described as being *intersex*.[49] There are well documented conditions where, for example, individuals with an XX karyotype are identified by their genitalia as males, and those with an XY karyotype are identified as females.[50] It is possible that intersex humans occur "about 1 to 3 times in every 2,000 births . . . (for comparison, the incidence of cystic fibrosis is about 1/2,000, Down's syndrome approx. 1/800)."[51] This estimate hides a large range in incidence arising from differences in the definition used for *intersex*, but even the most conservative estimate suggests that there were "about 50,000 true intersexuals living in the United States" in 2014.[52] Some specific types of intersex conditions are described in Appendix 2.

The assignment of sex has far-reaching implications, from psychological through to legal ramifications. Intersex conditions raise the challenging question of what should determine sex assignment and who should make the decision, both of which can result in dramatically different assignments. For example, if the gonads or chromosomes are considered to be the primary markers of sex, persons with Complete Androgen Insensitivity Syndrome (CAIS) are identified as "really" men. However, if external genitalia and personal gender identity are considered to be primary, persons with CAIS are labeled as "really" women.[53]

---

47 Anne Fausto-Sterling, "The Bare Bones of Sex: Part 1—Sex and Gender," *Signs* 30, no. 2 (Winter 2005): 1498.

48 Eliot, *Pink Brain, Blue Brain*, 3.

49 Rubin, "An Unnamed Blank That Craved a Name," 883–84.

50 Carlson, "The Body as a Biological and Genetic Entity," 356.

51 Douglas Allchin, "Male, Female and/or -? How Does Nature Define the Sexes?" *The American Biology Teacher* 68, no. 6 (August 2006): 375.

52 Megan DeFranza, "How Many Intersex Persons Are There?" in *Sex Difference in Christian Theology: Male, Female, and Intersex in the Image of God* (Grand Rapids and Cambridge, UK: Eerdmans, 2015), Kindle edition.

53 DeFranza "What Is Intersex? Types of Intersex Conditions," in *Sex Difference*.

One of the biggest challenges with regard to intersex is how best to help individuals born with one of these conditions that, until recently, have been viewed as "illnesses or diseases that may legitimately be rectified through corrective surgery."[54] Doctors and parents alike seem to have a desire to "fix" what has been viewed as an anatomical "error," as well as to "fix" the child into one sex.[55] In the 1950s, Money promoted early medical "correction" of intersex based on his belief that gender identity developed postnatally and was malleable in early childhood given the right conditions.[56] Although the case on which he based his view was subsequently shown to be far less successful than he claimed,[57] surgical intervention soon after birth remained the standard approach to managing infants with intersex conditions, whether or not the condition was life-threatening. It has been claimed that often the decision on which sex to assign was made based on the ease or difficulty of the surgical procedure and, because feminizing genital surgeries are easier to perform than masculinizing procedures, male infants born with deformed or unspecific genitals were almost always subjected to medical and surgical treatments to bring their anatomy into conformity with typical female morphology and reared as girls.[58]

> THE ASSIGNMENT OF SEX HAS FAR-REACHING IMPLICATIONS, FROM PSYCHOLOGICAL TO LEGAL RAMIFICATIONS.

Intersex activists have campaigned for a more "patient centered" approach, advocating the raising of children as male or female, not as an "in between" third category.[59] They argue that unusual sexual anatomy does not inevitably require surgical or hormonal intervention,[60] and that "doctors and parents should at least wait until a child is old enough to communicate their gender identity, which typically manifests around the age of three, or old enough to

54 Christian Institute, "Intersex Conditions – Why They Are Different to Transsexuality," Christian Institute, accessed February 5, 2016, www.christian.org.uk/transsexualism/intersex_briefing.pdf.

55 Bernice L. Hausman, "Do Boys Have to Be Boys? Gender, Narrativity, and the John/Joan Case," *NWSA Journal* 12, no. 3 (Autumn 2000): 129.

56 Elizabeth Reis, *Bodies in Doubt: An American History of Intersex* (Baltimore, MD: Johns Hopkins University Press, 2009), 135; DeFranza, "History of Intersex: From the Margins to Medicalization: Twentieth Century, from Medical Management to the Disappearance of Hermaphrodites," in *Sex Difference*.

57 As shown by Hausman, "Do Boys Have to Be Boys?"

58 Hausman, "Do Boys Have to Be Boys?" 114; DeFranza "What Is Intersex? Types of Intersex Conditions," in *Sex Difference*.

59 Reis, *Bodies in Doubt*, 152, 155.

60 Reis, *Bodies in Doubt*, 156.

decide whether they want surgery at all."[61] This wait-and-see approach, delaying the decision on whether surgery would be helpful until development and other factors can be taken into consideration, seems to be the most beneficial for the child, even if it presents challenges for the parents who may struggle with having a child with physical differences from what has traditionally been viewed as "normal" (see Box 1).

In 2005, a consortium was formed to develop clinical guidelines for the management of disorders of sex development in childhood.[62] The members of the Consortium have stated a preference to avoid the term *intersex* because of its imprecision, using instead the umbrella term *disorders of sex development* (DSD). However, it should be noted that some believe this term to be pejorative, arguing that *variation in sex development* (VSD) or *divergence of sex development* (retaining the acronym DSD) are preferable.[63]

Disorders of sex development (DSDs) include anomalies of the sex chromosomes, the gonads, the reproductive ducts, and the genitalia. More than twenty-five genes involved in DSDs have been identified since the 1990s.[64] However, the taxonomy for congenital sexual anatomies that has been utilized for the past 150 years still presents the "binary" model of male/female, accommodating the instances where, due to genetic and/or hormonal abnormalities, the sex of an individual fails to develop correctly, by dividing humans into five types based on the anatomy of the gonads:[65]

Females: standard female sexual anatomy

Female pseudohermaphrodites: some mixture or blurring of standard female and male sexual anatomy with the presence of ovaries (and not testes or ovotestes) and of an XX chromosomal complement

True hermaphrodites: at least one ovary and at least one testis, or at least one ovotestis

Male pseudohermaphrodites: some mixture of standard female and male sexual anatomy with the presence of testes (and not ovaries or ovotestes) and of an XY chromosomal complement

Males: standard male sexual anatomy

---

61 Claire Ainsworth, "Sex Redefined," *Nature* 518, no. 7539 (February 18, 2015), accessed February 15, 2016, www.nature.com/news/sex-redefined-1.16943.

62 Consortium on the Management of Disorders of Sex Development, *Clinical Guidelines for the Management of Disorders of Sex Development in Childhood*, Intersex Society of North America, accessed February 6, 2016, www.dsdguidelines.org/htdocs/clinical/index.html.

63 DeFranza "What Is in a Name? From Hermaphrodite to Intersex to Disorders of Sex Development (DSDs)," in *Sex Difference; Reis, Bodies in Doubt*, 159.

64 Ainsworth, "Sex Redefined."

65 Alice D. Dreger et al., "Changing the Nomenclature/Taxonomy for Intersex: A Scientific and Clinical Rationale," *Journal of Pediatric Endocrinology & Metabolism* 18 (2005): 729.

Although this model was challenged initially by Fausto-Sterling, she returned to this scale of five categories with male and female as the end-points.[66] However, some theologians, such as Cornwall[67] and DeFranza,[68] reject this model. In Cornwall's view, the existence of intersex, together with all of the issues surrounding it, is a reminder of the possibility that the definition of what it means to be human can change.[69]

DeFranza argues that "the ontological shifts allow for the multiplication of the sexes or their abandonment."[70] However, she points out the biggest difficulty in trying to expand the "number" of sexes is the problem of where to draw the line and who ultimately defines male, female, in-between, and other.[71] Her preferred option, therefore, appears to be to abandon the characterization of individuals by "sex."

Both DeFranza and Cornwall question what it means to be human. Their flawed reasoning suggests that because they consider male/female to be key to the definition of human, individuals with DSDs could be considered nonhuman if the binary model is retained. Their conclusion is therefore that the binary model has to be rejected. Both authors reject parts of the scriptural account of man created as male and female, and fail to consider the fact that some individuals with intersex conditions have lobbied against being described as a sex that is separate from male and female. In this world enslaved to the chaos of sin, there will always be exceptions to God's good order, but exceptions should not be used to create rules contrary to Scripture.

Male/female sex differentiation does not distinguish humanity from most animal and plant species. It is important that we help all who suffer with the effects of a DSD to see that the image of God and our being as humans relate not to our physical characteristics but to our relationships—with God and with our neighbor. This is what it means to be human. "The unity and distinction in God, with respect to the three persons of the Trinity and the two natures of Christ, provides a pattern for the unity and dis-

66 Anne Fausto-Sterling, *Sexing the Body: Gender Politics and the Construction of Sexuality* (New York: Basic Books, 2000).

67 Cornwall is the director of the Exeter Centre for Ethics and Practical Theology; see http://humanities.exeter.ac.uk/theology/staff/cornwall/.

68 "DeFranza is a Christian theologian, liberal-arts educator, author, speaker, and peace-maker . . ."; see http://0370025.netsolhost.com/wordpress1/sample-page/ (accessed February 13, 2016).

69 Susannah Cornwall, "Sex Otherwise: Intersex, Christology, and the Maleness of Jesus," *Journal of Feminist Studies in Religion* 30, no. 2 (Fall 2014): 39.

70 DeFranza "Postmodern Shifts: From Substance and Sex Dualism to Relational Ontology and the Multiplication of the Sexes," in *Sex Difference*, 144.

71 DeFranza "From Medical Management to Social Change: Questioning the Binary Sex Model," in *Sex Difference*. This is the challenge that Fausto-Sterling encountered as her thinking developed from a multiplicity of sexes, back to the five categories above in her more recent publications.

tinction in man as male and female, created in the image of God."[72] We are created for relationships as male and female, which describe our "situation before God."[73] Unfortunately, "the natural world, as it exists today, does not display a clean binary split of humanity that neatly includes every person."[74] While cautioning that "the church must not conclude that DNA is always the grand arbiter of human identity," Stiegemeyer emphasizes the importance of taking into account the need for male and female to reproduce in determining what is "normal" in relation to sex.[75] This is also the view of the social scientist Richardson, who points out that,

> In mammals there are two gametic sexes, and not more or fewer than two. Even intersex conditions do not change the assumptions of our genetic models of sexual reproduction and mating since they do not alter the two-gamete egg and sperm model of sexual reproduction. While it is essential to acknowledge the plurality and social contingency of sex and gender forms, the (present) necessity of male-female pairing for reproduction requires a different approach to the biological concept of sex.[76]

DeFranza encourages Christians, particularly those from more conservative traditions, "to reflect on their theologies and communal practices from the perspective of intersex people."[77] Like DeFranza, Stiegemeyer criticizes conservative churches for perhaps showing "little understanding for those individuals who are genuinely confused about where they fit into the traditional taxonomy"[78] and for approaching what are "at least partially medical issues with the same methodology as if it were simply discussing moral issues."[79]

72 Nathan Jastrum, "Man as Male and Female: Created in the Image of God," *Concordia Theological Quarterly* 68, no. 1 (January 2004): 63.

73 G. Kittel, G.W. Bromiley, and G. Friedrich, eds., *Theological Dictionary of the New Testament*, electronic ed., vol. 7 (Grand Rapids: Eerdmans, 1964), 135, 123.

74 Scott E. Stiegemeyer, "How Do You Know Whether You Are a Man or a Woman?" *Concordia Theological Quarterly* 79, nos. 1–2 (2015): 46.

75 Stiegemeyer, "How Do You Know?" 22, 26.

76 Richardson, *Sex Itself*, 199.

77 Teri Merrick, introductory comment in DeFranza, *Sex Difference*.

78 Stiegemeyer, "How Do You Know?" 43.

79 Stiegemeyer, "How Do You Know?" 46.

DSDS IN SCRIPTURE

DSDs do not represent a new medical condition. The word *hermaphrodite*, denoting "a person or animal having both male and female sex organs or other sexual characteristics,"[80] has been in use since ancient times. Its origins appear to rest in various Greek legends regarding the son of Hermes and Aphrodite.[81] Plato, Aristotle, Galen, Pliny, and Soranos of Ephesus all mention hermaphrodites, androgynes, or cases of gender ambiguity.[82]

Early rabbinic interpretations (AD 200–600) of Genesis 1:27 and 5:2, where mankind is described as "male and female," differ. Some rabbis understood this phrase to mean two individuals (a man and a woman), while others envisaged a single being that was both male and female—an androgyne. It seems that these rabbis thought that Adam's male and female parts were connected at either the front or the back (like conjoined twins).[83] They concluded that it was only after the original sin, when the woman and man were separated, that sexual differentiation came into being.[84]

The Bible refers to males and females who are unable to reproduce as "eunuchs" and "barren women." DeFranza argues that "by recovering the concept of the eunuch, theologians will find fresh avenues for rethinking the meanings of sex and gender for theological anthropology and a starting place to address the challenges and incorporate the insights learned from intersex."[85] The word סָרִיס (*saris*) occurs several times in the Old Testament, usually with the meaning of "(court) official," because of the practice of utilizing castrated men in key positions in Eastern courts.[86] Apart from the Book of Esther, Isaiah 56:3–5 "is one of the few places where we can be sure that *saris* refers to a sexually-mutilated male rather than a court official."[87] Eunuchs were forbidden to enter the temple by Mosaic Law

---

80 *Oxford Dictionaries*, s.v. "Definition of *hermaphrodite* in English," accessed February 9, 2016, www.oxforddictionaries.com/definition/english/hermaphrodite.

81 George Androutsos, "Hermaphroditism in Greek and Roman Antiquity," *Hormones* 5, no. 3 (2006): 215.

82 Androutsos, "Hermaphroditism in Greek and Roman Antiquity," 215–17; Fausto-Sterling, *Sexing the Body*, 33; DeFranza, "History of Intersex: From the Margins to Medicalization," in *Sex Difference*.

83 Kristen Kvam, Linda Schearing, and Valerie Ziegler, eds., *Eve and Adam: Jewish, Christian and Muslim Readings on Genesis and Gender* (Bloomington and Indianapolis: Indiana University Press, 1999), 78.

84 DeFranza, "History of Intersex: From the Margins to Medicalization" in *Sex Difference;* Androutsos, "Hermaphroditism," 214.

85 DeFranza, "Intersex: Medical and Sociological Challenges to the Two-Sex Model. Is Christianity to Blame?" in *Sex Difference*, 67.

86 R. D. Patterson, "סָרִיס." in R. L. Harris, G. L. Archer Jr., and B. K. Waltke, eds., *Theological Wordbook of the Old Testament* (electronic ed.) (Chicago: Moody Press, 1999), 1545; John D. W. Watts, *Word Biblical Commentary: Isaiah 34–66* (Waco, TX: Word Books, 1987), 249.

87 Joseph Blenkinsopp, "Reassurance for the Marginal," in *Isaiah 56–66 The Anchor Bible Volume 19B*. (Yale University Press, 2003), 137.

and were thus excluded from the worshiping community (Leviticus 22:24; Deuteronomy 23:2).[88]

With regard to females, עָקָר (*'aqar*) is used in the Old Testament to describe a woman as being sexually infertile and so not able to bear children.[89] In the New Testament, στεῖρος (*steiros*) describes a female who has been deprived of bearing children, one who is sterile, barren.[90] There is no way of knowing whether female barrenness was a result of a medical condition but, irrespective of the cause, the barren woman was viewed as having been cursed by God.[91]

THERE IS GOOD NEWS FOR EUNUCHS AND BARREN WOMEN IN SCRIPTURE. JESUS CAME FOR ALL, AND ESPECIALLY FOR THE OUTCAST.

Thus to be a eunuch or barren was to be an outcast. But there is good news for eunuchs and barren women in Scripture. Jesus came for all, and especially for the outcast. God makes the barren woman "the joyous mother of children" (Psalm 113:9) and promises that the barren women will have more children than fertile women (Isaiah 54:1). The acceptance of eunuchs into the congregation of Israel at the final redemption is foretold in Isaiah 56:3–5,[92] which makes clear that "it is not important that the eunuchs cannot engender children; they are truly the children of God because it is not genealogy but character that marks the servants of God."[93] This assurance given to eunuchs "carries weight because their memory will live on 'in my house and within my walls.' . . . God will not cut them off; they are not lifeless and fruitless."[94] The Ethiopian eunuch, who is even reading Isaiah, "the OT Gospel for outcasts,"[95] in Acts 8:27–39, is an example of this; "he has been remembered because of his faith far longer than if he had simply had sons and daughters."[96]

---

88 Patterson, "סָרִיס," P1545; John D. W. Watts, *Word Biblical Commentary: Isaiah 34–66*, 249.

89 J. Swanson, *Dictionary of Biblical Languages with Semantic Domains: Hebrew (Old Testament)*. (Oak Harbor: Logos Research Systems, Inc., 1997). Electronic edition.

90 S. Zodhiates, *The Complete Word Study Dictionary: New Testament* (Chattanooga, TN: AMG Publishers, 2000). Electronic edition.

91 Arthur A. Just Jr., *Luke 1:1–9:50*, Concordia Commentary (St. Louis: Concordia, 1996), 53.

92 W. D. Davies and Dale C. Allison Jr., *A Critical and Exegetical Commentary on the Gospel according to Saint Matthew* (Edinburgh: T & T Clark, 1997), 3:24.

93 John N. Oswalt, *The Book of Isaiah Chapters 40–66*, The New International Commentary on the Old Testament (Grand Rapids: Eerdmans, 1998), 457.

94 Blenkinsopp, "Reassurance for the Marginal," 139.

95 Frederick Dale Bruner, *Matthew: A Commentary* (Dallas: Word Publishing, 1990), 2:689.

96 Oswalt, *The Book of Isaiah. Chapters 40–66*, 458.

Jesus Himself describes three kinds of men who live as eunuchs (Matthew 19:11–12)[97]: those born with a congenital condition, those who have been rendered impotent through castration or other traumatic experience, and those who choose of their own free will not to marry.[98] Davies and Allison explain that the first two categories would have been "known entities": *seris hamma* (literally "eunuch of the sun," i.e., from the first seeing of the sun at birth—a male born with defective male organs or rendered impotent by the circumstances of his birth) and *seris adam* (literally "eunuch of man," i.e., a male who had been castrated or lost the power to reproduce).[99] The third category would have been an anathema at the time when the cultural expectation was that everyone would marry and bear children. Bruner explains that "Jesus dignified marriage; now he has dignified single life. Jesus sees both as gifts from God."[100] This raises the potentially sensitive question of whether individuals with a DSD can find a God-pleasing marriage partner. Given the importance of reproductive ability in the definition of male/female (as discussed above), the choice of a marriage partner may depend to a large extent on sexual anatomy. However, this is not a black and white issue; many factors will need to be taken into consideration, such as genetic makeup and what, if any, surgery may have been performed at an early stage of life. Irrespective of all these factors, it should be emphasized that God has dignified all human life and pours out His superabundant love on each one of us through Christ. "In Christ Jesus you are all sons of God. . . . There is no male and female, for you are all one in Christ Jesus" (Galatians 3:26, 28).

Conclusion

For Christians, the definition of "male" and "female" is a theological, not a sociological, question. Scripture clearly teaches that God has created man as two distinct sexes, male and female (Genesis 1:26–27), in His image, equal and interdependent (1 Corinthians 11:11–12) but not interchangeable.[101] God's good order, established at creation, placed male and female into relationship with each other and with Him, "united in their mutual dependence on each other and ultimately in their joint dependence

97 Jeffrey A. Gibbs, *Matthew 11:2–20:34*, Concordia Commentary (St. Louis: Concordia, 2010), 954.

98 Bruner, *Matthew*, 689.

99 Davies and Allison Jr., *Matthew*, 22.

100 Bruner, *Matthew*, 692.

101 Commission on Theology and Church Relations, *Women in the Church. Scriptural Principles and Ecclesial Practices.* (St. Louis: LCMS, 1985), 21, www.lcms.org/ctcr/document-library#.

on God."[102] Together male and female were also placed into relationship with the rest of creation. God said, "Let them have dominion . . . over all the earth" (Genesis 1:26). Thus *"man and woman are equal in having the same relationship to God and to nature;"*[103] "they are equally capable of the knowledge of God, righteousness, moral discernment, proper worship, adoption as the children of God, and immortality."[104]

Although male and female are equal, from the beginning, God created them as different and distinct. "Just as it is wrong to deny the distinctions between the three persons of the Trinity and merge them into one (Unitarianism), so it is wrong to deny the distinctions between the two sexes and merge them into one (androgyny). It would be as wrong to deny the distinction between the sexes as it would be to deny the unity that they form according to Scripture."[105]

THUS IN CREATING MALE AND FEMALE, GOD ALSO CREATED THE RELATION OF HUSBAND AND WIFE.

Adam was created from the dust of the ground and God's own breath. Eve, the mother of all the living (Genesis 3:20), came from the side of the First Adam to be his bride, just as the Church, the Bride of Christ, poured from the side of the Second Adam on the cross (John 19:31–34). Thus the First Adam, a type of Christ, was also the first pastor. The first female was Adam's bride and parishioner. This means we cannot define what it means to be male or female separate from Christ and the Church.[106] God's plan for salvation was in place before He breathed life into Adam (Ephesians 1:3–10; Matthew 25:34; Revelation 13:8). That plan was that God's own Son, Jesus Christ, would be incarnate as a male human (Luke 1:26–33), the Second (1 Corinthians 15:21–22, 44–49) and perfect Adam (Romans 5:14, 17–18) and that Jesus, the Bridegroom, would give His life for His Bride, the Church (Matthew 9:15; John 3:28–29; Ephesians 5:23–32; Revelation 19:6–8; 21:2, 9; 22:12–13, 17).

Thus in creating male and female, God also created the relation of husband and wife. The interdependence of man and woman is seen most obviously in relation to procreation. Male and female, sperm and egg, are required to form new life. Physically, the male and female reproductive

102 Jastrum, "Man as Male and Female," 29.

103 *Women in the Church*, 19–20. Italics original.

104 Jastrum, "Man as Male and Female," 63.

105 Jastrum, "Man as Male and Female," 69.

106 Stanley Hauerwas, *Matthew* (Grand Rapids: Brazos Press, 2006), 172.

organs were created to fit together, as part of the "one flesh" union, enabling the enjoyment of sexual intimacy within marriage. This union is a mystery, designed to "enflesh the great mystery of Christ's union with his bride and body, the church."[107] The beauty of the one-flesh union and its connection with Christ and His Bride is related in the Song of Songs, where Solomon is a type of Christ and the Shulammite prefigures the Christian Church.[108] It is precisely because the conjugal union of man and woman is God's most powerful image in the world that Satan attacks sexuality with such intensity.[109]

IT IS PRECISELY BECAUSE THE CONJUGAL UNION OF MAN AND WOMAN IS GOD'S MOST POWERFUL IMAGE IN THE WORLD THAT SATAN ATTACKS SEXUALITY WITH SUCH INTENSITY.

The relationship between male and female within the marriage union is also described in Ephesians 5:21–33. Each husband is required to love his wife to the point of sacrificing his own life for her, just as Christ sacrificed Himself for His Bride, the Church. Each wife is to respect and submit to her husband, not in a subservient way[110] but by receiving his love and trusting him to care for her, just as the Church submits to the love and care of Christ. It is important to note that "the New Testament does not speak of the general subordination of all women to all men but only their subordination in particular relationships, according to their station, such as wives to husbands."[111]

Woman was created to be a helper to man, as a necessary partner in achieving their God-given goals. There are many scriptural examples of the ways in which females fulfill the role of "helper" in Christ's Body, the Church, outside of marriage—for example, Miriam and Moses, Deborah and Barak, Phoebe and Paul, the women who supported Christ and His disciples. Jesus Himself elevated and honored women, treating them as equal members of the Christian community. He healed women (e.g., Luke 8:43–48; 13:10–17), talked with women (John 4:27), taught women (Luke 10:38–42), advocated for women (Luke 7:36–50; Matthew 26:13; John 8:1–11), told parables about women, (e.g., Luke 15:8–10; 18:1–8),

107 See the chapter by Christopher W. Mitchell, "What Is Marriage?," later in this volume.

108 Christopher W. Mitchell, *The Song of Songs*. Concordia Commentary (St. Louis: Concordia, 2003), 1154–55.

109 Stiegemeyer, "How Do You Know?," 47.

110 John Kleinig, "Ordered Community: Order and Subordination in the New Testament," *Lutheran Theological Journal* 17 (2004–5): 46.

111 Kleinig, "Ordered Community," 53.

and relied on women to care for His physical needs (Luke 8:1–3). Women cared for the body of Christ from His conception to His death and burial. Women were the first witnesses of the resurrection and the first to speak the Gospel message, "He is risen!" (e.g., Luke 24:1–12). They were also key members of the Early Church (e.g., Acts 1:14).

Sadly, sin permeates everything, distorting the original order created by God, resulting in disorder. The effects of the fall into sin are apparent in every aspect of human life. The fact that humans cannot all be categorized neatly in a binary system of "male/female" is merely one manifestation of this disorder (see Genesis 3:16–19; Romans 8:20–23).[112] But to simply dismiss individuals suffering with a DSD as demonstrating a manifestation of original sin is to leave them mired in the Law, alone with the unhelpful question, "Why me?" and with the impression that God is not in control of their lives, that He has abandoned them to chance or something worse. This is not the case, as declared by Martin Luther in his explanation of the First Article of the Creed: "I believe that God has made me and all creatures, that He has given me my body and soul, eyes, ears, and all my members."[113]

Clearly the fact that some individuals are born with a DSD does not mean that God was not in control of their conception and physical development—rather they, like all human beings, are "God's workmanship" (Isaiah 64:8; Ephesians 2:10). He formed their inward parts and knitted them together in their mother's womb (Isaiah 44:2, 21; Psalm 139:13), wrote all the days "formed for them" in His book "when as yet there were none of them" (Psalm 139:16), and, most important, sent His only Son to die for them. As Bruner reminds us, "What we were made genetically at birth and what we have become historically through experience is something attributable not only to human sin, social forces or demonic attacks but to the Creator who is sovereign over all genes, experiences, spirits and sins."[114] It is not helpful to ask why we were created as we are, as Job discovered (Job 40:6–41:11) and as Paul reminds us: "But who are you, O man, to answer back to God? Will what is molded say to its molder, 'Why have you made me like this?' Has the potter no right over the clay, to make out of the same lump one vessel for honorable use and another for dishonorable use?" (Romans 9:20–21).

---

112 Commission on Theology and Church Relations, *Gender Identity Disorder or Gender Dysphoria in Christian Perspective* (St. Louis: LCMS, May 17, 2014), www.lcms.org/search?q=intersex.

113 *Luther's Small Catechism with Explanation* (St. Louis: Concordia, 1986), 15.

114 Bruner, *Matthew*, 689.

God's ways are not our ways and His purposes are not always revealed to us. MacKenzie explains:

> God's good purposes may be invisible to us ("Many things seem, and are, very good to God, which seem, and are, very bad to us"), but Luther offers "Christ and the gospel" as a premier example of how God operates. The world cannot see—it "abominates" them both—but in truth nothing is better. So recognizing God's goodness is not a matter of sight but of faith. From Luther's perspective, therefore, God is responsible for what happens and employs it for His own good purposes, but Satan and man are responsible for the sinful character of what they do.[115]

Thus, even though the effects of the fall are apparent in all aspects of our humanity, God has plans for everyone, "for welfare and not for evil, to give you a future and a hope" (Jeremiah 29:11). As Bayer reminds us, "We are humans precisely because God has given us life, because he has addressed us, because we can hear him, and because we can and must respond to him. God's addresses and our human response are the essence of worship. . . . Every human being as such belongs to the church, as an order of creation. In fact, this is what defines us as humans."[116] Thus it is our relationships, to God and to one another, that reflect the image of God and our humanity, whether we were created as male or female, with or without a disorder of sexual development. In Baptism, God puts His seal on us, marking us as His own dear, redeemed children, united in Christ. We have new life in Christ, sharing in His suffering, death, and resurrection. Just as "[Christ's] strength was shown in human weakness, so . . . in our weakness we find strength in Him."[117] Even in the midst of a lack of clarity regarding the definition of "male" and "female," it is comforting to be reminded by Stiegemeyer that "our sex/gender is so constitutive to our identity that we continue as male and female in the resurrection . . . that means every person has a 'true sex', even when we are unable to ascertain it in our fallenness. God knows."[118]

115 Cameron A. MacKenzie, "The Origin and Consequences of Original Sin in Luther's *Bondage of the Will,*" *Concordia Journal* 31, no. 4 (2005): 392–93.

116 Oswald Bayer, Jeffry G. Silcock, and Mark C. Mattes, eds. and trans. *Theology the Lutheran Way* (Grand Rapids: Eerdmans, 2007), 86.

117 Robert C. Baker and Charles P. Schaum, eds. *Lutheran Spirituality: Life as God's Child* (St. Louis: Concordia, 2010), 135.

118 Stiegemeyer, "How Do You Know?," 46–47.

APPENDIX 1 • GLOSSARY OF TERMS

Disorders of Sex Development (DSD)	Conditions involving any of the following elements:[1] • congenital development of ambiguous genitalia; • congenital disjunction of internal and external sex anatomy; • incomplete development of sex anatomy; • sex chromosome anomalies; or • disorders of gonadal development.
Epigenetic	"Refers to external modifications to DNA that turn genes 'on' or 'off.' These modifications do not change the DNA sequence, but instead, they affect how cells 'read' genes."[2]
Gamete	"A reproductive cell or sex cell that contains the haploid set of chromosomes, e.g., spermatozoon or sperm cell (male reproductive cell) and egg cell or ovum (female reproductive cell)."[3]
Gender	"The state of being male or female (typically used with reference to social and cultural differences rather than biological ones)"[4]; "a social construct, the sum of all the attributes typically associated with one sex. It is not fixed and binary but a fluid spectrum between masculinity and femininity."[5]
Gender Identity	"A concept recognizing that any individual, regardless of his or her biological gender, can and does exhibit some cognitive characteristics of the opposite gender."[6]
Gonad	"The part of the reproductive system that produces and releases eggs (ovary) or sperm (testicle/testis)."[7]
Hormones	"The chemical agents that transmit signals from one cell to another, acting at a distance to create metabolic changes in cells and tissues."[8]
Intersex	"A group of conditions where there is a discrepancy between the external genitals and the internal genitals (the testes and ovaries). Increasingly this group of conditions is being called disorders of sex development (DSDs)."[9]
Karyotype	"An individual's collection of chromosomes. The term also refers to a laboratory technique that produces an image of an individual's chromosomes . . . used to look for abnormal numbers or structures of chromosomes."[10]
Mosaicism	"A condition in which cells within the same person have a different genetic makeup. This condition can affect any type of cell . . . [and is] caused by an error in cell division very early in the development of the unborn baby."[11]
Phenotype	"An individual's observable traits, such as height, eye color, and blood type. The genetic contribution to the phenotype is called the genotype. Some traits are largely determined by the genotype, while other traits are largely determined by environmental factors."[12]
Primary Sex Characteristics	"Any of the body structures directly concerned in reproduction, as the testes, ovaries and external genitalia."[13]
Secondary Sex Characteristics	"Any of the external physical characteristics of sexual maturity secondary to hormonal stimulation that develop in the maturing individual. These characteristics include adult distribution of hair and development of the penis or breasts and the labia."[14]
Sex	"Either of the two main categories (male and female) into which humans and most other living things are divided on the basis of their reproductive functions;"[15] "a biological attribute, defined by chromosomes and anatomic characteristics. It is a binary, either/or trait."[16]
Sexual Dimorphism	"The differences in appearance between males and females of the same species, such as in color, shape, size, and structure, that are caused by the inheritance of one or the other sexual pattern in the genetic material."[17]

APPENDIX 2 • TYPES OF INTERSEX CONDITIONS

CONDITION	TYPE	DESCRIPTION[18]	OCCURRENCE
Androgen Insensitivity Syndrome (AIS)		Born with XY chromosomes but cells lack receptors to process male hormones (androgens)	
	Complete AIS (CAIS)	Appear "unambiguously" female Develop female external genitals; retain undescended or partially descended testes Usually have short or no vagina and no cervix Not usually discovered until puberty—do not menstruate Develop secondary sex characteristics typical of pubescent females because some of the testosterone released at puberty converts back to estrogen[19]	1 in 13,000 births[20]
	Partial AIS (PAIS)	Have bodies that fall anywhere along the spectrum between male and female, with 7 grades, ranging from "1. Male genitals, infertility" through "7. Female genitals, little or no pubic/underarm hair"	1 in 130,000 births[21]
Congenital Adrenal Hyperplasia (CAH)		Inherited enzyme deficiency causes the fetus's adrenal gland to overproduce fetal androgen Can be life-threatening due to severe dehydration, leading to death within the first weeks of the infant's life	1 in 13,000 births[22]
	XX Individuals	Have androgen levels similar to typical males; can have larger than average clitoris, clitoris that looks like a penis, labia that look like a scrotum May be misidentified as males at birth Retain female internal reproductive organs and are capable of reproducing Can have secondary sex characteristics typical of male puberty At puberty, additional medical intervention is needed because "the internalized vagina may be a source of urine pooling and infection if left uncorrected."[23] Virilization on a scale of "I. normal female genitals" through "V. mild to medium hypospadias"	
	XY Individuals	Can have higher than average androgen levels May require counseling and/or treatment as puberty can occur early, which stops children from growing taller and can cause them to be very sexual at a young age Not considered an intersex condition	
Ovotestes		Individual is born with one ovary and one testis or a combination of gonads that contains both ovarian and testicular tissue (true hermaphrodite) Sometimes produces ambiguous external genitals but not always	Less than 1/20,000[24]

Gonad Dysgenesis	Swyer Syndrome	XY individuals look female and have functional female genitalia and structures including a vagina, uterus, and fallopian tubes Lack sex glands (ovaries) Instead, have "gonadal streaks," in which the ovaries do not develop properly (aplasia) and are replaced by functionless scar (fibrous) tissue Do not produce sex hormones and will not undergo puberty (unless treated with hormone replacement therapy) Children typically reared as girls and given hormone replacement therapy	
	Turner Syndrome	All or part of one sex chromosome is missing (XO) Causes ovarian failure and other physiological abnormalities Most present as female Many have a mosaic karyotype	1 in 2,500 births; about 10% of spontaneously aborted fetuses have Turner's[25]
Klinefelter Syndrome		Atypical chromosome patterns – XXY, XXYY "A group of chromosomal disorders in males in which one or more extra X chromosomes are present. Males with the classic form of the disorder have one extra X chromosome. Males with other X and Y variations have additional X and/or Y chromosomes. The extra X and/or Y chromosome can affect physical, developmental, behavioral, and cognitive functioning. Common physical features may include tall stature, lack of secondary pubertal development, small testes (hypogonadism), delayed pubertal development, and breast development (gynecomastia) in late puberty. These features may be associated with low testosterone level and elevated gonadotropin levels."[26]	1 in 1,000 births[27]
5-Alpha Reductase Deficiency Syndrome (5-ARDs)		Baby with female or ambiguous genitals at birth whose body is transformed at puberty into that of a male	Rare condition; the exact incidence is unknown. Large families with affected members have been found in several countries, including the Dominican Republic, Papua New Guinea, Turkey, and Egypt.[28]

1 Consortium on the Management of Disorders of Sex Development, "Definition of DSDs," *Clinical Guidelines for the Management of Disorders of Sex Development in Childhood.*

2 Rachael Rettner, "Epigenetics: Definition and Examples," *Livescience* (June 24, 2013), accessed March 20, 2016, www.livescience.com/37703-epigenetics.html.

3 *Biology Online Dictionary*, accessed January 23, 2016, www.biology-online.org/dictionary/Gamete.

4 *Oxford Dictionaries*, s.v. "Gender," accessed February 2, 2016, www.oxforddictionaries.com/definition/english/gender.

5 Eliot, *Pink Brain, Blue Brain*, 3.

6 Judith Marley, "Gender Differences and Distance Education: Major Research Findings and Implications for LIS Education," *Journal of Education for Library and Information Science* 48, no. 1 (Winter 2007): 14.

7 NIH National Cancer Institute, "NCI Dictionary of Cancer Terms," accessed January 19, 2016, www.cancer.gov/publications/dictionaries/cancer-terms.

8 Richardson, *Sex Itself*, 63.

9 Medline Plus Medical Encyclopedia, "Intersex," US National Library of Medicine, accessed January 22, 2016, www.nlm.nih.gov/medlineplus/ency/article/001669.htm.

10 NIH National Human Genome Research Institute, "Talking Glossary of Genetic Terms," accessed January 19, 2016, www.genome.gov/glossary.

11 US National Library of Medicine Medline Plus, "Mosaicism," accessed February 6, 2016, www.nlm.nih.gov/medlineplus/ency/article/001317.html.

12 NIH National Human Genome Research Institute, "Talking Glossary of Genetic Terms," accessed January 19, 2016, www.genome.gov/glossary.

13 Dictionary.com, "Primary Sex Characteristic," accessed February 15, 2016, http://dictionary.reference.com/browse/primary-sex-characteristic.

14 *Mosby's Medical Dictionary*, 8th edition, s.v. "Secondary Sex Characteristic," accessed February 15, 2016, http://medical-dictionary.thefreedictionary.com/secondary+sex+characteristic.

15 *Oxford Dictionaries*, s.v. "Sex," accessed February 14, 2016, www.oxforddictionaries.com/definition/english/sex.

16 Eliot, *Pink Brain, Blue Brain*, 3.

17 *Encyclopaedia Britannica*, s.v. "Sexual Dimorphism," accessed January 19, 2016, www.britannica.com/science/sexual-dimorphism.

18 Megan DeFranza, "I.1. What Is Intersex? Types of Intersex Conditions," in *Sex Difference in Christian Theology*. National Organization for Rare Disorders, "Swyer Syndrome," accessed February 6, 2016, http://rarediseases.org/rare-diseases/swyer-syndrome.

19 ISNA, "Androgen Insensitivity Syndrome," accessed February 6, 2016, www.isna.org/faq/conditions/ais.

20 ISNA, "How Common Is Intersex?" accessed February 6, 2016, http://www.isna.org/faq/frequency.

21 ISNA, "How Common Is Intersex?"

22 ISNA, "How Common Is Intersex?"

23 Consortium on the Management of Disorders of Sex Development, "DSDs and Related Conditions," in *Clinical Guidelines for the Management of Disorders of Sex Development in Childhood*, 6.

24 NORD, "Ovotesticular Disorder of Sex Development," accessed March 20, 2016, http://rarediseases.org/rare-diseases/ovotesticular-disorder-of-sex-development.

25 Colorado State University, "Turner's Syndrome (X Monosomy, Gonadal Dysgenesis)," accessed February 6, 2016, www.vivo.colostate.edu/hbooks/genetics/medgen/chromo_eg/turners.html.

26 National Organization for Rare Disorders, *Klinefelter Syndrome*, accessed February 6, 2016, http://rarediseases.org/rare-diseases/klinefelter-syndrome.

27 ISNA, "How Common Is Intersex?"

28 National Library of Medicine, "5-Alpha-Reductase Deficiency," in *Genetics Home Reference*, accessed February 6, 2016, http://ghr.nlm.nih.gov/condition/5-alpha-reductase-deficiency.

FIGURE 1 • CHROMOSOMES OF THE HUMAN GENOME

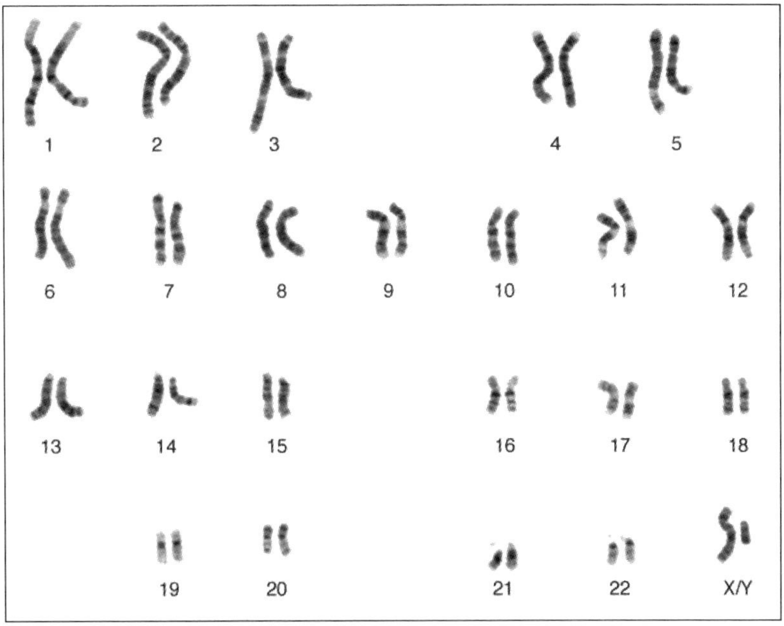

Courtesy: National Human Genome Research Institute and the Smithsonian National Museum of Natural History. "Chromosome" Genome. Unlocking Life's Code, accessed February 21, 2016, https://unlockinglifescode.org/media/images/458?page=1#468.

BIBLIOGRAPHY

(References preceded by * contain descriptions of male/female sex differences.)

Ainsworth, Claire. "Sex Redefined." *Nature* 518 (7539) (February 18, 2015). Accessed February 15, 2016. www.nature.com/news/sex-redefined-1.16943.

*Allchin, Douglas. "Male, Female and/or -? How Does Nature Define the Sexes?" *The American Biology Teacher* 68, no. 6 (August 2006): 372–75.

*Alonso-Nanclares, L., J. Gonzalez-Soriana, J. R. Rodriguez, and J. DeFelipe. "Gender Differences in Human Cortical Synaptic Density." *Proceedings of the National Academy of Sciences of the United States of America* 105, no. 38 (September 2008): 14615–19.

Androutsos, George. "Hermaphroditism in Greek and Roman Antiquity." *Hormones* 5, no. 3 (2006): 214–17.

Bainbridge, David. *The X in Sex: How the X Chromosome Controls Our Lives.* Cambridge, MA and London: Harvard University Press, 2003.

Baker, Robert C., and Charles P. Schaum, eds. *Lutheran Spirituality: Life as God's Child.* St. Louis: Concordia, 2010.

Bancroft, John. "Biological Factors in Human Sexuality." *The Journal of Sex Research* 39, no. 1 (February 2002): 15–21.

Bayer, Oswald, Jeffry G. Silcock, and Mark C. Mattes, eds. and trans., *Theology the Lutheran Way.* Grand Rapids: Eerdmans, 2007.

Berchtold, Nicole C., David H. Cribbs, Paul D. Coleman, et al. "Gene Expression Changes in the Course of Normal Brain Aging Are Sexually Dimorphic." *National Academy of Sciences* 105, no. 10 (October 7, 2008): 15606–10.

Bianconi, Eva, A. Piovesan, F. Facchin, A. Beraudi, et al. "An Estimation of the Number of Cells in the Human Body." *Annals of Human Biology* 40, no. 6 (November–December 2013): 463–71.

Biology Online Dictionary. Accessed January 23, 2016. www.biology-online.org/dictionary.

Blenkinsopp, Joseph. "Reassurance for the Marginal." In *Isaiah 56–66*. The Anchor Bible Volume 19B. New York: Doubleday, 2003.

Bruner, Frederick Dale. *Matthew: A Commentary*. Vol. 2. Dallas: Word Publishing, 1990.

Carlson, Elof Axel. "The Body as a Biological and Genetic Entity." *Social Research* 28, no 2. (Summer 2011): 349–58.

Christian Institute. "Intersex Conditions—Why They Are Different to Transsexuality." (2004) Accessed February 5, 2016. www.christian.org.uk/transsexualism/intersex_briefing.pdf.

Colorado State University. "Turner's Syndrome (X Monosomy, Gonadal Dysgenesis)." www.vivo.colostate.edu/hbooks/genetics/medgen/chromo_eg/turners.html.

Commission on Theology and Church Relations. *Creator's Tapestry: Scriptural Perspectives on Man-Woman Relationships*. St. Louis: LCMS, 2010. www.lcms.org/ctcr/document-library#content-filter:value=tapestry.

———. *Gender Identity Disorder or Gender Dysphoria in Christian Perspective*. St. Louis: LCMS, 2015. www.lcms.org/search?q=intersex.

———. *Women in the Church: Scriptural Principles and Ecclesial Practices*. St. Louis: LCMS, 1985. www.lcms.org/ctcr/document-library#.

Consortium on the Management of Disorders of Sex Development. *Clinical Guidelines for the Management of Disorders of Sex Development in Childhood*. Intersex Society of North America (2006). Accessed February 6, 2016. www.dsdguidelines.org/htdocs/clinical/dsds_defined.html.

Cornwall, Susannah. "Sex Otherwise: Intersex, Christology, and the Maleness of Jesus." *Journal of Feminist Studies in Religion* 30, no. 2 (Fall 2014): 23–39.

———, ed. *Intersex, Theology, and the Bible: Troubling Bodies in Church, Text and Society*. New York: Palgrave MacMillan, 2015.

Davies, W. D., and Dale C. Allison Jr. *A Critical and Exegetical Commentary on the Gospel According to Saint Matthew*. Vol. 3. Edinburgh: T&T Clark, 1997.

Davis, Devra Lee, Pamela Webster, Hillary Stainthorpe, et al. "Declines in Sex Ratio at Birth and Fetal Deaths in Japan, and in US Whites but Not African Americans." *Environmental Health Perspectives* 115, no. 6 (June 2007): 941–46.

*de Vries, Geert J., and Nancy G. Forger. "Sex Differences in the Brain: A Whole Body Perspective." *Biology of Sex Differences* 6, no. 15 (2015). http://bsd.biomedcentral.com/articles/10.1186/s13293-015-0032-z.

DeFranza, Megan. *Sex Difference in Christian Theology: Male, Female, and Intersex in the Image of God*. Grand Rapids: Eerdmans, 2015. Kindle edition.

Dictionary.com, s.v. "Primary Sex Characteristics." Accessed February 15, 2016. http://dictionary.reference.com/browse/primary-sex-characteristic.

Drea, Christine. "Endocrine Mediators of Masculinizaton in Female Mammals." *Current Directions in Psychological Sciences* 18, no. 4 (August 2009): 221–26.

Dreger, Alice D., Cheryl Chase, Aron Sousa, Philip A. Gruppuso, and Joel Frader. "Changing the Nomenclature/Taxonomy for Intersex: A Scientific and Clinical Rationale." *Journal of Pediatric Endocrinology & Metabolism* 18 (2005): 729–33.

Eagleman, David. *The Brain: The Story of You*. Edinburgh and London: Canongate, 2015.

Eliot, Lise. *Pink Brain, Blue Brain*. Oxford: OneWorld Publications, 2010.

Encyclopaedia Britannica. "Sexual Dimorphism." Accessed January 19, 2016. www.britannica.com/science/sexual-dimorphism.

*Fausto-Sterling, Anne. "The Bare Bones of Sex: Part 1—Sex and gender." *Signs* 30, no. 2 (Winter 2005): 1491–1527.

———. *Sexing the Body: Gender Politics and the Construction of Sexuality*. New York: Basic Books, 2000.

*Fausto-Sterling, Anne, Cynthia Garcia Coll, and Meghan Lamarre. "Sexing the Baby: Part I—What Do We Really Know about Sex Differentiation in the First Three Years of Life?" *Social Science & Medicine* 24 (2012): 684–1692.

Ferdenzi, Camille, Jean-François Lemaître, Juan David Leongómez, and S. Craig Roberts. "Digit Ratio (2D:4D) Predicts Facial, but Not Voice or Body Odour, Attractiveness in Men." *Proceedings: Biological Sciences* 278 (1724) (December 7, 2011): 3551–57.

Fujimura, Joan H. "Sex Genes: A Critical Sociomaterial Approach to the Politics and Molecular Genetics of Sex Determination." *Signs* 32, no. 11 (Autumn 2006): 49–82.

*Gabory, Anne, Tessa Roseboom, Tom Moore, Lorna Moore, and Claudine Juniene. "Placental Contribution to the Origins of Sexual Dimorphism in Health and Diseases: Sex Chromosomes and Epigenetics." *Biology of Sex Differences* 4 (2013): 4–14.

Gibbs, Jeffrey A. *Matthew 11:2–20:34*. Concordia Commentary. St. Louis: Concordia, 2010.

Godlee, Fiona. "Two More Genes Are Discovered. 1. The Sex Determining Gene." *BMJ* 301 (1990): 195.

*Goldschmidt, Orly Turgeman, and Leonard Weller. "'Talking Emotions': Gender Differences in a Variety of Conversational Contexts." *Symbolic Interaction* 23, no. 2 (2000): 117–34.

Graham, Kerrie Lewis, and Gordon M. Burghardt. "Current Perspectives on the Biological Study of Play: Signs of Progress." *The Quarterly Review of Biology* 85, no. 4 (December 2010): 393–418.

Harris, R. L., G. L. Archer Jr., and B. K. Waltke, eds. *Theological Wordbook of the Old Testament*. Chicago: Moody Press, 1999. Electronic edition.

Hauerwas, Stanley. *Matthew*. Grand Rapids: Brazos Press, 2006.

Hausman, Bernice L. "Do Boys Have to Be Boys? Gender, Narrativity, and the John/Joan Case." *NWSA Journal* 12, no. 3 (Autumn 2000): 114–38.

Healy, Mary. *Men & Women Are from Eden: A Study Guide to John Paul II's Theology of the Body*. Cincinnati, OH: Servant Books, 2005.

*Hines, Melissa, Mihaela Constantinescu, and Debra Spencer. "Early Androgen Exposure and Human Gender Development." *Biology of Sex Differences* 6, no. 3 (2015). Accessed February 1, 2016. www.bsd-journal.com/content/6/1/3.

Hollinger, Denis P. *The Meaning of Sex: Christian Ethics and the Moral Life*. Grand Rapids: Baker Academic, 2009.

Jastrum, Nathan. "Man as Male and Female: Created in the Image of God." *Concordia Theological Quarterly* 68, no. 1 (January 2004): 5–96.

Joel, Daphne, and Anne Fausto-Sterling. "Beyond Sex Differences: New Approaches for Thinking about Variation in Brain Structure and Function." *Philosophical Transactions of the Royal Society B* (371: 20150451). Accessed February 1, 2016. http://rstb.royalsocietypublishing.org.

Johnson, Olive Skene. *The Sexual Spectrum: Exploring Human Diversity*. Pacific Place Publishing Smashwords Edition, 2004.

Just, Arthur A., Jr. *Luke 1:1–9:50*. Concordia Commentary. St. Louis: Concordia, 1996.

Kleinig, John. "Ordered Community: Order and Subordination in the New Testament." *Lutheran Theological Journal* 17 (2004–5): 45–59.

Kvam, Kristen, Linda S. Schearing, and Valerie H. Ziegler, eds. *Eve and Adam: Jewish, Christian, and Muslim Readings on Genesis and Gender*. Bloomington and Indianapolis, IN: Indiana University Press, 1999.

Lebacqz, Karen. "Difference or Defect? Intersexuality and the Politics of Difference." *Annual of the Society of Christian Ethics* 17 (1997): 213–29.

Lebedev, I. N. "Genomic Imprinting and Human Reproduction." in *Epigenetics and Epigenomics*, edited by Christopher Payne. Rijeka, Croatia: InTech, 2014. Accessed January 25, 2016. www.intechopen.com/books/epigenetics-and-epigenomics/genomic-imprinting-and-human-reproduction.

MacKenzie, Cameron A. "The Origin and Consequences of Original Sin in Luther's *Bondage of the Will*." *Concordia Journal* 31, no. 4 (2005): 384–97.

*Marley, Judith. "Gender Differences and Distance Education: Major Research Findings and Implications for LIS Education." *Journal of Education for Library and Information Science* 48, no. 1 (Winter 2007): 13–20.

Medline Plus Medical Encyclopedia. "Intersex" US National Library of Medicine. Accessed January 22, 2016. www.nlm.nih.gov/medlineplus/ency/article/001669.htm.

Mitchell, Christopher W. *The Song of Songs*. Concordia Commentary. St. Louis: Concordia, 2003.

Mosby's Medical Dictionary, 8th edition. (2009). Accessed February 15, 2016. http://medical-dictionary.thefreedictionary.com/secondary+sex+characteristic.

National Library of Medicine. "5-Alpha-Reductase Deficiency." In *Genetics Home Reference*. Accessed February 6, 2016. http://ghr.nlm.nih.gov/condition/5-alpha-reductase-deficiency.

National Organization for Rare Disorders. "Ovotesticular Disorder of Sex Development." Accessed March 20, 2016. http://rarediseases.org/rare-diseases/ovotesticular-disorder-of-sex-development/.

———. "Swyer Syndrome." Accessed February 6, 2016. http://rarediseases.org/rare-diseases/swyer-syndrome.

NIH National Cancer Institute. *NCI Dictionary of Cancer Terms*. Accessed January 19, 2016. www.cancer.gov/publications/dictionaries/cancer-terms.

NIH National Human Genome Research Institute. Accessed January 19, 2016. *Talking Glossary of Genetic Terms* www.genome.gov/glossary/.

Offner, Susan. "The Y Chromosome." *The American Biology Teacher* 72, no. 4 (April 2010): 235–40.

Oswalt, John N. *The Book of Isaiah: Chapters 40–66*. The New International Commentary on the Old Testament. Grand Rapids: Eerdmans, 1998.

Oxford Dictionaries. "Definition of *hermaphrodite* in English." Accessed February 9, 2016. www.oxforddictionaries.com/definition/english/hermaphrodite.

———. "Gender: Usage." Accessed February 2, 2016. www.oxforddictionaries.com/definition/english/gender.

———. "Sex." Accessed February 14, 2016. www.oxforddictionaries.com/definition/english/sex.

Patterson, R. D., R. L. Harris, G. L. Archer Jr., and B. K. Waltke, eds. *Theological Wordbook of the Old Testament*. Chicago: Moody Press, 634–35. Electronic edition.

Pinker, Steven. *The Blank Slate*. London: Penguin Books, 2002.

Reis, Elizabeth. *Bodies in Doubt: An American History of Intersex*. Baltimore, MD: Johns Hopkins University Press, 2009.

Rettner, Rachel. "Epigenetics: Definition and Examples." *Livescience* (June 24, 2013). Accessed March 20, 2016. www.livescience.com/37703-epigenetics.html.

*Richardson, Sarah S. "How the X Became the 'Female Chromosome.'" *Signs* 37, no. 4 (Summer 2012): 909–33.

———. *Sex Itself: The Search for Male & Female in the Human Genome*. Chicago and London: University of Chicago Press, 2013.

Robcis, Camille. "Catholics, the 'Theory of Gender,' and the Turn to the Human in France: A New Dreyfus Affair?" *The Journal of Modern History* 87, no. 4 (December 2015): 892–923.

Rubin, David A. "'An Unnamed Blank That Craved a Name': A Genealogy of Intersex as Gender" *Signs* 37, no. 4 (Summer 2012): 883–908.

Sato, Takashi, Takahiro Matsumoto, Hirotaka Kawano, et al. "Brain Masculinization Requires Androgen Receptor Function." *Proceedings of the National Academy of Sciences of the United States of America* 101, no. 6 (February 10, 2004): 1673–78.

Small, Chanley M. "Reinventing Sex: The Construction of Realistic Definitions of Sex and Gender." *The American Biology Teacher* 60, no. 8 (October 1998): 590–93.

Soares, Marta C., Redouan Bshary, Leonida Fusani, et al. "Hormonal Mechanisms of Cooperative Behavior." *Philosophical Transactions: Biological Sciences*. 365 (1553) (September 12, 2010): 2737–50.

Society for Women's Health Research. Accessed February 1, 2016. http://swhr.org/.

Stiegemeyer, Scott E. "How Do You Know Whether You are a Man or a Woman?" *Concordia Theological Quarterly* 79 (2015): 19–48.

Swanson, J. *Dictionary of Biblical Languages with Semantic Domains: Hebrew (Old Testament)*. Oak Harbor: Logos Research Systems, Inc. Electronic edition.

US National Library of Medicine. "Mosaicism." In *Medline Plus*. Accessed February 6, 2016. www.nlm.nih.gov/medlineplus/ency/article/001317.htm.

Van Honk, Jack, Dennis J. Schutter, Peter A. Bos, et. al. "Testosterone Administration Impairs Cognitive Empathy in Women Depending on Second-to-Fourth Digit Ratio." *Proceedings of the National Academy of Sciences of the United States of America* 103, no. 8 (February 22, 2011): 3448–52.

Warnke, Georgia. *Debating Sex and Gender*. New York and Oxford: Oxford University Press, 2011.

Watts, John D. W. *Word Biblical Commentary: Isaiah 34–66*. Waco, TX: Word Books Publisher, 1987.

Zhao, Roseanne F. "The Y Chromosome: Beyond Gender Determination" *NIH National Human Genome Research Institute*. Accessed February 15, 2016. www.genome.gov/27557513.

Zodhiates, S. *The Complete Word Study Dictionary: New Testament*. Chattanooga, TN: AMG Publishers, 2000. Electronic edition.

CHAPTER 2

WHAT IS MARRIAGE?

Christopher Wright Mitchell

What is marriage? Answering that question on the basis of Scripture establishes a foundation for the theology and practice of sexual ethics. In short, marriage is a divine institution, a holy estate created by God to enflesh the great mystery of Christ's union with His Bride and Body, the Church.[1] This article will start with the protology, Christology, and eschatology of the marriage theme, drawing on passages from the beginning, "middle," and end of Scripture, then turn to how marriage might be (or has been) called a sacrament, type, prophetic sign, and vocation. After considering divorce, a pastoral conclusion will be offered.[2]

Even aside from Scripture, the natural knowledge of God, attested by the human conscience and general revelation in creation, supports what seems to be an almost universal recognition, not only by adherents of other religions but even by the most strident of pagans, that sexual intimacy transcends ordinary human activity and somehow involves the sacred, contact with the divine, even a mode of worship.[3] Hence marriage is customarily conducted by some kind of representative of a higher authority in a place deemed hallowed (even if only by natural beauty) and with some manner of liturgy in a communal setting.

Divine Institution

Genesis 1 and 2 record the establishment of marriage by God, and even though those chapters take place before the fall into sin (ch. 3), marriage remains the divine institution depicted therein. In Genesis 1:26–28, in one of the first unmistakable revelations of the Trinity ("Let *Us* make . . . Our . . . Our"), God creates man as male and female and inaugurates marriage

1 Here and throughout this essay, unless otherwise stated, the author speaks of "marriage" as the exclusive (monogamous, faithful) lifelong union of one man and one woman, and refers to a "husband," "wife," or "spouse" in such a marriage.

2 Scripture's marriage theme is the principal concern of this author's *The Song of Songs*, Concordia Commentary (St. Louis: Concordia, 2003). Particularly helpful are Richard Batey, *New Testament Nuptial Imagery* (Leiden: Brill, 1971); Ernest Best, *One Body in Christ* (London: SPCK, 1965); and J. Paul Sampley, *"And the Two Shall Become One Flesh": A Study of Traditions in Ephesians 5:21–33* (Cambridge University Press, 1971).

3 In the sexualized pagan culture of modern America, this is evident in popular sacrilegious songs ranging from "Closer (to God)" by Nine Inch Nails (1994) to "Take Me to Church" by Hozier (2013).

as the means by which mankind will fulfill His mandate to propagate and subdue the earth. Then the close-up of that event in the Garden of Eden provided in the following chapter elaborates that the woman was built from the side of Adam, taken from his own flesh, and that in marriage the original unity is surpassed as the two become one flesh (2:22–24).[4] Immediately after the fall into sin, God issues the promise of salvation through the Seed to be born of the woman (3:15), and (marital) procreation will be the means of continuance for the *Protevangelium* until the advent of the (betrothed) Virgin Mary's Son, who crushes Satan and redeems mankind from the curse.[5] Thus marriage cannot be confined to the order of creation (First Article of the Creed) or civil order ("left-hand kingdom") since it serves a vital role in the accomplishment of God's redemption, preservation, and extension of His Church (Second and Third Articles of the Creed; "right-hand kingdom").[6] This is evident when marriage is a means through which God brings about salvation.[7]

The Great Sacramental Mystery

Ephesians 5 reveals the Christological basis and intent of marriage. The relationship between husbands and wives is (to be) patterned after that between Christ and His Church. Yet, Paul goes beyond saying that henceforth marriage is (to be) an imitation of the relationship Christ has now established with His Church through His sacrificial death and resurrection (in the order of redemption). He cites Genesis 2:24 in such a way as to intimate that in the order of creation, marriage was originally insti-

---

4 The Trinity is the Father, Son, and Spirit in eternal union. Genesis 1–2 leaves open the possibility that the Tri-unity of the one God may, in some way, set the pattern for the unity of male and female in marriage. Thomas Winger, *Ephesians*. Concordia Commentary (St. Louis: Concordia, 2015), 618–19, plausibly explains the citation of Genesis 2:24 in Ephesians 5:31 by noting that the Son left His heavenly Father and distanced Himself from His mother (the Virgin Mary) in order to cleave to His wife (the Church). Some other attempts, however, to develop analogies between marriage and the Trinity have strayed into heresy; see Mark W. Elliott, *The Song of Songs and Christology in the Early Church [AD] 381–451* (Tübingen: Mohr Siebeck, 2000), passim.

5 See Genesis 3:15; the patriarchal promises (Genesis 12:1–3; 18:18; 22:17–18; 26:3–4; 28:13–14); Romans 16:20; Galatians 3.

6 The Old Testament genealogies demonstrate that marriage preserved and enlarged the Old Testament Church until the advent of the Seed. Marriage also plays a role in the preservation and extension of the New Testament Church, perhaps most clearly as couples bear children, bring them to Holy Baptism, and raise them in the faith (often through Christian schools) to become the next generation of the Church's members and leaders.

7 That God can and has accomplished salvation through marriage is a historical truth evident in Scripture, not an assertion that marriage itself is a sacrament or means through which God promises to bestow the forgiveness of sins. As scriptural examples, the marriage of a woman is key to the accomplishment of salvation in three Old Testament wisdom books. Through Ruth's marriage she became a progenitor of the Son of David (Ruth 4:17; Matthew 1:5). Esther's marriage to King Ahasuerus enabled her to persuade him to save the Judeans. In the Song of Songs, the Shulammite's marriage to Solomon embodies the salvific love that is stronger than death and is "the flame of Yah" (8:6). In the New Testament, St. Paul may allude to such Old Testament passages, and certainly to Genesis 3:15, when, in his apostolic teaching about Christian women, he declares that the woman "will be saved through childbearing" (*sōthēsetai de dia tēs teknogonias*, 1 Timothy 2:15).

tuted to embody that relationship between Christ and the Church. The one-flesh union of Christ and His Church is in fact "this mystery" that is "great" (Ephesians 5:32).[8] This Christological mystery was already latent in the Old Testament passage. Thus God's institution in Genesis 1–2 had a predictive purpose already in the Old Testament era as a model of the salvific union between Yahweh and Israel that would be fulfilled and clearly revealed at the first advent of Christ. Subsequently in the church age, Christian marriage continues to serve the purpose of enfleshing the love of Christ for His Bride and Body. The husband's life of sacrificing self for his wife displays the love of Christ for her, and their mutual love is a testimony to the world of the mutual love of Christ and His Church.[9]

Ephesians 5:21–33 is laden with sacramental language, most clearly the baptismal "washing of water with the Word" (Ephesians 5:26) made possible by His giving up of Himself for her (5:25).[10] In the context of His death, His feeding and nourishing of her (5:29) alludes to His giving of His flesh as true food and His blood as true drink (John 6:55).[11] In Ephesians 5:22–27, Paul focuses on the wife and Church as "Bride." This hints at partially realized eschatology.[12] But in Ephesians 5:28–31, his emphasis is on the wife/Church as the "Body" of the husband/Christ. The transition to "body" facilitates his sacramental language in these verses, both for Baptism, in which the baptized is bodily washed with water as the Word is spoken, and for the Lord's Supper, wherein the communicant receives the true body

THE RELATIONSHIP BETWEEN HUSBANDS AND WIVES IS TO BE PATTERNED AFTER THAT BETWEEN CHRIST AND HIS CHURCH.

8 See Winger, *Ephesians*, 617–23.

9 This assertion is consistent with John 13:35 but goes beyond it.

10 Biblical allusions to Baptism and the Lord's Supper sometimes use overlapping imagery that may be understood as an indication that both Sacraments bestow the same salvation earned by the death of Christ on the cross. Thus Scripture depicts the saints as those who have "washed their robes and made them white in the blood of the Lamb" (Revelation 7:14; cf. Leviticus 6:27; Isaiah 1:18; Revelation 1:5; 13:4–5; 19:8, 14–15; 22:14), a kind of mixed metaphor, as washing in blood would not naturally render a garment white. Luther similarly connected the blood of Christ with Holy Baptism; see, e.g., his "Sermon on Matt. 3:13–17 at the Baptism of Bernhard von Anhalt," preached in Dessau, April 2, 1540 (AE 51:315–29), particularly AE 51:325.

11 The connection between the baptismal washing of the Bride and her nourishment by the Supper may be compared to the eschatological fulfillment in Revelation 19:7–9, where the Bride is first clothed in bright linen (Baptism; Galatians 3:26) and then invited to partake of the marriage supper of the Lamb. The historic practice of the Church is to administer Baptism before admittance to the Supper.

12 See the discussion of Revelation 21–22 below under "The Eschatological Consummation."

and blood of Christ.[13] It is through these Means of Grace (Word, Baptism, Supper) that the Church enters into her betrothal to Christ and is sustained as His Bride and Body until the wedding supper and consummation of the marriage upon the return of Christ (Revelation 19–22).

The Early Church Father Augustine drew on Ephesians 5:21–33 (also John 19:34–37 and possibly 1 John 5:6–8) to draw a sacramental comparison between the creation of Eve from Adam and the creation of the Church through the Sacraments of Christ.[14] The Greek term *mustērion*, "mystery," which Paul applies to the union between Christ and the Church in Ephesians 5:32, was commonly translated into Latin as *sacramentum*, and that probably facilitated Augustine's association between the Sacraments and the marriage motif:

SEDUCTIVE DALLIANCE IN FALSE DOCTRINE AND ENGAGEMENT IN SYNCRETISTIC WORSHIP LEAD TO INFIDELITY AND ADULTERY.

> And since the Lord has enlightened us through the apostle, to show us what we were in search of, by this one sentence, "The two shall be one flesh; a great mystery concerning Christ and the Church;" [Ephesians 5:31–32] we are now permitted to seek Christ everywhere, and to drink wine from all the water-pots. Adam sleeps, that Eve may be formed [Genesis 2:21]; Christ dies, that the Church may be formed. When Adam sleeps, Eve is formed from his side; when Christ is dead, the spear pierces His side [John 19:34], that the mysteries [*sacramenta*, "Sacraments," referring to the "blood" and "water" in John 19:34] may flow forth whereby the Church is formed.[15]

13 For the Supper, see, e.g., 1 Corinthians 10:16–17; 11:23–27. The point above is supported by additional passages such as 1 Corinthians 6:9–20. There the basis for Christian sexual ethics is that the Christian has been "washed" (bodily in Baptism), "sanctified," and "justified" (6:11); therefore "the body is not for sexual immorality" (6:13), but instead is "a temple of the Holy Spirit" (6:19). Through baptismal union with Christ and reception of His body and blood in the Supper, Christians are "members of Christ" in body and spirit (6:15–17). Sexual immorality severs that holy union by desecrating the body and uniting the flesh to an unlawful partner (6:9, 16, 18; note the quotation of Genesis 2:24 in 1 Corinthians 6:16).

14 This author is not sure which hermeneutical term might be best to characterize Augustine's exegesis, and hence what term might be applied to marriage in his view. Perhaps an "analogy" is best for his method of figuration, although "typology" or marriage as a "sacrament" might also be possible.

15 Augustine, *Homilies on the Gospel of John*, tractate 9.10 (PL 35:1463; *NPNF*[1] 7:66–67), commenting on John 2:6. Compare Augustine's fuller statement of the same idea in *The City of God*, 22:17 (*NPNF*[1] 2:496; PL 41:778–79), and his comments on John 19:34 (tractate 120.2; *NPNF*[1] 7:434–35; PL 35:1953).

The Eschatological Consummation

The first advent of Christ "fulfills" the promises latent in the Old Testament, including the sacramental ("one flesh," Ephesians 5:31) union of Christ and His Church, which is the profound mystery embodied in Christian marriage. At His second advent, Christ "consummates" His relationship with His Church and brings to completion the purpose of Christian marriage.[16] Revelation 19 envisions the wedding supper of the Lamb, and then in Revelation 21 the Church, the holy "Bride" (*numphē*, 21:2), finally becomes Christ's "wife" (21:9).[17]

A central aspect of marriage, then, is the eschatological tension between the "now" (what we already have in Christ) and the "not yet" (fully realized only at the consummation).[18] The Church is the virgin Bride now "betrothed" to Christ, but in the present era she risks forfeiting her place in the future marriage. Seductive dalliance in false doctrine and engagement in syncretistic worship lead to infidelity and adultery.[19] With "divine jealousy" the apostle Paul betrothed the Church in Corinth "to one husband . . . as a pure virgin to Christ," but feared that "as the serpent deceived Eve," she might be seduced away from Christ (2 Corinthians 11:2–3). In the present era, then, the Church must guard her "virginity" (both her purity of faith and her sexual behavior),[20] lest she be excluded from the marriage at Christ's return. This is the main theme of the parable of the wedding (Matthew 22:1–14) and the parable of the ten virgins (Matthew 25:1–13), as they are applicable both to individual Christians and to the corporate Church.[21]

This eschatological tension is vital for sexual ethics. Since "the present form of this world is passing away" (1 Corinthians 7:31), those who are

16 Jesus states that after the resurrection the redeemed "neither marry nor are given in marriage" (Matthew 22:20; see also Mark 12:25; Luke 20:34–36). The earthly purpose of human marriage will have been completed and thus the institution shall end. Yet this does not imply that marriage and conjugal relations in this life are somehow sinful unless they serve the purpose of procreation (as held by some pietists).

17 Revelation 21:9 depicts the Church Triumphant as the glorious new Jerusalem who is "the bride, *the wife* of the Lamb" (*tēn numphēn tēn gunaika tou arniou*). This is the only New Testament passage in which the Church is designated Christ's "wife"; thus, the consummation takes place only at His return. Earlier throughout the New Testament, the Church is depicted as the betrothed Bride of Christ, awaiting the consummation.

18 This tension extends throughout the themes of the New Testament. Exegetes may refer to the "now" as proleptic, inaugurated, or realized eschatology, and the "not yet" as future eschatology.

19 Throughout the Scriptures, idolatry and other forms of apostasy are depicted as adultery. See, e.g., Ezekiel 16 and 23. This is both a spiritual and a physical description of pagan religions (ancient and modern) in which sexual immorality is practiced; thus the spiritual and the literal may overlap in Revelation 21:8; 22:15.

20 That the Church's "virginity" involves both theological purity and sexual fidelity is evident in, e.g., 1 Corinthians 6:9–20. The baptized communicant believer must abstain from idolatry and sexual immorality.

21 In neither parable is there an explicit mention of a bride. How can a wedding take place without one? The implication is that those who attended in (baptismal) wedding garments (Matthew 22:1–14) and the vigilant virgins admitted to the wedding feast (25:1–13) constitute the Bride of Christ.

unmarried are called to lead a life of chastity, and the married are to live in exclusive fidelity until the end of natural life (ch. 7). The ever-present danger is that our sinful human nature will be seduced by the sexual enticements ubiquitous in our culture. Not only does promiscuity physically violate our union with Christ (6:9–20), it also robs the single of their virginity and destroys the holy bond of matrimony; it is the sole grounds allowed by Jesus for divorce (Matthew 5:32; 19:9). Christians, then, are called to live in this tension by mortifying the flesh while drawing new life from our baptismal death and resurrection with Christ (Romans 6) as we await His final deliverance (7:24–25) from our constant battle against sin (*simul iustus et peccator*, ch. 7).[22]

The final chapter of Scripture, Revelation 22, draws together and completes[23] many of these themes. The garden imagery of Eden returns, but the new "paradise" (Luke 23:43; Revelation 2:7) surpasses the original.[24] The "water of life" therein (22:1, 17) recalls the "living waters" in the bridal garden imagery and marital consummation in Song of Songs 4:12–5:1.[25] Jesus elaborates those waters for the marital situation of the woman by the well in John 4[26] and further explicates the "rivers of living water" in terms of His glorification and the baptismal gift of the Spirit in John 7:37–39. The communal wedding banquet (Revelation 19:7–9) along with the eating from the tree of life (22:2, 14; cf. Genesis 2:9 and contrast Genesis 3:22–24) are the feast of which the Lord's Supper is a present foretaste. It is no coincidence that Jesus was buried and raised in a garden, that the Virgin's Son was laid in a virgin tomb (John 19:41), and that He was taken to be the gardener (20:15); where the first gardener (Genesis 2:8) failed, the second One triumphed (cf. Romans 5:12–21). The Scriptures end with eschatological yearning for the eternal bliss of this consummation: "The Spirit and the

22 Romans 7 depicts the daily, ongoing battle against sin experienced by Paul (and every Christian) after his conversion; it does not simply portray Paul's struggle prior to his conversion. See "Who Is the 'I' in Romans 7:14–25? Christian or Non-Christian?" in Michael Middendorf, *Romans*. Concordia Commentary (St. Louis: Concordia, 2013), 584–97.

23 "Completes" attempts to express the verbal idea of *anakephalaiōsasthai* in Ephesians 1:10, where God's eternal goal is for all things be united and subsumed under the headship of Christ, to be accomplished at His return.

24 In the Song of Songs, marital intimacy is portrayed protologically as a return to the paradise of the Garden of Eden, and eschatologically as a proleptic enjoyment of the paradise to come; see "The Garden Paradise" in Mitchell, *The Song of Songs*, 263–74.

25 In the Song of Songs, the virgin bride with these waters is called the "garden locked ... a spring locked, a fountain sealed" (Song of Songs 4:12). She has long been interpreted as a figure of the church as the virgin bride of Christ. See Mitchell, *The Song of Songs*, 837–40, 844–47, 868–73.

26 See William Weinrich, *John 1:1–7:1*. Concordia Commentary (St. Louis: Concordia, 2015), 465–506. See also below under "What about Divorce?"

bride say, 'Come!' . . . Amen. Come, Lord Jesus!" (Revelation 22:17, 20), or in Aramaic, *Maranatha* (1 Corinthians 16:22).[27]

If this Christological, sacramental, ecclesiastical, and eschatological portrait of marriage holds water, then further questions may be asked to flesh out its implications for Christian ethics.

Is Marriage a Sacrament?

The preceding discussion raises the question of whether marriage should be called a sacrament. One simple definition in the Confessions is that "sacraments" are "rites which have the command of God and to which the promise of grace has been added" (Ap XIII 3).[28] Marriage certainly was instituted by God (Genesis 1–2). It involves visible, physical participants—the husband and wife. Normally the pastor speaks the words, "I now pronounce you husband and wife," and God Himself joins the couple together (Matthew 19:6).[29] Marriage has also received God's blessing and promise (Genesis 1:28). But one searches in vain for a divine promise that the forgiveness of sins is conferred on a husband and/or wife by virtue of being united in marriage, so marriage is not a sacrament as defined. In Ephesians 5:21–33, it is Christ's love, not the husband's, that saves. The redemptive love of Christ comes through the baptismal "washing of water with the Word" (5:26), not through the institution of marriage itself.

Another Pauline passage that addresses marriage from a different perspective confirms the preceding. In 1 Corinthians 7:14, St. Paul says that in a marriage of a believer to an unbeliever, the unbelieving spouse has been "sanctified" (*hēgiastai*, the perfect tense of *hagiazō*) by the believing spouse, so that even the children are "holy" (*hagia*), a possible allusion to infant Baptism.[30] The apostle goes on to say that the believing spouse may yet "save" (*sōzō*, 1 Corinthians 7:16) the unbelieving partner. That hope *for the future* implies that the unbeliever is not already saved by virtue of the

27 The Song of Songs concludes with this same eschatological yearning for the Bridegroom to return (Song of Songs 8:13–14).

28 The definition in the 1991 LCMS Explanation (*Luther's Small Catechism with Explanation* [St. Louis: Concordia, 1986, 1991], 197) that a "sacrament is a sacred act instituted by God in which God Himself has joined His Word of promise to a visible element and by which He offers, gives, and seals the forgiveness of sins earned by Christ" is not a direct quote of the Confessions or Luther, but can be inferred from Luther's explanations of Baptism and the Lord's Supper in his Small and Large Catechisms (SC IV 9–10; VI 7–8; LC IV 14, 17–19; V 8–11).

29 One can debate exactly when and how the couple is married. On the one hand, the oral pronouncement in the wedding ceremony is an efficacious speech act, as the pastor speaks on behalf of God. After this word, the couple may consummate the marriage with the blessing of God. Usually the state considers the couple legally married after the completion of the ceremony (along with the signing of the state-required documents). On the other hand, the one-flesh union does not take place until the consummation. It is best, then, to consider the marriage union to be accomplished through the ceremony and the consummation together, not by either apart from the other.

30 See the commentary on 1 Corinthians 7:12–16 by Gregory Lockwood, *1 Corinthians*. Concordia Commentary (St. Louis: Concordia, 2000), 240–44.

state of being "sanctified" (7:14) through his or her marriage to a believer. Therefore, Paul's statement that the unbeliever in the mixed marriage is "sanctified" (7:14) may mean that the marriage has God's blessing and approval; that through the baptized Christian spouse, the sanctifying Word of the Gospel is present in the marriage; and/or that through the initiative of the Christian spouse the children may have been baptized into Christ. But Paul's statement does not mean that the forgiveness of sins comes to the unbeliever through marriage itself. However, at some future time the unbeliever may be brought to faith in Christ and to Baptism by the power of the Holy Spirit, who works through the Gospel proclaimed by the Christian spouse, and then the presently unbelieving spouse would most assuredly receive the forgiveness of sins.[31]

> CHRISTIAN MARRIAGE IS A PUBLIC WITNESS TO THE WORLD OF GOD'S SALVATION IN CHRIST, OF WHAT IS, WHAT WAS, AND WHAT IS TO COME.

The younger Luther did call marriage a sacrament in that he considered it a sign of "the union of the divine and human natures in Christ":

> [The doctors say] that it [marriage] is a sacrament. A sacrament is a sacred sign of something spiritual, holy, heavenly, and eternal, just as the water of baptism, when the priest pours it over the child, means that the holy, divine, eternal grace is poured into the soul and body of that child at the same time, and cleanses him from his original sin. This also means that the kingdom of God, which is an inestimable benefit, in fact immeasurably greater than the water which conveys this meaning, is within him. In the same way the estate of marriage is a sacrament. It is an outward and spiritual sign of the greatest, holiest, worthiest, and noblest thing that has ever existed or ever will exist: the union of the divine and human natures in Christ. The holy apostle Paul says that as man and wife united in the estate of matrimony are two in one flesh, so God and man are united in the one person Christ, and so Christ and Christendom are one body. It is indeed a wonderful sacrament, as Paul says [Ephesians 5:32]. . . . Is it not a wonderful thing that God is man and

31 Cf. 1 Peter 3:1–2, where the apostle holds out the hope that Christian wives may win over their husbands through the purity and reverence of their lives; husbands who do not believe "the Word" may be persuaded "without words" (1 Peter 3:1).

> that he gives himself to man and will be his, just as the husband gives himself to his wife and is hers? But if God is ours, then everything is ours.[32]

Writing this in 1519, Luther appeals more to the doctors of the Church than to Scripture itself. His description of Baptism as conveying the forgiveness only of "*original* sin" plus the concessions to works-righteousness in the surrounding context[33] are further indications that not too much weight should rest on this early view.

In some places, the Lutheran Confessions allow for the inclusion of marriage among "sacraments," but only under a more general definition of a sacrament as a rite instituted by God and accompanied by certain divine promises, not necessarily the forgiveness of sins. Thus Melanchthon, representing the Lutheran viewpoint, allowed that marriage "has the command of God as well as certain promises that pertain . . . to the bodily life. Therefore, whoever wishes to call it a sacrament should still distinguish it from the preceding ones,[34] which are . . . testimonies of grace and the forgiveness of sins" (Ap XIII 14).

The Roman Catholic tradition counts seven sacraments, including matrimony, which are said to convey grace and salvation.[35] Similarly, the Eastern Orthodox tradition also considers marriage to be a sacrament that conveys grace.[36] However, the Roman tradition defines the sacramental nature of marriage as being of a different kind: "Two other sacraments, Holy Orders and Matrimony, are directed towards the salvation of others; if they contribute as well to personal salvation, it is through service to others that they do so."[37] That statement is to be applauded insofar as it emphasizes that Christian marriage is to be characterized by the selfless, sacrificial giving of oneself for the benefit of the other—as Paul says most directly to husbands in Ephesians 5:21–33. Most certainly, the Christian should be

---

32 "A Sermon on the Estate of Marriage" (1519), AE 44:10. Compare the discussion of this and other statements by Luther in Thompson, "Toward a Confessional Practice of Pre-Marriage Pastoral Care" (*Logia* 6/2 [Eastertide 1997]: 11–15). Luther denies that marriage should be called a sacrament in *The Babylonian Captivity of the Church* (1520), AE 36:94–95 (cited in Winger, *Ephesians*, 622 note 106). Johann Gerhard (1582–1637), "De conjugio," *Loci*, 7:1–468, affirms that the personal union in Christ is a kind of marriage attested in Scripture. Gerhard also recognizes the marriage of husband and wife; the sacramental or mystical marriage of Christ and the corporate Church; the spiritual marriage of God and the soul of the individual believer; but rejects the idea in Roman canon law that a bishop is married to his church or diocese.

33 AE 44:12–14.

34 By "the preceding ones" Melanchthon refers to "baptism, the Lord's Supper, and absolution" (Ap XIII 4).

35 *Catechism of the Catholic Church*, §§ 774–76.

36 John Karmiris, "Concerning the Sacraments," in *Eastern Orthodox Theology: A Contemporary Reader*, ed. Daniel B. Clendenin (Grand Rapids: Baker, 1995), 22, 30–31.

37 *Catechism of the Catholic Church*, § 1534

concerned for the salvation of the spouse and the children. But to ascribe to the institution of marriage itself the ability to "contribute . . . to . . . salvation" exceeds what can be supported by the Scriptures and distorts the biblical doctrine of justification.[38]

More satisfactory than *sacrament*, in this author's opinion, is the hermeneutical terminology that marriage may serve as a *type* or a *prophetic sign* of the salvific relationship between God and His people, and specifically that of Christ and His Church. Most readily applicable is *vocation*.

Is Marriage a Type?

While *sacrament* is inadvisable for reasons given above, the broader category of typology is helpful, and some biblical scholars speak of types as sacramental. That is to say, biblical types are salutary works of God that have a physical dimension or element accompanied by interpretive words. Old Testament types are commonly identified as persons and offices (e.g., prophet, priest, king), places (the Promised Land; Jerusalem), events (the exodus), and institutions (the temple and its worship) that prefigured and are fulfilled in the incarnation, ministry, death, and resurrection of Jesus Christ, and that will be consummated upon His return.[39] Marriage fits well in this framework.

A type is a miniature "working model," imperfect and yet efficacious for a divine purpose, of what was or is to come, and/or of what is above. Scripture refers to "horizontal types," which function diachronically in history, relating the past to the present and toward the future.[40] Marriage serves in this way as a sacred institution established by divine words spoken over people at creation, reenacted throughout human history, instantiated now in Christian marriages and the betrothal of Christ to His Church, to be consummated at the eschaton. Christ, the heavenly Bridegroom, visibly came (Matthew 9:15; John 3:29); the Church is betrothed now, awaiting His return. What is more, these realities are visibly typified by the one-flesh unions of Christian couples. As they live in loving fidelity, they enact what God intended and what He has and will restore in Christ. Christian

38 The view that marriage is a sacrament seems inseparable from a transformational doctrine of justification. Cf. Michael Lawler, *Marriage and Sacrament: A Theology of Christian Marriage* (Collegeville: Liturgical Press, 1993), 14.

39 For treatments of typology and related hermeneutics see, e.g., Horace Hummel, *The Word Becoming Flesh* (St. Louis: Concordia, 1979), 16–18 and Richard Davidson, *Typology in Scripture* (Barrien Springs, MI: Andrews University Press, 1981). Particularly helpful is Sidney Greidanus, *Preaching Christ from the Old Testament* (Grand Rapids: Eerdmans, 1999).

40 See, e.g., Adam as a type of Christ in Romans 5:14; Old Testament events that serve as types for the Church in 1 Corinthians 10:6, 11; and Baptism as the saving "antitype" of the Noahic flood in 1 Peter 3:21.

marriage is a public witness to the world of God's salvation in Christ, of what is, what was, and what is to come.

Is Marriage a Prophetic Sign?

Old Testament prophets often acted out dramatizations that signified their divine messages.[41] For some, their marriages were intended to portray the dynamics of God's own relationship with His people, either in judgment or in grace, in which case they prophesied the union of Christ and His Church. Each situation was unique. For Isaiah, the repetition of Hebrew terminology might suggest that the child naturally conceived and born by his wife (Isaiah 8:3–4) could be a sign of the future virgin birth of Immanuel (7:14; 9:6–7).[42] More clearly developed is the symbolism of Ezekiel's marriage: his delightful wife signifies the delightful Jerusalem temple and dies to portend the Babylonians' destruction of the sanctuary. The prophet is told not to mourn his wife as a sign to the Israelites that the temple's judgment was just (Ezekiel 24:15–27). Three chapters (Hosea 1–3) are devoted to the marriage of Hosea and Gomer, a prostitute whose whoredom dramatizes that of Israel, and their three children bear names prophesying the divine judgment of the apostate people. Yet, instead of divorcing her, God then instructs Hosea to redeem her and keep her as his wife to signify that God will once again betroth to Himself a people forever and call them His own (Hosea 2:19–23; see Romans 9:25–26). A literal marriage laden with Gospel motifs is that of Solomon in the Song of Songs; see also the messianic royal marriage in Psalm 45.

> HOLY MATRIMONY IS THEN RIGHTLY CALLED A SIGN, AN EVANGELICAL WITNESS TO THE WORLD OF THE FIDELITY, LOVE, AND FORGIVENESS THAT CHARACTERIZES CHRIST'S ATTACHMENT TO HIS CHURCH.

One married Roman Catholic theologian references Old Testament prophetic dramas to contend that marriage is

> a religious, prophetic symbol, proclaiming, revealing and celebrating in the human world the communion between

41 See, e.g., Jeremiah 19 and Ezekiel 4–5.

42 She is called *hannebi'ah,* "the prophetess," in Isaiah 8:3 not because she prophesied but because of her union to the prophet. The Hebrew vocabulary from 7:14, repeated in 8:3, includes the feminine verbs "conceive" and "give birth," the noun "son," and the formula for naming, "to call his name." In any case, Isaiah's sons and their names had prophetic significance: "Behold, I and the children Yahweh gave to me for signs and portents in Israel" (8:18; cf. also 7:3).

> God and God's people. . . . Lived within this context of grace, lived within faith . . . marriage appears as a two-tiered reality. On one tier, it signifies the mutually covenanted love of this man and this woman. . . . On another, more profound level, it proclaims, makes explicit and celebrates the intimate communion of life and love and grace . . . between Christ and Christ's people, the Church.[43]

The *Catechism of the Catholic Church* declares that "by their own faithfulness" Christian spouses "can be witnesses to God's faithful love."[44] That marriage is a "witness," as the spouses faithfully *show* love, is in keeping with passages such as 1 Corinthians 7 and Ephesians 5:21–33, and avoids the claim that marriage itself is a means through which spouses *receive* God's love. The *Catechism* also uses the terms *image* and *sign*: "Since God created . . . man and woman, their mutual love becomes an image of the absolute and unfailing love with which God loves man."[45] As for John 2:1–11, which narrates Jesus' first "sign" at the wedding in Cana, the Church "sees in it the confirmation of the goodness of marriage and the proclamation that thenceforth marriage will be an efficacious sign of Christ's presence."[46]

> A JOYFUL CHRISTIAN MARRIAGE IS LIKELY TO PROVIDE BOTH SPOUSES WITH AN ABUNDANCE OF EXUBERANT LOVE THAT SPILLS OVER INTO ALL OF THEIR OTHER VOCATIONS IN LIFE.

On the one hand, it would be tenuous to suppose all marriages have the same prophetic significance as those in Scripture. Isaiah, Ezekiel, and Hosea received verbal revelations of how and why they were to interact with their wives as they did as part of their preaching to Israel. On the other hand, we certainly may affirm that a pastor who combines sound doctrine with a vibrant and healthy marriage will be a model of faithfulness, both to the congregation he serves and to the unbelieving world. His marriage will help confirm his sincerity and the genuineness of the Christian faith he preaches. More broadly, every Christian marriage, insofar as the spous-

43 Lawler, *Marriage and Sacrament*, 13–14.

44 *Catechism of the Catholic Church*, § 1648.

45 *Catechism of the Catholic Church*, § 1604.

46 *Catechism of the Catholic Church*, § 1613. "Efficacious" would need careful definition in this context.

es live by grace,[47] serves as a prophetic sign that portends the present betrothal between Christ and His Church, and that joyfully yearns for the consummation at Christ's second coming. Holy matrimony is then rightly called a sign, an evangelical witness to the world of the fidelity, love, and forgiveness that characterizes Christ's attachment to His Church. A marriage that lasts attests that "love bears all things, believes all things, hopes all things, endures all things" (1 Corinthians 13:7).

Scripture can also ascribe a prophetic significance to singleness, celibacy, and the foregoing of children, as for Jeremiah and Paul. God mandated Jeremiah to remain celibate and childless to portend the impending judgment that would destroy the world order in which God's people lived (Jeremiah 16:2), the fall of Jerusalem (587 BC) and exile to Babylon. Paul's celibacy apparently was by choice, not by divine command (1 Corinthians 7:7–9), and through him God provides an explanation of the prophetic significance of a celibate life chosen by Christians who have the gift of continence (7:29–35). Celibacy is a sign that the present world is passing away (7:31) and the Christian's hope is for "the life of the world to come" (Nicene Creed), where marriage will have passed away.[48]

Marriage as a Vocation

Marriage certainly is a *vocation* or calling in life to which the Gospel applies.[49] "God who created man out of love also calls him to love—the fundamental and innate *vocation* of every human being."[50] Each believer is to "love your neighbor as yourself" (Leviticus 19:18; Matthew 19:19; 22:39), and this begins with the closest "neighbors," those who are fellow members of the household of faith (Galatians 6:10) and heirs of the grace of life (wives in 1 Peter 3:7). A joyful Christian marriage is likely to provide both spouses with an abundance of exuberant love that spills over into all of their other vocations in life.

The Lutheran tradition considers marriage a holy estate instituted by the Creator upon which His favor rests as Christian spouses live in love and fidelity, but also a vocation that is not intrinsically superior or inferior to

47 An excellent practical and pastoral treatment of this topic is given by Peter Kurowski, *The Lifelines of Love* (Pleasant Word, A Division of WinePress Publishing, 2007).

48 See "The Outstanding Service of Single and Childless Christians in 'the Things of the Lord' " in Lockwood, *1 Corinthians*, 260–61.

49 The term *vocation*, derived from Latin, reflects the Greek vocabulary of "call" and "calling" (*kaleō, klēsis*) as in 1 Corinthians 7:15–24, in a context where the apostle speaks of the divine callings of singlehood and marriage. Cf. Gene Edward Veith Jr. and Mary J. Moerbe, *Family Vocation* (Wheaton, IL: Crossway, 2012).

50 *Catechism of the Catholic Church*, § 1604; emphasis added.

other stations in life. That is a predominant theme in Luther's discussions of marriage.[51] Similarly, in the Lutheran Confessions, the theme of Apology XXIII, "The Marriage of Priests," is that the Word of God, received in faith, hallows the marriage relationship, as indeed it hallows the entirety of the Christian's life of faith:

> Marriage is pure in believers because it is sanctified by the Word of God, that is, it is a matter that the Word of God permits and approves, as Scripture testifies abundantly. For Christ calls marriage a divine union when he says [Matthew 19:6], "What God has joined together . . ." And Paul says about marriage, foods, and similar things [1 Timothy 4:5] that they are "sanctified by God's Word and by prayer," that is, through the Word, by which the conscience is made certain that God approves, and through prayer, that is, through faith, which uses marriage with thanksgiving as a gift of God. . . . In every human creature a good work of a particular calling ought to follow faith. This work pleases God on account of faith.[52]

What about Divorce?

As sinners living in a broken world, Christians too may suffer a host of failed relationships, such as the inability to find a suitable spouse, infertility, infidelity, and widowhood, just to mention some. The Torah of Moses includes provisions designed to restrict divorce and protect women from abuse, but the "hardness of heart" that remains even among God's people still causes it.[53] God hates divorce (Malachi 2:16), yet permits it in some circumstances (Matthew 19:9; 1 Corinthians 7:15), although Christians may nevertheless find themselves divorced outside of those circumstances and against their will.

On the one hand, we must not minimize the evil of rending asunder what God has joined together (Matthew 19:6). Throughout Scripture, there is a correlation between sexual infidelity, idolatry, and "divorce" from

51 See, for example, "A Sermon on the Estate of Marriage" (1519; AE 44:7–14); the section on marriage in *The Babylonian Captivity of the Church* (1520; AE 36:92–106); and "The Estate of Marriage" (1522; AE 45:17–49).

52 Ap XXIII 28–30, 32.

53 See Jeffrey Gibbs, *Matthew 11:2–20:34*, 949–53, commenting on Matthew 19:3–9. Contrary to Pharisaic and modern misconceptions of the Torah, it does not command or sanction divorce. Rather, it allows for divorce in case of infidelity and furnishes a number of protections for women (e.g., Exodus 20:17; 21:3–10; 22:16; Leviticus 18:8, 14–20; Deuteronomy 20:7; 22:13–19, 25–30; 24:1–4). The Torah was "countercultural" since it opposed ancient Near Eastern cultures that sanctioned infidelity and spousal abuse.

God.[54] Divorce is a breaking of a divine covenant (Malachi 2:14–16).[55] If marriage embodies the mutual love of Jesus Christ and His Church, then divorce exhibits a deficiency or absence of Christian faith and love.

On the other hand, God has provided plenary forgiveness in Christ, the ever-faithful Bridegroom (cf. 2 Timothy 2:13), for the worst of sinners (1 Timothy 1:15) and all manner of sins. The biblical marriage paradigm includes abundant provision for pardon and restoration to full participation in the marital love of Christ for His Church. Once again, Hosea 1–3 illustrates this as a human marriage simultaneously signifies the marital relationship of God and His people.[56] Gomer's harlotry was grounds for divorce,[57] but Hosea, acting on the divine command, redeems her and reclaims her as his wife (3:2–3) as a prophetic sign of what God will do for His harlot people (2:1–23).[58] The same truth is portrayed prophetically (verbally, absent an actual human marriage) in Jeremiah 2–3. Since Yahweh's "wife" has gone awhoring, he asks (3:1), "A man divorces his wife and she goes from with him and becomes [the wife of] another man, will he return to her again?"

God sent Israel away with a certificate of divorce (Jeremiah 3:8), yet, astonishingly, He promises to restore the people as His own (3:14–18). Ezekiel 16 and 23 are notoriously explicit sexual allegories of the harlotries of Yahweh's wife that have severed her marriage covenant, and yet the first concludes with an even more shocking great reversal: the Gospel promise that not only Israel but even her "sisters" Sodom and Gomorrah (!) shall be restored and given to her as her daughters when Yahweh establishes an everlasting covenant and makes atonement (16:53–63).

Christ's interaction with the Samaritan woman in John 4 serves as a paradigm for the forgiveness and restoration of those who have endured broken marriages. The marriage theme of Christ the Bridegroom now

---

54 Many biblical passages associate sexual immorality with idolatry and exclusion from the people of God. See, e.g., the golden calf incident in Exodus 32 and its ecclesiastical application in 1 Corinthians 10:1–13; the worship of Baal of Peor in Numbers 25 (Psalm 106:28); and New Testament texts such as Acts 15:20, 29; Colossians 3:5; Jude 7; Revelation 2:20–21; 21:8. "Antonymous Texts with Adulterous Language" in Mitchell, *The Song of Songs*, 62–64, cites in particular Ezekiel 16 and 23; Hosea; and Babylon the harlot in Revelation 17–19.

55 See Gordon Hugenberger, *Marriage as Covenant: Biblical Law and Ethics as Developed from Malachi* (Grand Rapids: Baker, 1998).

56 The Old Testament paradigm differs somewhat from that of the New (see the "betrothal" theme above under "The Great Sacramental Mystery" and "The Eschatological Consummation" above). The Old Testament picture is that Yahweh "married" Israel by the exodus redemption and subsequently she was His "wife" (see Jeremiah 2:2; Ezekiel 16:8–10; also the Jewish Midrash on the Song of Songs, *Shir HaShirim Rabbah*), not simply His betrothed bride.

57 If the Hebrew of Hosea 1:2 ("woman/wife of harlotries") suggests that Gomer had already been involved in prostitution, then Hosea's initial action of marrying her is an additional sign of the forgiving love of the God who "marries" Himself to sinners. Cf. Romans 5:6–10.

58 Thus the Old Testament prophecy is not just verbal; the prophetic Word is attached to physical elements, people, in a way that might be called sacramental.

come for His Bride is a subtext throughout chapters 2–4 of this Gospel, each time associated with the baptismal image of water, and it resurfaces in 4:7–18.[59] This woman's admission of five previous husbands may allude to the five heathen nations who, with their false gods, inhabited Samaria after God punished the Northern Kingdom of Israel for her adulteries (1 Kings 17). Her current lack of a husband (true Bridegroom) is apropos for an adherent of the syncretistic Samaritan religion. Jesus, however, in effect, extends to her an invitation to marriage.[60] This discourse in John 4 also looks forward to Jesus' words at the Feast of Tabernacles that foretell of living water that will flow from His side (7:37–39) and to the death of Jesus, when Jesus hands over the Spirit (19:30), and water and blood flow from His side (19:34).[61] The wedding supper of the Lamb is by invitation only (Revelation 19:7–9). God graciously extends this invitation to all through the bridal washing of Baptism and until the consummation He sustains His betrothed through the sacramental foretaste of this feast.

Conclusion

The Christological, sacramental, ecclesiastical, and eschatological contours of Christian marriage explored above may be summarized by affirming that it is a holy estate, created by God to enflesh the great mystery of Christ's union with His Bride and Body, the Church, who is now His betrothed Bride, called to live in exclusive fidelity to Him as she awaits His return, when she will become "the wife of the Lamb" (Revelation 21:9). This conception is no novelty, for it underlies the Lutheran marriage liturgy: "Marriage is an honorable estate instituted and blessed by God in Paradise, before humanity's fall into sin. In marriage we see a picture of *the communion between Christ and His bride, the Church.*"[62]

Fittingly, the closing benediction recalls Eden and, by way of reference to the end of natural life, encourages the couple to live in anticipation of the eschaton:

---

59 At the wedding in Cana (John 2:1–11), an abundance of water was turned into wine, and John 3:29 is in the context of baptizing with water (3:22–26). See Weinrich, *John 1:1–7:1*, 488–92.

60 William Weinrich, *John 1:1–7:1*, p. 492: "When the woman says about the 'living water' (Jn 4:10), 'Give me this water' (Jn 4:15), Jesus invites the woman to the true marriage between God and his people. This marriage will be celebrated and characterized by the eschatological worship 'in Spirit and Truth' (Jn 4:23–24)."

61 See the role of John 19:34 in Augustine's sacramental marriage analogy described above in "The Great Sacramental Mystery." See further Weinrich, *John 1:1–7:1*, 469–71.

62 "Holy Matrimony" in *Lutheran Service Book: Agenda* (St. Louis: Concordia, 2006), 65; emphasis added. This pastoral address is well supported by the rite's traditional Epistle Reading from Ephesians 5. The Christological, sacramental, and ecclesiastical aspects of marriage are implicitly affirmed by the rubrics (p. 64) for the marriage rite to be incorporated into the Divine Service with Holy Communion.

> The almighty and gracious God abundantly grant you His favor and sanctify and bless you with the blessing given to Adam and Eve in Paradise, that you may please Him in both body and soul and live together in holy love until your life's end.[63]

The Church displays the plenary forgiveness of sins showered by the Bridegroom upon all baptized and communicant members of His Body by conducting this same wedding liturgy for the remarriage of those divorced and for all who purify themselves in hopeful expectation of the Bridegroom's return no matter what sins may lie in their past (1 John 3:2–3; cf. 1:8–9).

63 *Lutheran Service Book: Agenda*, 69.

CHAPTER 3

POLYGAMY AND ITS CONTEMPORARY VARIATIONS IN BIBLICAL PERSPECTIVE

David A. Kind

Introduction

The practice of polygamy has made a comeback in popular culture. No longer is the idea of having multiple spouses or of having multiple committed sexual partners met with the same kind of outrage and revulsion it used to evoke. Once the secret practice of a few isolated, aberrant groups, polygamy has burst onto the popular scene through television series, such as HBO's *Big Love*, TLC's *Sister Wives* and *My Five Wives*, and National Geographic's *Polygamy USA*, all of which portray the practice in a relatively positive light.[1] This is not to say that there haven't been popular critiques of the practice—LMN's *Escaping Polygamy* for example. But for the most part, the practice of polygamy has been treated as a positive lifestyle choice, much as the popular media has portrayed and promoted homosexuality and the LGBTQ culture.

In the great debate over the definition of marriage, the fact that polygamy was practiced by prominent figures in the Bible has been used to help dismantle the strict definition of marriage as "one man and one woman" by those who wished to open marriage to homosexual couples. The homosexual movement has now moved on to promote polygamy among their own ranks as well, as is evidenced by the relatively new phenomenon of "throupling."[2] The general argument for all such arrangements and sexual practices follows the tired lines of "who am I to judge," and "people should be free to love whomever they choose to love."

Christians, with good reason, are often confused by the arguments of popular culture, especially when those arguments make use of biblical po-

1 Practitioners of polygamy cite many benefits, including a sense of sorority among multiple wives, a greater division of domestic labor, and a broader skill set among wives, better socialization of children who often have multiple siblings in their own age group, etc.

2 Throupling refers to the practice of having three mutually committed partners in a homosexual relationship.

lygamy.[3] That polygamy features prominently in the Old Testament, and without clear statements of condemnation, is troublesome to many and is an issue that even the finest theologians of the Church, men such as St. Augustine and Martin Luther, struggled over. A few Christians nowadays even argue that polygamy is a more God-pleasing practice than monogamy, that having multiple wives is a better reflection of God and His Church.[4]

So what are Christians to make of this matter? How does one properly understand what the Bible has to say about polygamy or other polyamorous relationships? From where does the practice of polygamy arise in the Bible? Does the fact that patriarchs such as Abraham, Jacob, Gilead, David, and Solomon had multiple wives teach Christians that polygamy is an acceptable, or even blessed, practice? What should we make of the regulation of certain aspects of polygamy in the Mosaic Law? What, if anything, does Jesus have to say about the matter?

Hermeneutics

To begin any discussion concerning what the Bible teaches about a matter, one must apply a consistent and faithful hermeneutic to the biblical text. Without such a hermeneutic, one can make the Scriptures appear to teach whatever one wishes them to teach. Such hermeneutics must flow from the text of Scripture itself first. It is not the intent of this essay to give an exhaustive set of rules for biblical interpretation. However, there are several points that will be important to understand if one is to deal properly with the issue of polygamy in the Scriptures.

If one honestly believes the Holy Scriptures to be inspired by God and without error, then one cannot simply dismiss what the Scriptures teach nor can one temper that teaching because of external factors, such as one's own contemporary culture or private desires. Popular arguments, such as "freedom of choice" or "freedom to love whomever one wishes to love," will therefore have no bearing against the biblical texts or the overarching theology presented in Scripture about this subject, as such concepts do not flow from Scripture, but rather from contemporary postmodern thought.

3 Biblical polygamy is more properly termed *polygyny* (the practice of having multiple wives simultaneously). The practices of polyandry (having multiple husbands) or of any other form of polyamory are not found in the Scriptures. The term *polygamy* will be used throughout this essay according to its common usage, indicating the practice of polygyny, not polyandry or homosexual polyamory. This essay will not deal with other forms of polygamy, such as clerical bigamy, digamy, or successive polygamy. John Witte Jr. offers a chart helpful in understanding the various forms of polygamy on page 28 of his excellent book *The Western Case for Monogamy over Polygamy* (Cambridge University Press, 2015).

4 See, for example, the website christianpolygamy.com.

Rather, one will allow Scripture to interpret itself, the clearer passages informing one's understanding of the passages that are more ambiguous. Moreover, one must not take passages or even entire stories of the Bible out of context. One must pay attention both to the immediate context in which the passage is found and the broader context of the whole of Scripture and its overarching themes and teaching. One must also interpret the passage with its literary genre in mind. A historical passage must be read as history, while a poetic passage must be interpreted as such. One must also be careful to avoid eisegesis, the practice of reading an idea or presuppositions into a text. Moreover, one ought not make an argument solely on the basis of what one does *not* find in Scripture, but on the basis of what one *does* find.

> POLYGAMY IS NOT ORIGINAL TO THE CREATED ORDER ESTABLISHED BY GOD.

The Origins of Polygamy in the Scriptures

To understand what the Scriptures teach concerning polygamy, it will be helpful to examine the origins of the practice according to the biblical record. Polygamy is not original to the created order established by God. Adam was not given multiple wives, but one wife, Eve. The *sedes doctrina* of marriage is found in Genesis 2:24: "Therefore a man shall leave his father and his mother and hold fast to his wife, and they shall become one flesh." This passage is cited both by Jesus and by St. Paul as the determinative statement about what constitutes a marriage. The Septuagint version of Genesis, which both Jesus and St. Paul quote, makes it clear that the "they" of "they shall become one flesh" is defined as "two": *kai esontai oi duo eis sarka mian*. No provision is made here for polygamous marriage.

There is no evidence of polygamy being practiced among prediluvian man until the seventh generation of mankind. "And Lamech took two wives. The name of the one was Adah, and the name of the other Zillah" (Genesis 4:19). Moreover, Lamech is the only prediluvian who is mentioned as having had more than one wife. Who was this Lamech and what is his significance in the biblical record?

It has already been stated that Lamech is among those of the seventh generation. His descent from Adam, however, is not through the line of Seth (in which there are no recorded cases of polygamous marriages), but through the line of Cain. This is no minor point. That the line of Cain is included in the Genesis genealogies seems strange at first, for his line presumably dies out with the great flood of Genesis 6 in which the entire race is exterminated by God, with the exception of the family of Noah, who is a descendant not of Cain, but of Seth. Why is Cain's line recorded at all? This is not simply a stub that was included in Moses' account from an earlier source document, but was included for a specific reason. It is generally recognized that Moses includes this brief excursus into Cain's line as a record of the degeneration into sin and unbelief of those who had rejected the faith prior to the flood.[5] The record of Cain's line is characterized not by godliness and piety, but by human achievement and self-sufficiency.

THE LACK OF EXPLICIT CONDEMNATION HERE (AND ELSEWHERE) SHOULD NOT BE TAKEN AS A TACIT ACCEPTANCE OF POLYGAMY BY MOSES OR BY GOD.

The record of the line of Cain begins with Cain building a city and ends with the achievements of Lamech's sons, two of whom are called "fathers" of "those who dwell in tents and have livestock," and of "all those who play the lyre and pipe," and the third called: "the forger of all instruments of bronze and iron." It is implied from the use of the term *father* in relation to Lamech's sons that there were further generations in this line that are not recorded. Moses was not interested in giving an exhaustive genealogy, but rather in portraying the idolatry of man, showing mankind's sin and rebellion in the form of human accomplishment apart from faith in God. The blessed Martin Luther writes concerning this:

> The Holy Spirit relates these things that we may realize that at the very beginning there were two kinds of churches: the one, that of the children of Satan and of the flesh, which quickly makes great increases; the other, that of the children of God, which makes slow gains and is weak. Although Scripture does not relate how they lived with each other, nevertheless, because it is stated: "I shall put enmity between you and her Seed," it is certain that Cain's church was most hostile toward the church of Adam. Our text also indicates very plainly that the children of men became so predominant in power that they destroyed almost the entire

5 This is not the only explanation that has been offered for the inclusion of Cain's line in Genesis 4. Some have speculated that Lamech's daughter, Namaah, became the wife of Noah. While this opinion would explain the reason that her name is identified by Moses (and besides the names of Lamech's wives, no other female name is recorded after Eve's), there is no evidence whatsoever that connects her to Noah, or to anyone else for that matter.

> church of the sons of God. In the Flood only eight people were saved. All the rest of the race perished in the waters because of their sin.[6]

Luther's thoughts here flow also from the summary of the prediluvian civilization provided by Moses in Genesis 6:1–5:

> When man began to multiply on the face of the land and daughters were born to them, the sons of God saw that the daughters of man were attractive. And they took as their wives any they chose. Then the Lord said, "My Spirit shall not abide in man forever, for he is flesh: his days shall be 120 years." The Nephilim were on the earth in those days, and also afterward, when the sons of God came in to the daughters of man and they bore children to them. These were the mighty men who were of old, the men of renown. The Lord saw that the wickedness of man was great in the earth, and that every intention of the thoughts of his heart was only evil continually.

It is the great, ruthless renown of men and their sinfulness that characterizes the line of Cain and its influence on the earth.

At the culmination of the record of this lineage, as stated above, sits Lamech and his sons. Lamech is famous not only for his polygamy, but for his murderous and prideful heart. In the first piece of Old Testament poetry, he declares to his wives:

> Adah and Zillah, hear my voice;
> you wives of Lamech, listen to what I say:
> I have killed a man for wounding me,
> a young man for striking me.
>
> If Cain's revenge is sevenfold,
> then Lamech's is seventy-sevenfold. (Genesis 4:23–24)

This bit of poetry is commonly known as Lamech's "Sword Song" on the assumption that having gotten a forged weapon created by his son Tubal-cain the smith, he either has killed two men, or now has the power to kill them; and that whereas God promised to avenge the slaying of Adam sevenfold, Lamech would avenge any harm done to himself seventy-sev-

6 AE 1:311.

en-fold.[7] Here we see the complete rejection from any notion of dependence upon God. Lamech's declaration is that he will depend on his own might and will claim his own vengeance. Lamech, then, is portrayed by Moses as an unrighteous man, perhaps even the very image of mankind's unbelief and sin come to its full ripening.

This is the first polygamist in the biblical record. It is true that Genesis does not condemn his polygamy. Neither does it condemn his "Sword Song." The lack of explicit condemnation here (and elsewhere) should not be taken as a tacit acceptance of polygamy by Moses or by God. That the polygamous marriage of Lamech is noted, whereas the presumably monogamous marriages of his ancestors after Adam are passed over in silence, shows that it was out of the ordinary. This points rather to polygamy being one of Lamech's sins, and one aspect of the culmination of man's wickedness before God, that mankind as a whole was bent on being "only evil, all the time," to the extent that God condemns the world to the destruction of the flood (Genesis 6:5).

Polygamy among the Patriarchs

The practice of polygamy in the Scriptures is not limited to unbelievers. Many of the patriarchs, judges, and kings of Israel practiced polygamy. The historical record of these prominent leaders of God's people again contains no explicit prohibition or condemnation of their polygamy. The historical accounts of the Old Testament rarely declare moral judgments on the acts of their subjects. It is up to the reader to apply the biblical Law (as found especially in the created order and in the Mosaic Code) to arrive at any moral conclusions about specific acts or practices described. We are not told, for example, when Abraham attempted to pass off his wife Sarai as his sister that it was a sinful act on his part, an act flowing from a lack of faith in God when confronted with a perceived threat to his life on account of Sarai's beauty. Moses simply records the event. The task of providing a moral or ethical judgment is most often left to the reader.

But can the reader rightly make moral or ethical judgments concerning the acts of those recognized in Scripture as holy men of faith? Many commentators throughout the history of the Church's engagement with these

7 C. F. Keil and F. Delitzsch, *Commentary on the Old Testament* (Grand Rapids: Eerdmans, 1976), 1:118–19; H. C. Leupold, *Exposition of Genesis* (Columbus: The Wartburg Press, 1942), 222–24; Francis A. Schaeffer, *Genesis in Space and Time* (Downers Grove, IL: InterVarsity Press, 1972), 114.

texts have been hesitant to do so.[8] Here Luther's understanding of the man of faith as *simul justus et peccator* must be brought to bear.[9] Because all of the faithful are at the same time sinners, one should expect to find sinful acts and even sinful practices in the annals of the faithful if these annals are true and faithful accounts. Ethical and moral judgments of the actions of the saints must, therefore, be a component of a true exegesis of the biblical histories. That one finds men such as Abraham or David engaging in sinful activity should not discourage Christians in regard to the holiness of such men, but encourage them both in regard to the grace of God and with regard to the veracity of sacred history.

ABRAHAM'S POLYGAMOUS ACTION WAS A CAUSE OF STRIFE BETWEEN THE RIVAL WIVES AND RIVAL HEIRS WITHIN HIS FAMILY.

Polygamy is first recorded among the saints in the Genesis account of the life of Abraham.[10] Abraham had at least three wives: Sarah (Sarai), Hagar, and Keturah.[11] Abraham took Keturah as his wife after the death of Sarah, so this marriage was not necessarily a case of polygamy.[12] That Sarah gave her maid Hagar to Abraham for the sake of raising up an heir was a polygamous act. Whether or not a polygamous relationship continued after the conception of Ishmael is unknown, but appears doubtful due to the fact that Abraham had no other children by Hagar after Ishmael. Hagar certainly continued to live among Abraham's household for many years.

This arrangement, however, was anything but peaceful or happy. Genesis records the strife that Abraham's act of polygamy caused.

> And [Abraham] went in to Hagar, and she conceived. And when she saw that she had conceived, she looked with contempt on her mistress. And Sarai said to Abram, "May the

8 John Chrysostom, Augustine of Hippo, Martin Luther, and others taught that God permitted polygamy among the patriarchs for the purpose of either enlarging the nation of Israel or of providing Old Testament types for New Testament antitypes (Sarah and Hagar, for example).

9 This phrase, though coined by Luther, describes a thoroughly biblical concept. That the faithful struggle against sin, and do so imperfectly such that they actually sin, is taught throughout the Scriptures. See, for example, Psalms 14:3; 53:3; Isaiah 64:6; Romans 7:7–25; 1 John 1:8–10, etc.

10 Although we are told little of his story, Nahor, the brother of Abraham, also practiced polygamy. See Genesis 22:20–24.

11 Hagar is called Abraham's concubine. Keturah is called both Abraham's wife (Genesis 25:1) and his concubine (1 Chronicles 1:32). Practically speaking, the two terms are used synonymously to indicate a spouse who is not the first wife. It is possible that Abraham had other concubines as well (Genesis 25:6).

12 Some have labeled consecutive marriages, even after the death of the first wife, as a form of polygamy (successive polygamy, bigamy, digamy or sequential polygamy). If Abraham had other concubines along with Keturah, then this marriage, too, would be a case of real polygamy.

> wrong done to me be on you! I gave my servant to your embrace, and when she saw that she had conceived, she looked on me with contempt. May the LORD judge between you and me!" But Abram said to Sarai, "Behold, your servant is in your power; do to her as you please." Then Sarai dealt harshly with her, and she fled from her. (Genesis 16:4–6)

Hagar is returned to Abraham's household through the intercession of the Angel of the Lord who, for Abraham's sake, promises to make a great nation of Ishmael. This return did not alleviate the internecine tensions in Abraham's household. Some fifteen years later, after the birth and weaning of Isaac, Sarah again turns on Hagar and her child.[13]

> But Sarah saw the son of Hagar the Egyptian, whom she had borne to Abraham, laughing. So she said to Abraham, "Cast out this slave woman with her son, for the son of this slave woman shall not be heir with my son Isaac." And the thing was very displeasing to Abraham on account of his son. But God said to Abraham, "Be not displeased because of the boy and because of your slave woman. Whatever Sarah says to you, do as she tells you, for through Isaac shall your offspring be named. And I will make a nation of the son of the slave woman also, because he is your offspring." (Genesis 21:9–13)

Abraham's polygamous action was a cause of strife between the rival wives and rival heirs within his family. The Lord, nevertheless, made use of Abraham's polygamy to raise up great tribes and nations, peoples that continue to be in conflict with one another to this very day!

Abraham's polygamous relationship with Sarah and Hagar must also be examined in terms of its cause. Long before the conception of Ishmael, the Lord had promised to make of Abraham a great nation (Genesis 12:2). When Sarah gave Hagar to Abraham for the sake of procreation, she did so despairing of her own ability to conceive, for she had long been barren. It was an attempt on the part of Sarah to bring to fulfillment what the Lord had promised to Abraham. By consenting to Sarah's plan, Abraham was taking matters into his own hand, so to speak. Here we see the *simul jus-*

---

13 David A. Kind, "A Timeline of Biblical and Early Christian Events," University Lutheran Chapel, http://ulcmn.org/wp-content/uploads/2016/04/Bible-Timeline-Septuagint.pdf.

tus et peccator principle at work. Sarah and Abraham believed the Lord's promise that Abraham would father a great nation. At the same time, they did not trust the Lord to bring this about by His own power by means of Sarah's previously barren womb. The polygamous act of Sarah's offering, and Abraham's receiving, Hagar into the marriage bed flowed not from faith in the Lord's promise but from unbelief regarding the Lord's ability to perform what had been promised through their own bodies in marital union.

Abraham's son Isaac was not a polygamist, but his son Jacob had four wives.[14] In Jacob's case, his initial polygamy resulted from his having been deceived by his uncle Laban into marrying Laban's eldest daughter, Leah, rather than his younger daughter, Rachel, whom Laban had promised to Jacob. On the night of the wedding, Laban, unbeknownst to Jacob, had Leah take Rachel's place. The deception was not discovered by Jacob until after the marriage had been consummated. Jacob, having unwittingly taken Leah as his wife, renegotiates his contract with Laban and takes Rachel as his wife as well. The resultant tensions between the hated but fertile Leah and the beloved but barren Rachel are well known. So strong was the rivalry between the two that they each offer their maids as concubines to gain prominence over the other in their contest of producing children. The offspring of these four women become the twelve tribes of Israel. Strife in the family between Leah and Rachel gives birth to strife among their offspring, culminating in the sale into slavery of Joseph, the favorite son born of the favorite wife, by his brothers who were envious of him. Polygamy in this family, though used by God to lay the foundation of Israel's family as a future nation, led directly to great strife, great sin, and great suffering.

> ONE CAN SAY THAT WHILE POLYGAMY WAS NOT THE ONLY CAUSE OF ALL OF THE SINS THAT POLYGAMISTS AND THEIR CHILDREN COMMITTED, IT WAS CERTAINLY A CONTRIBUTING CAUSE AND FACTOR OF MANY OF THEM.

14 In Hebrew thought, and for the sake of this essay, concubines are considered secondary wives. Jacob's four wives were Leah, Rachel, Bilhah, and Zilpah (Genesis 35:22–26).

Polygamy among the Israelites appears to have caused similar problems among Jacob's descendants.[15] Gideon, a judge of Israel, had many wives. Abimelech, his son by a concubine he kept at Shechem, murdered seventy of his brothers (sons of Gideon's other wives) in order to wrest power away from his rivals in the family and gain kingship over Israel (Judges 9:1–6). David's having had children by multiple wives led to much sin and strife, including acts of incest, murder, and treason (see, for example, 2 Samuel 13). Solomon, famous not just for being wise but also for his large-scale polygamy, became an idolater as a result.

> Now King Solomon loved many foreign women, along with the daughter of Pharaoh: Moabite, Ammonite, Edomite, Sidonian, and Hittite women, from the nations concerning which the LORD had said to the people of Israel, "You shall not enter into marriage with them, neither shall they with you, for surely they will turn away your heart after their gods." Solomon clung to these in love. He had 700 wives, princesses, and 300 concubines. And his wives turned away his heart. For when Solomon was old his wives turned away his heart after other gods, and his heart was not wholly true to the LORD his God, as was the heart of David his father. For Solomon went after Ashtoreth the goddess of the Sidonians, and after Milcom the abomination of the Ammonites. So Solomon did what was evil in the sight of the LORD and did not wholly follow the LORD, as David his father had done. Then Solomon built a high place for Chemosh the abomination of Moab, and for Molech the abomination of the Ammonites, on the mountain east of Jerusalem. And so he did for all his foreign wives, who made offerings and sacrificed to their gods. (1 Kings 11:1–8)

Can every failure of these patriarchs be laid at the feet of polygamy? To claim this is to claim too much. But one can say that while polygamy was not the only cause of all of the sins that polygamists and their children committed, it was certainly a contributing cause and factor of many of them. Had these patriarchs maintained monogamous marriage according to the created order as explicitly stated in Genesis 2:24, much of their

15 Not every instance of polygamy has a story attached to it. Some instances receive no more attention than a brief note that someone had more than one wife. In those instances where a fuller story is given, those stories invariably involve strife and sin resulting at least in part from the tensions polygamy creates within the family unit.

heartache and suffering as parents, as families, and as a nation might have been averted.

Polygamy in the Mosaic Law Code

That being the case, one might be surprised to find polygamy regulated to a certain degree in the Law of Moses. That God gave legislation governing polygamy has led some to argue that polygamy must indeed be pleasing to Him, or at the very least not contrary to His will. Legislation that deals explicitly with polygamy is found in Exodus 21, Leviticus 18, Deuteronomy 17, and Deuteronomy 21.[16]

Exodus 21:7–11 deals with the woman who has been sold as a slave in order to serve as wife to the owner or the owner's son. The concern here is the welfare of the woman who is sold: that she not be sold to foreigners and thus be cut off from Israel, that she enjoy the full rights of a wife, and that she not be treated as mere chattel:

> And if a man sells his daughter to be a female slave, she shall not go out as the male slaves do. If she does not please her master, who has betrothed her to himself, then he shall let her be redeemed. He shall have no right to sell her to a foreign people, since he has dealt deceitfully with her. And if he has betrothed her to his son, he shall deal with her according to the custom of daughters. If he takes another wife, he shall not diminish her food, her clothing, and her marriage rights. And if he does not do these three for her, then she shall go out free, without paying money.[17]

Leviticus 18:18 forbids as an act of incest the practice of taking one's wife's sister as a wife. Here the wife and her sister are protected from rivalry like that which existed between Leah and Rachel, and from shame. "And you shall not take a woman as a rival wife to her sister, uncovering her nakedness while her sister is still alive."

Deuteronomy 21:15–17 regulates the inheritance of children of polygamous marriages to protect the rights of the firstborn:

---

16 John Witte Jr. argues that polygamy is implicit in other parts of the Mosaic Code dealing with slave ownership, levirate marriage, and seduction. Witte cites various rabbinical authors to prove this. I am not convinced that the interpretations of rabbinical authors should be taken as authoritative, especially in light of Christ's having proven the Pharisees ignorant concerning marriage and divorce in the Mosaic Code. While these regulations would certainly have been applied to polygamous relationships, they do not necessarily either presuppose or condone such relationships.

17 The NKJV translation is used here for clarity regarding the intention to wed the slave girl.

> If a man has two wives, the one loved and the other unloved, and both the loved and the unloved have borne him children, and if the firstborn son belongs to the unloved, then on the day when he assigns his possessions as an inheritance to his sons, he may not treat the son of the loved as the firstborn in preference to the son of the unloved, who is the firstborn, but he shall acknowledge the firstborn, the son of the unloved, by giving him a double portion of all that he has, for he is the firstfruits of his strength. The right of the firstborn is his.

These regulations should in no way be interpreted as promoting polygamy. Rather, each is put in place to mitigate its potential negative effects. The concern expressed in these laws is not for the polygamist husband, but for the wives and children, that they not be mistreated, put in danger, or denied their familial rights. Far from promoting polygamy, these regulations illuminate the problems and confusion introduced by it.

Deuteronomy 17:16–17 warns kings not to take multiple wives. The intent here is that the king of Israel put his trust in God rather than putting trust in strength, influence, or wealth. "Only he must not acquire many horses for himself or cause the people to return to Egypt in order to acquire many horses, since the LORD has said to you, 'You shall never return that way again.' And he shall not acquire many wives for himself, lest his heart turn away, nor shall he acquire for himself excessive silver and gold." Polygamy in this context is seen as a cause of temptation away from faithfulness to the Lord. We see in Solomon the results of ignoring the Lord's command in this regard.

FAR FROM PROMOTING POLYGAMY, THESE REGULATIONS ILLUMINATE THE PROBLEMS AND CONFUSION INTRODUCED BY IT.

Although upheld by many rabbis as an endorsement of polygamy, the regulation of the practice in no way should be read as such, but rather as an effort to diminish the damage polygamy might cause. In a similar manner, the Law of Moses also legislates divorce. The rabbis of the New Testament era took this legislation as divine permission.[18] They were corrected, however, by Jesus, who said of it: "Because of your hardness of heart Moses

18 John Witte Jr., *The Western Case for Monogamy over Polygamy* (Cambridge: Cambridge University Press, 2015), 52–55.

allowed you to divorce your wives, but from the beginning it was not so" (Matthew 19:8). Legislation and regulation of practice do not necessarily imply divine endorsement of it. In the case of divorce, Christ refers the rabbis back to the created order: "from the beginning it was not so." By the created order, one may say the same of polygamy.

Polygamy was not, and is not, however, the most severe marital or sexual sin, which perhaps helps to explain the lack of explicit condemnation of it in the Old Testament. It is, in fact, one of the milder violations of created order in that, while it departs from the divine ordinance of marriage, it does so only to a relatively moderate degree, not rejecting marriage itself, but misusing it. Other sexual sins fall further from the mark. Leviticus 18 and 20, for example, label the more severe sin of homosexuality as an abomination, something detestable to God; the sin of bestiality is labeled as a perversion or confusion, something that completely violates the boundaries between creatures within the divinely created order. Other sexual sins related to varying degrees of incest these passages classify as causing uncleanness, and adultery with the spouse of another an act of wickedness.[19] These sins are explicitly condemned to one degree or another because they present a serious assault on the created order and on the institution of marriage itself; whereas polygamy upholds the created order, but misuses marriage by wrongful multiplication of the gift.

Similar distinctions regarding gradation of sexual sins are found in the canons of the Early Church and in the penitential manuals of the early medieval Church. For example, the Council of Ancyra (AD 314) assigned a penance of seven years for an adulterer, fifteen years for a fornicator who aborted her child conceived of fornication, and twenty years for one who has engaged in bestiality.[20] Likewise, the penitential manuals of the Medieval Church typically assign penalties to sexual sins in relation to their departure from the ideal of monogamous marriage.[21] Generally speaking, the further from the ideal, the greater the penalty.[22] Hence, according to

19 John W. Kleinig, *Leviticus*, Concordia Commentary (St. Louis: Concordia, 2003), 379–80. Kleinig further explains, "bestiality violates the order of the species, homosexuality violates the order of the sexes, and incest violates the order of kinship" (p. 388).

20 Canons 16, 20, and 21 of the Council of Ancyra in *The Seven Ecumenical Councils*, ed. Henry R. Percival, Nicene and Post-Nicene Fathers, Second Series, Volume 14, ed. Philip Schaff and Henry Wace (New York: Charles Scribner Sons, 1900), 70–73.

21 A summary of how these manuals handle sexual sins can be found in James A. Brundage, *Law, Sex, and Christian Society in Medieval Europe* (Chicago: University of Chicago Press, 1987), 165–69, 600.

22 A notable exception to this rule is the sin of bestiality, which, strangely, is treated rather leniently in many of the penitential manuals. Brundage (*Law, Sex, and Christian Society*, p. 168) opines that this may be because of the challenges of rural life where livestock were abundant, but women were not. In some manuals, however, it was treated as severely as were homosexual acts with a penance of up to twenty-five years (p. 600).

John Witte, "canon law did not prohibit [polygamy] outright until the fourth century. Even then, the few canon laws on point treated real polygamy rather lightly. Adultery was punished nearly four times more severely; simple fornication between single parties at nearly double the rate."[23]

Polygamy in the Wisdom Literature

It is perhaps more surprising that one does not find polygamy promoted in the Psalms or Proverbs, especially when one considers the Davidic and Solomonic authorship of the greater portions of those books. In the Psalter, Psalms 127 and 128 in particular deal with family life. While Psalm 127 extols the blessings of having many children, it does not promote the idea of gaining them through the wombs of many wives. Likewise Psalm 128, describing the blessedness of the man who fears the Lord, speaks in monogamous terms: "Your wife will be like a fruitful vine within your house; your children will be like olive shoots around your table. Behold, thus shall the man be blessed who fears the Lord" (vv. 3–4).

Throughout the Proverbs, every description of marriage and of the relationship of husband to wife, whether positive or negative, speaks of the wife as a singular entity. Rather than promoting polygamy anywhere in this collection of wise sayings, Solomon discourages it, urging instead a strict and unadulterous monogamy: "Drink water from your own cistern, and running water from your own well. Should your fountains be dispersed abroad, streams of water in the streets? Let them be only your own, and not for strangers with you. Let your fountain be blessed, and rejoice with the wife of your youth. As a loving deer and a graceful doe, let her breasts satisfy you at all times; and always be enraptured with her love. For why should you, my son, be enraptured by an immoral woman, and be embraced in the arms of a seductress?" (Proverbs 5:15–20 NKJV). Drinking from one's own cistern and refraining from letting others drink from its waters signify faithfulness to one spouse in marriage, which is made clear when Solomon equates the fountain to the "wife of one's youth."

THROUGHOUT THE PROVERBS, EVERY DESCRIPTION OF MARRIAGE AND OF THE RELATIONSHIP OF HUSBAND TO WIFE, WHETHER POSITIVE OR NEGATIVE, SPEAKS OF THE WIFE AS A SINGULAR ENTITY.

23 Witte, *The Western Case for Monogamy over Polygamy*, 140–41.

In Ecclesiastes, Solomon contrasts the vanity of seeking pleasure from having many concubines to the blessedness of the man who enjoys a simple life, which includes having but one wife.[24] In the Song of Songs, Solomon acknowledges his own polygamy, but does so in passing and in the context of speaking of his love for the one wife who is, with him, the subject of the poem (6:8–9). That Solomon mentions multiple queens and concubines could be interpreted in various ways. The context seems to indicate, at the very least, the inferiority of polygamy when compared to the love and unity of monogamy; for in the following verse the queens and concubines give place to the singular Shulammite bride, whose singularity is a particular point of emphasis. Rather than a promotion of polygamy, these verses appear to reject it for something better, namely the monogamous love between Solomon and the Shulammite, who, according to the majority of Christian exegetes throughout history, represent Christ and the Church.

Polygamy in the New Testament

Although practiced by some Jews at the time of the writing of the New Testament and later, polygamy was not practiced among the Christians of that era, nor is it promoted in the New Testament Scriptures.[25] When speaking of marriage, the authors of the New Testament generally refer to the union of husband and wife as given in Genesis 2:24.[26] St. Paul explains the theological underpinnings of the institution of marriage and its place in the created order in Ephesians 5. He explains that the marriage of husband and wife is intended to reflect the primary union of Christ with His Bride, the Church. In this relationship, polygamy has no place (vv. 22–33). Elsewhere, St. Paul calls the Church the Body of Christ, a phrase that brings to mind Adam's declaration concerning Eve: "This *is* now bone of my bones and flesh of my flesh." In Romans 12, St. Paul emphasizes the unity of the Church as the one Body of Christ: "For as in one body we have many members, and the members do not all have the same function, so we, though many, are one body in Christ, and individually members one of another" (vv. 4–5). Here he is not describing polygamy, as if each Christian individually were a bride to Christ, but monogamy, that there is but one Body and one Bride, of which all Christians are members. He repeats this point in 1 Corinthians 10 and 12. "For in one Spirit we were all baptized into

---

24 Compare Ecclesiastes 2:1–11 with 9:7–10, especially in light of the injunction of Deuteronomy 17:17 against kings taking many wives for themselves.

25 For more on Jewish polygamy, see Witte, *The Western Case for Monogamy over Polygamy*, 50–64.

26 Matthew 19:5–6; Mark 10:8; Ephesians 5:31; 1 Corinthians 6:16.

one body" (12:13).[27] Christ is no polygamist. Marriage, therefore, which was given to mankind in order to portray the deeper reality of Christ and the Church, ought not be polygamous. Polygamy is not only foreign to the image of Christ and the Church, but destroys the image of the Church as the singular Bride/Body of Christ.

For this reason, polygamists were excluded from the Office of the Holy Ministry (1 Timothy 3:1–13; Titus 1:5–9). Some have taken the prohibition of polygamy as something that applied only to the bishops and deacons (and perhaps elders) of the Church. When one examines the requisites of the Office, however, one finds that in every other item but one, what is required of the bishop or deacon is also enjoined upon Christians in general.[28] The qualities listed by St. Paul are given because the bishop and deacons are to exemplify the life all Christians are expected to live. They themselves are to bear witness to the truth not just in their preaching, but by their example as well.

Polygamy was of concern to our Lord when dealing with the issue of divorce. Because God had joined husband and wife in marriage, improper divorces, while severing the bonds of husband and wife under civil law, could not sever those bonds according to divine Law. What of those who were wrongly divorced who then married someone else? The fact that the divorcee was, in God's eyes, still married would lead to a polygamous second marriage. Jesus does not, however, use the term *polygamy* to describe the resultant situation, but calls it *adultery*.[29] This goes a step beyond simply stating that the divorcee who remarries in reality has more than one spouse, but clearly labels the resultant polygamous marriage as sin.[30] If this is so in the case of a polygamous marriage resulting from divorce and remarriage, other polygamous unions (and to an even greater degree homosexual throupling, *ménage à trois* arrangements, spouse swapping, and other marital or sexual practices that depart from the standard set in Genesis 2:24) must also, by their very nature, be considered adulterous and, therefore, sinful.

---

27 See also the surrounding verses in 1 Corinthians 12:12–27 and 1 Corinthians 10:17, which make the same point.

28 The one exception is the ability to teach.

29 Matthew 5:22; 19:9; Mark 10:11–12; Luke 16:18.

30 This concern is echoed by St. Paul in 1 Corinthians 7:10–16. The LCMS Commission on Theology and Church Relations in their document *Divorce and Remarriage* states: "In light of Jesus' confirmation of the original institution of marriage, polygamy, like divorce, must be regarded as evidence of Israel's refusal to be bound by the constraints of God's will expressed in the pattern set down at creation." (Commission on Theology and Church Relations, *Divorce and Remarriage* [St. Louis: The Lutheran Church—Missouri Synod, 1984], footnote 16).

Patristic Thoughts on Polygamy

Based on the teachings of the New Testament, the Christian Church has never sanctioned polygamy for its followers. The great theologians and Fathers of the Church were unanimous in their rejection of the practice, but for varying reasons.

The second-century apologist, Justin Martyr, held that polygamy, while used for the divine purpose of prefiguring the rivalry between the synagogue and the church, came about through lust; and castigated the Jews of his day for practicing it still:

> You should obey God rather than your blind and stupid teachers, who even now permit each of you to have four or five wives; and if any of you see a beautiful woman, and desire to have her, they cite the example of Jacob, who is Israel, and other Patriarchs to prove that there is no evil in such practices. How wretched and ignorant they are even in this respect! For as I have said, in each such action certain divine plans were mysteriously fulfilled . . . your teachers never considered the more divine purpose for which each thing was done, but rather what concerned base and corruptible passions. Give me your attention, therefore, and heed my words. The marriages of Jacob were types of what Christ would do. It was not lawful for Jacob to marry two sisters at the same time.[31]

In his First Apology, Justin equates bigamy with adultery: "All who according to human law make second marriages are sinners in the sight of our Master, as are those who look on a woman to lust after her. For not only the man who in act commits adultery is condemned by Him, but also the man who desires to commit adultery."[32]

Tertullian, writing in the third century, likewise held that polygamy was contrary to the created order and was first brought about by lust. In his book "On Monogamy," he complains of those who reject marriage altogether and of those who practice polygamy: "Heretics snatch away mar-

---

31 Justin Martyr, "Dialogue with Trypho," in *The Fathers of the Church: A New Translation*, vol. 6, trans. Thomas B. Falls (Washington DC: Catholic University of America Press, 1965), 355–56. Justin goes on to show how Leah represents the synagogue, but Rachel the true Bride, the Church. Christ, he says, will save both if the synagogue comes to faith in Him. It seems that figuratively Leah must become Rachel in order to be a proper bride for Jacob. And so Laban had to deceive Jacob into thinking Leah was Rachel.

32 Justin Martyr, "The First Apology," in *The Fathers of the Church*, 32.

riages. Those of the flesh[33] pile them up. The former don't marry once, the latter marry more than once. . . . The one blasphemes; the other revels in excess. The former destroys the God of marriages; the latter confounds. . . . We recognize one marriage, just as we recognize one God."[34] A contemporary of Tertullian, Clement of Alexandria likewise taught that polygamy was an overindulgence of the flesh. "Those who indulge in excess violate the laws of nature and harm themselves in illegitimate unions." The following, capturing his attitude toward sexuality in general, seems especially to apply to polygamy: "Our Lord wanted humanity to multiply, but He did not say that people should engage in licentious behavior, nor did he intend for them to give themselves over to pleasure as if they were born for rutting."[35]

Lactantius equated polygamy with adultery in *The Divine Institutes*: "The man who has a wife may not wish to have a mistress, either slave or free, and he must keep the marriage contract. For it is not the case that only the woman who has taken another is guilty of adultery, whereas the husband is free of the charge of adultery, even if he has several concubines. No, divine law joins the two under equal legal obligation in marriage, which is in one body. Therefore, either partner who divides the unity of the body is considered an adulterer."[36] John Chrysostom, preaching on the polygamous marriages of Jacob, allowed that polygamy was permitted for a time in order to increase the race,[37] but also said of the thing itself: "since the practice itself was evil, see how it has been rooted out, and no one is free now to propose it. Consequently, I beseech you, far from seeking to adopt it in any way, search rather what is useful, not what is spiritually harmful."[38] St. Jerome taught that the evilness of the polygamy is in its departure from created order and from the image of Christ and the Church. "The creation of the first man should teach us to reject more marriages than one. There

---

33 Tertullian uses the Gnostic term *psychici*, sometimes translated "psychics," to indicate Christians who are morally lax. I've translated this term with "of the flesh" so as to avoid confusion with the modern definition of "psychic."

34 Tertullian, "De monogamia," in *Patrologia Latina*, vol. 002, ed. Jacques-Paul Migne (Paris: Apud Garnier, 1844), 950–51. The translation is my own.

35 Clement of Alexandria, "The Instructor," in *Marriage in the Early Church*, ed. David G. Hunter (Minneapolis: Fortress Press, 1992), 44.

36 Lactantius, "The Divine Institutes," in *Marriage in the Early Church*, ed. David G. Hunter (Minneapolis: Fortress Press, 1992), 74–75.

37 So did Augustine, who saw polygamy as necessary among the patriarchs for the increase of the nation. But Augustine also argued that polygamy "is certainly not allowed today." See Hunter, *Marriage in the Early Church*, 116. Many of the Church Fathers portrayed the supposed shift from Old Testament polygamy to New Testament monogamy as a growth in virtue from the Old to the New. For more on this see Witte, *The Western Case for Monogamy over Polygamy*, 85–93.

38 Chrysostom, "Homily 56 on Genesis," in *The Fathers of the Church: A New Translation*, vol. 87, trans. Robert C. Hill (Washington DC: Catholic University of America Press, 1992), 124.

was but one Adam and one Eve . . . 'the two shall be one flesh,' not three or four. . . . Paul in explaining this passage refers it to Christ and the church; making the first Adam a monogamist in the flesh, and the second a monogamist in the spirit."[39]

What the Early Fathers taught on the matter laid the groundwork for the opinions of the later theologians of the Church. By the end of the Middle Ages, the question of polygamy among Christians had been settled, and had been codified in the canon law of the Church.[40] With a few exceptions, polygamy has been rejected by the vast majority in the Church ever since.[41]

So what should Christians of today make of the increasing prominence of polygamy (and by extension polyamory, and other deviant marital arrangements and sexual practices involving multiple partners) in our culture? Although found in the Old Testament, and used by God for His own purposes, it is evident that polygamy is ultimately contrary to God's will. Not only is polygamy contrary to the created order, not only does it bring harm to the polygamist and his family, but it also does violence to the institution of marriage, which is intended by God as an icon of Christ and His Church. We must confess with Christ, St. Paul, and the Fathers of the Church that polygamy is sin; sin that should in no way be approved among Christians or sanctioned by the Church.

MARRIAGE, THEREFORE, WHICH WAS GIVEN TO MANKIND IN ORDER TO PORTRAY THE DEEPER REALITY OF CHRIST AND THE CHURCH, OUGHT NOT BE POLYGAMOUS.

39 Jerome, "Letter 123," quoted in Witte, *The Western Case for Monogamy over Polygamy,* 85.

40 See Witte, *The Western Case for Monogamy over Polygamy,* 145–95.

41 An entire essay could be written on Martin Luther and polygamy. In brief, Luther held that polygamy had been allowed in the Old Testament and was not expressly forbidden in the New Testament, and that it could be practiced in cases of extreme need. In general, however, he stood against the practice. In 1526 he wrote in a letter, "Although the patriarchs had many wives, Christians may not follow their example, because there is no necessity for doing this, no improvement is obtained thereby, and, especially, there is no word of God to justify this practice, while great offense and trouble may come from it. Accordingly, I do not believe that Christians any longer have this liberty." Quoted in W. T. Dau, *Luther Examined and Reexamined: A Review of Catholic Criticism and a Plea for Reevaluation* (St. Louis: Concordia, 1917), 103.

CHAPTER 4

CONTRACEPTION: AN EMBRYO'S POINT OF VIEW

Donna J. Harrison

Introduction

Issues surrounding the creation and care of children touch almost every married couple. The marital one-flesh relationship forms the context in which God creates new human beings. These new beings make demands of the parents, challenging and stretching their ability to love, to forgive, to be consistent, and to provide for their children's physical, emotional, and spiritual needs. In this practical, immediate care for their children, parents are given an opportunity for character growth.

In the last century, the ability to separate the act of physical intimacy from the birth of children has brought difficult theological and scientific issues into the heart of every marital relationship. Until the 1930s, couples generally understood and accepted that sexual intercourse could very likely lead to conception and birth of children, and married couples mainly faced the challenges of faithfulness to one's spouse and the willingness to give oneself in sacrificial love to each other and to their children. Today's married couples face even more questions: "Do we want to have children?" "Why should we have children?" "How many?" "When is the right time?" "Is there any God-pleasing way to structure our family size and timing?"

Faithful couples faced with these theological and practical questions turn to pastoral counselors for answers. The pastoral counselor seeking scientific information about contraception will find a lot of information designed to sell a particular device or pill. The marketing discussion centers on how effective the drug or device may be in preventing a recognized pregnancy. Little or no discussion is given to the way in which such pills or devices alter or change the natural physiological processes of a woman's body. Rarely is any information given on the effect of that drug or device on interpersonal relationships, long-term fertility, or the effect on an embryo created when the drug fails. The pastor is then left to counsel couples about decisions that have a profound impact on their interpersonal relationships, without the foundational knowledge of normal physiological processes, how those processes are altered by contraceptives currently on the market, and the effects such alterations could have on interpersonal relationships.

The purpose of this essay is to equip the reader to better understand how different methods of contraceptives function in relation to the working of the reproductive system. Although each method affects not only the reproductive system and the woman's long-term health but also the couple's relationship as a whole, this essay will focus only on what is currently known about the effects of contraceptive methods on embryos. Whether or not an embryonic human being faces harm from the use of a contraceptive method is often the single most important question to faithful couples. When pastors and parishioners understand the biological reality of various contraceptive methods, they can then begin to address the deeper theological issues and provide those answers urgently needed to bridge the gap from "What we know" to "What should we then do?"

GOD DESIGNED THE BODIES OF BOTH THE HUSBAND AND THE WIFE TO BRING NEW HUMAN LIFE INTO THE WORLD IN THE MOST PROTECTED AND NURTURING WAY POSSIBLE.

Normal Physiology of Reproduction: The Symphony of Procreation

In the symphony of human procreation, God designed the bodies of both the husband and the wife to bring new human life into the world in the most protected and nurturing way possible. The biology of procreation is a marvelous illustration of the reality of the one-flesh relationship: It is the only instance in which cells from one person's body fulfill their physiological function inside another person's body![1] The woman's body provides the safe and nurturing context to receive procreative cells from a man, to stimulate procreation, and for new human life to begin and flourish.

Understanding human procreation starts with understanding a woman's monthly cycles. A woman's monthly cycle is counted from the first day she bleeds (day 1) and ends on the day before she starts to bleed again, approximately twenty-eight days later (ranges 26–32 days). Between day 1

1 Sperm cells cannot fertilize an egg as they are when they leave the man's body. Sperm cells become capable of fertilization as they travel through the woman's body, and only here can these male cells finish their maturation and fulfill their purpose.

and day 7 (the first week) of the woman's cycle, her brain[2] releases Follicle Stimulating Hormone (FSH) that causes the egg sacs (follicles) in her ovaries to grow and produce the natural hormone "estradiol." Estradiol makes the lining of her womb begin to grow again (after being shed in her monthly period).

In the second week of her cycle, one of these follicles will grow faster, as the egg inside gets ready to be released and fertilized. For this reason, the first two weeks of a woman's cycle spent preparing for egg release is called the "follicular phase" of the cycle.

Near the end of the follicular phase, the woman's brain senses that one (or sometimes two) eggs are nearly ready to be released. Her brain stops releasing so much FSH and begins a different hormone called Luteinizing Hormone (LH). Then, around day 12, her brain releases a very large amount of LH, called the "LH surge." The "LH surge" is what causes the woman's ovary to release an egg. If there is not enough LH, the egg will not be released from the ovary, but rather will stop growing, and eventually be reabsorbed into the ovary. But if the LH surge is high enough, the egg will be released and gently swept up into the fallopian tube, ready to meet sperm.

In addition to causing the ovary to release an egg, LH has another very important job in the symphony of procreation. LH reprograms the cells of the ruptured follicle into cells that become yellow (luteus) and begin making a very important natural hormone called "progesterone." In this way, LH transforms the follicle that once held the egg into a "corpus luteum" (yellow body). The amount of LH in the LH surge determines the number of cells in the follicle that will later go on to produce progesterone. So the amount of LH in the LH surge and the amount of progesterone produced later in the luteal phase of the cycle are directly related. Once egg release happens, the second half of a woman's cycle is called the "luteal phase" because all the action depends on the corpus luteum producing the right amount and timing of progesterone.

2 A special part of the woman's brain (hypothalamus) conducts this symphony. The hypothalamus drums out a beat (GnRH pulse frequency), which evokes the release of specific hormones from her pituitary gland, which in turn controls the woman's ovary. The rate of this hypothalamic beat in the first two weeks of her cycle causes release of Follicle Stimulating Hormone (FSH). FSH causes eggs to mature and make estradiol, and a different hypothalamic beat frequency in the second half of her cycle causes release of Luteinizing Hormone (LH) from her pituitary that then tells the woman's ovary to release an egg and make progesterone. The precise timing of estradiol and progesterone production by the ovary in the woman's body not only causes the egg to be released at a precise time, but also prepares the lining of her womb to embrace and nurture a new human being. Knowing the basic details of this symphony reveals the implications of interfering at different points with contraceptive drugs, devices, and surgeries.

Just as its name implies ("pro" = for; "gest" = pregnancy; "one" = hormone), progesterone is the "for-pregnancy-hormone" that changes the woman's reproductive tract to be able to care for the embryo. Progesterone causes the woman's fallopian tube to gently sweep the newly formed embryo toward and into the womb. Progesterone also prepares the lining of the woman's womb to embrace and nurture the embryo, allowing the embryo to implant. After the embryo has implanted, progesterone causes the womb's tissues to be able to feed the embryo. So progesterone is absolutely essential to the survival of the early embryo, and LH is the hormone that enables the ovary to produce progesterone. Both LH and progesterone are the targets for hormonal contraception.

SCIENTIFICALLY SPEAKING, THERE IS NO SUCH THING AS A "FERTILIZED EGG."

One note about the "LH surge": it is possible to have enough LH to cause the egg to be released, but not enough LH to change a sufficient number of follicular cells to make progesterone, leading to insufficient progesterone to prepare the lining of the uterus to receive and nurture an embryo. This condition is known in infertility research as "Luteal Phase Defect" (LPD). Women who have Luteal Phase Defect have a very difficult time with embryo implantation and early miscarriage.

Once the egg is released, the egg must be fertilized within twenty-four hours; after this time the egg can no longer be fertilized, and no embryo will be created. Understanding the changes that happen in a woman's body in preparation for egg release forms the basis of Fertility Awareness Based Methods (FABMs) of avoiding fertilization. By identifying the time of egg release, and knowing that sperm can last up to five days in a woman's body, couples can time intercourse to either achieve or avoid pregnancy. Since most women have very predictable physiological changes that are relatively easy to recognize, FABMs can be highly effective in preventing fertilization but require the cooperation of both husband and wife to time intercourse.

If there are sperm present in the fallopian tube to meet the egg when it is released, then fertilization and the procreation of a human embryo can occur. At the moment of fertilization, the sperm and egg fuse together. At the moment of sperm-egg fusion, which happens in milliseconds, an entirely new human being is formed. This new human being has the special scientific name "zygote," another name for a one-celled embryo. This embryo exhibits all the scientific characteristics of a unique human organism,[3] and he or she will continue through all the stages of human existence until death.

In order to avoid the reality that a new human being exists at sperm-egg fusion, and to allow for in vitro fertilization research, some researchers began in the 1960s to refer to the zygote as a "fertilized egg." Scientifically speaking, there is no such thing as a "fertilized egg." The moment that the sperm fuses with the egg, the sperm cease to exist and the egg ceases to exist. Scientifically, what exists is a unique human embryo at the beginning of that human being's life.

After fertilization, the one-celled embryo is brushed gently down the tube toward the womb. On the way through the tube, the embryo grows rapidly[4] and prepares to implant in the womb. The trip through the fallopian tubes into the womb takes about five to seven days. The cells of the tube move the embryo response to precise amounts of the hormone progesterone made by the corpus luteum. When the embryo arrives in the womb, he or she arrives at a perfect time, ready to implant. The lining of the womb has also been perfectly prepared to embrace and nurture the embryo as he or she emerges from the covering that protected him or her while traveling in the tube. This precise timing comes from the correct amount and timing of progesterone made by the corpus luteum of the ovary.

SCIENTIFICALLY, WHAT EXISTS IS A UNIQUE HUMAN EMBRYO AT THE BEGINNING OF THAT HUMAN BEING'S LIFE.

Once the embryo has implanted, the embryo herself or himself starts to make a special hormone called Human Chorionic Gonadotropin (hCG). Pregnancy tests available at pharmacies and grocery stores test for the presence of hCG in a mother's urine. When a woman has a positive pregnancy test, that means that her embryo has produced enough hCG to be detected in the mother's urine. This usually occurs about a week after implantation, when the embryo is around fourteen days old.

By the time hCG is high enough to give a positive pregnancy test, the mother misses her period. A missed period is usually the signal to the mother to consider her embryo might be present. Often at the point of the

3 Maureen Condic, "When Does Human Life Begin? A Scientific Perspective," *Westchester Institute White Paper* 1, no. 1 (2008): 1, www.bdfund.org/whitepapers. Reprinted in: *National Catholic Bioethics Quarterly* 9, no. 1 (2009): 127–208.

4 All the stages of embryonic development are available at www.visembryo.com and www.ehd.org/prenatal-images-index.php (accessed July 22, 2016).

positive pregnancy test, the mother begins to emotionally bond to her unborn child, weeks after the physical bonding has already occurred.

But hCG does more than trigger the mom's awareness of her embryo. The hCG produced by the embryo stimulates the corpus luteum to continue making progesterone[5] in exactly the same way that LH stimulated the corpus luteum. As the LH signal from the woman's brain slowly disappears, hCG takes its place to ensure continuous production of progesterone so that the embryo can survive and grow.

Progesterone continues to stimulate the lining of the mother's womb to provide nourishment to the implanted embryo. Without progesterone produced by the corpus luteum of the ovary, nourishing and sustaining the embryo for the first ten weeks of his or her life, the embryo would die.[6] If for some reason during that time the corpus luteum were damaged or surgically removed, the fetus would die unless the mother is given supplemental progesterone. After approximately thirteen weeks of life, the placenta itself will produce enough progesterone to sustain the unborn child until birth.

During the nine months of pregnancy, and for several months after birth, if she is exclusively breastfeeding, the mother typically will not release additional eggs. If she exclusively breastfeeds for at least six months, and if she does not resume her monthly cycles during that time of breastfeeding, a woman will naturally tend to bear children on average roughly about once every two years. However, a woman can become pregnant during breastfeeding even if she has not resumed her periods.

In summary, the song of human procreation starts with the intricately timed symphony of pituitary and ovarian hormones, which in turn prepare the woman's body to receive and nurture new human life. The ovary responds to the pituitary by maturing an egg during the follicular phase of the cycle and then releasing that egg in response to LH. After egg release, the ovary produces progesterone. Progesterone then stimulates the tube to move the embryo toward the womb at the right time for implantation and ensures that the lining of the woman's uterus develops with such precision that, at the point when

CONTRACEPTIVES PREVENT OUR BODIES FROM DOING SOMETHING OUR BODIES WERE DESIGNED TO DO.

5 Tulay Ozlu, Aysenur Cakir Gungor, Melahat Donmez, and Bulent Duran, "Use of Progestogens in Pregnant and Infertile Patients," *Archive of Gynecology and Obstetrics* 286, no. 2 (2012): 495–503.

6 Ozlu, "Use of Progestogens," 495–503.

her embryo enters the endometrial cavity, her uterus is perfectly ready to receive, embrace, and nurture that new life. The mother's ovary responds to the presence of her unborn child (as signaled by hCG) by continuing to produce progesterone, which sustains the maternal-fetal embrace, until such time as the unborn baby's placenta has grown and can produce enough progesterone on its own. The placenta will then support the needs of the baby until birth. If she exclusively breastfeeds, a woman's body will tend not to resume making eggs for several months after birth.

Contraception: An Overview

The scientific and medical concept of "contraception" is a curious one. Usually, drugs, surgeries, and implants are given to cure or prevent a disease. But contraceptives do not prevent or cure any disease. In fact, contraceptives prevent our bodies from doing something our bodies were designed to do, i.e., procreate. Contraceptive drugs, devices, and surgeries induce a state in which the normal function of the body is altered. Why would someone want to alter the normal function of his or her body? Perhaps more significant: ought we be inducing an abnormal physical state in our bodies to make our bodies function the way we want as opposed to the way that our bodies were designed to function? Considering some aspects of contraception may give insight into these questions. This chapter will consider three aspects of contraception: the advent of the term *contraception,* the concept of "efficacy," and the reasons for concern about the environment that embryos face when they are created during the use of contraception.

The Advent of the Term *Contra-ception*

Contra-ception is a term coined in the 1960s for drugs, devices, and surgeries that prevent a sexually active woman from obtaining a positive pregnancy test at the end of her cycle. The term was designed to be the opposite of *conception.*

The term *conception* is understood by most people to be the moment of fertilization—the moment when the sperm penetrates the egg. The term *conception* is used interchangeably with the term *fertilization* in many biology textbooks, as well as current medical dictionaries.

In the 1960s, researchers discovered that giving large amounts of artificial estrogens and progestins could interfere with a woman's reproductive system and keep her from having a positive pregnancy test. But some people were concerned about how these artificial hormones actually worked. Could these hormones harm a human life at the beginning? The general public understood that ending an unborn human life is generally called an "abortion." Many people were worried that these drugs and devices were "abortifacient"—things that end the life of an unborn human being. Manufacturers recognized that this thinking could interfere with the marketability of the drugs or devices and felt a need to reassure the public that contraceptives did not cause abortions.

The solution to the problem of public concern about whether or not contraceptives caused early abortions was developed in 1965 by the American Congress of Obstetricians and Gynecologists (ACOG),[7] which is heavily financed by the contraceptive drug industry. ACOG acknowledged that the term *abortion* is understood to be the ending of a pregnancy. Everyone knows that pregnancy begins at conception. But ACOG recognized that the term *conception* had no scientific definition. (The scientific definition for the beginning of any organism, including human beings, is "fertilization"—the moment of sperm-egg fusion.) So, ACOG decided to legally define the word *conception* as "the completion of implantation."[8] Now, legally speaking, pregnancy begins at conception, but conception is an event that takes place ten days to two weeks *after* fertilization.

Using the ACOG definition of conception as the beginning of pregnancy, the accusation against contraceptives as abortifacient is easily dismissed. Since abortion is defined as the ending of a pregnancy and since pregnancy does not begin until the completion of implantation, then legally, drugs and devices that kill an embryo *before* implantation is complete cannot be classified as abortifacients.[9] Voilà! Problem solved!

Thus the term *abortifacient* is rendered meaningless in discussions about most contraceptive mechanisms of action. But the fact remains that some drugs, devices, and surgeries labeled as "contraceptive" can and do

7 "Terms Used in Reference to the Fetus," American Congress of Obstetricians and Gynecologists *Terminology Bulletin* 1 (1965).

8 ACOG, "Facts Are Important," (June 12, 2014) www.acog.org/-/media/Departments/Government-Relations-and-Outreach/FactsAreImportantEC.pdf?dmc=1&ts=20160722T1510227981. Note that ACOG commits many logical fallacies in this document, and also includes some factually inaccurate statements, such as the timing of fertilization which actually takes place in milliseconds, not twenty-four hours. See footnote 3. Rachel Benson Gold, "The Implications of Defining When a Woman Is Pregnant," *Guttmacher Policy Review* 8 (2005), www.guttmacher.org/about/gpr/2005/05/implications-defining-when-woman-pregnant.

9 The ACOG acknowledges the distinction between fertilization and the ACOG definition of conception and the implications on the difference in their recent press release on personhood amendments: "Although the individual wording in these proposed measures varies from state to state, they all attempt to give full legal rights to a fertilized egg by defining 'personhood' from the moment of fertilization, before conception (i.e., pregnancy/implantation) has occurred. This would have wide-reaching harmful implications for the practice of medicine and on women's access to contraception, fertility treatments, pregnancy termination, and other essential medical procedures." See www.acog.org/About-ACOG/News-Room/News-Releases/2012/Personhood-Measures.

have actions that harm or kill embryos. Thus the difficult moral question for faithful couples is not whether or not a contraceptive is abortifacient but whether or not the contraceptive is *embryocidal*—does it have an action that can kill an embryo if the embryo is formed during the use of that contraceptive drug, device, or surgery?

THE CONCEPT OF EFFICACY OF A CONTRACEPTIVE

In order to determine whether or not some drug or device works as a contraceptive, scientists see if the user has a positive pregnancy test at the end of the cycle in which she used that particular contraceptive drug or device (i.e., day 28 of her cycle). That positive pregnancy test is the detection of the hormone "beta hCG" made by a living embryo that implanted in her womb a week before. If no beta hCG is found, then the contraceptive worked. But *how* did it work? This is the core of the huge controversy surrounding contraceptives. Day 28 of a woman's cycle is two weeks after an embryo is created. Did something happen during the first twelve days of an embryo's life to make the embryo not able to survive to produce a positive pregnancy test?

There are three reasons to consider the environment of embryos conceived during the use of a contraceptive:

1. All contraceptive drugs, devices, and surgeries "fail" at a certain rate.[10] As noted in a recent paper: "Unintended pregnancies occur with all contraceptive methods, including IUDs. This provides incontrovertible evidence that fertilization and implantation can occur, albeit rarely, with modern methods of contraception."[11]
2. The fact that pregnancy can happen with all contraceptive drugs and devices proves that embryos can be and in fact are created during the use of all contraceptive drugs, devices, and surgeries, because all pregnancies begin with creation of an embryo.

10 "Failure rate" is a particularly negative term. Each of those "failures" is a unique human being, made in the image of God. Each "failure" is an embryo that has survived the conditions inside his or her mother's womb caused by the contraceptive; survived to the point of being able to be recognized as a pregnancy. The remainder of this essay will consider what conditions the embryo faces in his or her mother's womb when a couple uses a particular kind of contraceptive.

11 Roberto Rivera, Irene Yacobson, and David Grimes, "The Mechanism of Action of Hormonal Contraceptives and Intrauterine Contraceptives Devices," *American Journal of Obstetrics and Gynecology* (1999): 1263–69.

3. When that embryo is created, the contraceptive drug, device, or surgery will create a certain environment for the embryo that either helps or hinders that embryo's life. Understanding the way contraceptive methods work in the woman's body makes clear the environment that the embryo will face during the beginning of his or her life.

Quantifying the extent of embryo destruction or survival during the use of a particular contraceptive method requires knowing how often eggs are released during the use of a particular contraceptive method, knowing how often those eggs are fertilized and therefore produce embryos, and knowing the environment the embryo will face in the woman's reproductive tract. The question to be answered: Is there likely to be an increase in embryo death for women using a particular method of contraception when compared to embryo death in women not using any method of contraception?

How often are eggs released on a particular contraceptive?

Researchers can easily answer this question, because the place in the ovary where an egg grows—the follicle—is easily seen by ultrasound. The follicle ruptures to release the egg, and this rupture is also easily seen by ultrasound. So it is very easy to determine how often eggs are released during a normal cycle (normal is about 60 percent ovulation rate[12]) and compare that to how many are released using a particular method of contraception.

How often are those eggs fertilized, producing embryos, and is there an increase in embryo death for women using a particular method of contraception when compared to embryo death in women not using any method of contraception?

This is a more difficult question. Currently it is not known even how often embryos are formed in natural cycles without contraception, because there is no direct scientific test for fertilization and embryo formation. If a reliable test for fertilization inside a woman's body were developed, it would be simple to determine the rate of fertilization to pregnancy in normal women and then compare that normal rate with the rate of women using various methods of contraception. But money for contraceptive research comes from contraceptive manufacturers, and the answer to this very important question would likely not be financially profitable. There is a tremendous need for funding the basic research to find a marker for

12 Jerilynn Prior, Marit Naess, Arnulf Langhammer, and Siri Forsmo, "Ovulation Prevalence in Women with Spontaneous Normal-Length Menstrual Cycles—A Population-Based Cohort from HUNT3, Norway," *PLoS One* 10, no. 8 (2015), http://journals.plos.org/plosone/article?id=10.1371/journal.pone.0134473.

fertilization[13] in order to directly answer the question of the effect of contraceptive methods on embryos.

Although a direct test for fertilization occurring inside a woman's body is not currently available, there is an indirect way to provide a crude estimate of embryo formation. For an embryo to form, an egg must be released. Researchers can measure egg release. When an embryo survives through implantation, the woman will have a positive pregnancy test. Researchers routinely measure the number of positive pregnancy tests at the end of a cycle. This gives a ratio of egg release (ovulation) to pregnancy ratio.

In one hundred normal women not using any kind of contraception, sixty of those women will release eggs in any given cycle. That gives a normal ovulation rate of 60 percent. In one hundred sexually active couples who do not use any contraception, eighty-five of those couples will be able to achieve a pregnancy within a year. These facts yield a normal monthly ovulation to yearly pregnancy ratio of 60 percent/eighty-five pregnancies in couples using no contraception.

SOME DRUGS, DEVICES, AND SURGERIES LABELED AS "CONTRACEPTIVE" CAN AND DO HAVE ACTIONS THAT HARM OR KILL EMBRYOS.

If contraceptives have no effects after an egg is released, then the ovulation to pregnancy ratio should be the same whether or not a woman is using contraception. It would be expected that she would *ovulate* less frequently than women not using contraceptives, all other things being equal, but should ovulation occur, then fertilization of the released egg should occur at the same rate regardless of the use of contraception. The normal ratio of ovulation to pregnancy (60 percent ovulation/eighty-five pregnancies) should be maintained.

If it were true that there were no other effects of a contraceptive drug, device, or surgery other than preventing egg release, then measuring the degree to which that contraceptive method prevented egg release should reliably predict the number of pregnancies (i.e., "failure rate") in a year. For example, if the contraceptive method results in reducing ovulation by half (i.e., 30 percent ovulation rate) and if that contraceptive drug or device only works by preventing ovulation, the result should be forty-three preg-

13 See www.melisainstitute.org. The MELISA Institute is actively seeking an easily usable test for women to determine when fertilization occurs in order to facilitate the best environment for early embryonic life, and to allow for healthy interventions at the beginning of life. This fertilization marker would also clearly answer the question of whether or not embryos are harmed during the use of contraceptives.

nancies at the end of the year. If there are fewer pregnancies, then the drug or device must work in ways other than preventing ovulation to explain the reduction in pregnancies. Many hormone-based contraceptives have large discrepancies between ovulation rate and the rate of expected pregnancies, leading researchers to conclude that other mechanisms of action must be at work.

What are those other ways that a contraceptive might use to prevent a recognized pregnancy test at the end of a woman's cycle? There are five points where a contraceptive drug or device can interfere with the human reproductive system and prevent the woman from having a positive pregnancy test on day 28 of her cycle:

1. prevent the ovary from making and/or releasing an egg
2. prevent the sperm from meeting the egg in the tube
3. prevent the embryo from surviving the passage through the tube to the lining of the uterus
4. prevent the embryo from implanting in the lining of the uterus
5. prevent the embryo who has already implanted from surviving to day 28.

If a contraceptive drug, device, or surgery worked only by mechanism number 1 or number 2, then no embryo would be formed. Action at points 3–5 will kill embryos. But many methods work by interfering at several different points in the reproductive process. The more points of interference, the more "effective" the contraceptive.

For example, the drug Ella (ulipristal) was approved by the FDA as an "emergency contraceptive." The manufacturer claims that Ella works as an emergency contraceptive by delaying egg release from the ovary for up to five days. And Ella does work this way. But Ella works by this mechanism *only if* taken several days *before the woman releases an egg*.

What the manufacturer *does not mention* is that Ella can also prevent a positive pregnancy test if taken *after* egg release. It is obvious that Ella cannot possibly prevent the release of an egg that has already been released. So, what is the mechanism by which Ella "works" after egg release?

Ella (ulipristal) is a second generation of the abortion drug RU-486 (Mifeprex). Both drugs are "hormone-blockers"/"anti-hormones." Both drugs effectively block the actions of natural progesterone. Without sufficient progesterone, an embryo is unable to implant in the womb, and will also die after implantation due to the uterine lining not sufficiently nourishing the embryo. Ella is as effective in blocking progesterone as is the abortion drug RU-486.[14] Yet, Ella is called an emergency contraceptive because that is the indication for which the manufacturer sought approval from the FDA.

For faithful couples to make an informed decision regarding the use of Ella or any other method of contraception requires the couple to have basic information about how those methods are known to work. The documented fact that all contraceptive drugs, devices, and surgeries "fail" to prevent pregnancy at a certain rate proves that embryos can be and in fact are created during the use of all contraceptive drugs, devices, and surgeries, because all pregnancies begin with the creation of an embryo.

When that embryo is created, the contraceptive drug, device, or surgery will create a certain environment for the embryo that either helps or hinders that embryo's life. The important question facing faithful couples is this: When embryos are created during the use of a certain method of contraception, is there any reason to suspect that the particular method creates conditions inside the mother's body that will make it more likely that these embryos will die? The unique way each contraceptive method functions determines whether an embryo "unintentionally" created will find his or her mother's body a safe haven or a hostile environment.

Contraceptive Methods: Evaluating the Risk to the Embryo

There are basically five different methods currently used to avoid a positive pregnancy test at the end of a woman's cycle: (1) fertility awareness based methods [FABMs], (2) barrier methods, (3) hormone-based methods, (4) IUDs, and (5) emergency contraception. Some methods work exclusively by preventing fertilization and have no effect after fertilization. Some work by sometimes preventing fertilization and sometimes making it difficult or impossible for the embryo to survive. Some methods will directly kill the embryo. Many methods work by a combination of all three. We will look at these five methods from the least to the most harmful for the embryo.

14 Jerry Reel, Sheri Hild-Petito, and Richard Blye, "Antiovulatory and Postcoital Antifertility Activity of the Antiprogestin CDB-2914 When Administered as Single, Multiple, or Continuous Doses to Rats," *Contraception* 58, no. 2 (1998): 129–36. (During development of the drug ulipristal, the original experimental names for ulipristal were CBD-2914, VA2914, HRP2000, or RTI 3021-012.)

1. FERTILITY AWARENESS BASED METHODS (FABMS)

Based on the biological fact that the egg can only be fertilized during the twenty-four hours after egg release, FABMs time intercourse so that sperm are not present during the twenty-four hours after the egg has been released. Since sperm can live in a woman's reproductive tract for up to five days, the timing of intercourse takes into account sperm survival times. The details on these methods are easily available online,[15] and space does not allow a full discussion here of details. But a brief review below will help with understanding of their effects on embryos conceived during the use of FABMs.

> THE CONTRACEPTIVE DRUG, DEVICE, OR SURGERY WILL CREATE A CERTAIN ENVIRONMENT FOR THE EMBRYO THAT EITHER HELPS OR HINDERS THAT EMBRYO'S LIFE.

Most women have many physical signs that the egg is beginning to mature and getting ready to release. One example is a woman's vaginal mucus, which is produced in direct response to the amount of natural estrogen produced by the follicles in the woman's ovary during the first half of the cycle. When the follicles are small, very little estrogen is produced, and the woman has very little mucus. As the follicles mature, more natural estrogen is produced, resulting in more clear mucus. Since sperm live up to five days in the woman's reproductive tract, the beginning of clear mucus formation is the signal to avoid intercourse. When an egg is about to be released, copious amounts of clear vaginal mucus are produced. Within two days after ovulation, the consistency of the mucus changes from clear to white and sticky, due to progesterone now produced by the corpus luteum of the ovary after egg release. This change happens more than twenty-four hours after egg release, when the egg is no longer able to be fertilized. So, intercourse after this time under normal circumstances does not result in embryo formation.

Embryos formed during the use of FABMs do not face any increased risk of death. There is no interference with the woman's reproductive tract. The embryo will not face any interference with transport through the fallopian tube, with implantation, or with the ability of the ovary to make progesterone to support the early pregnancy. Fertility Awareness Based Methods pose no risk to embryos.

---

15 See www.factsaboutfertility.org.

2. BARRIER METHODS

Like fertility awareness methods, barrier methods work by trying to prevent the sperm from reaching the egg when the egg can be fertilized. However, unlike fertility awareness methods, this prevention is accomplished by putting up a barrier to sperm transport. This barrier can be temporary (condom, diaphragm, cervical cap) or permanent (male vasectomy, female tubal ligation, or tubal occlusion). The location of the barrier is key to identifying whether or not there is potential harm to the embryo.

In general, reversible barrier methods and vasectomy in men are fairly safe for the embryo. These methods do not affect the ability of the ovary to release an egg because there is no known hormonal interference with the processes of reproduction in the woman's body. Egg release is not affected, LH surge is intact, and the ovary can produce normal amounts of progesterone during the luteal phase of the cycle. The lining of the womb matures normally, and if an embryo reaches the womb, these methods are not known to interfere with implantation.

However, permanent female sterilization procedures place barriers inside the woman's fallopian tubes, which result in permanent damage that increases the risk that any embryo conceived will not be able to successfully travel through the tube to the womb. This damage to the tube increases the risk that the embryo will implant in the tube (ectopic pregnancy), further discussed below.

2A. Reversible Barrier Methods

Condoms, diaphragms, and cervical caps provide a temporary physical barrier that seals off sperm from entering the womb, preventing the sperm from being present when the egg is released. However, sperm are mighty swimmers and can frequently escape from these barriers. So, most of the time these methods are used with a spermicide—a chemical (cream, foam, or gel) designed to kill sperm in order to kill sperm managing to escape the barrier.

There was some concern in the past that these spermicides might cause an increase in birth defects, by damaging sperm instead of killing them. This would theoretically allow a damaged sperm to fertilize the egg. Some small reports indicated a possible increase in various birth defects after the use of spermicides, but large studies did not find an increase in birth defects in children born to parents who used spermicides for contraception.

2B. Permanent Barrier Methods: Vasectomy

A vasectomy is a permanent male sterilization procedure that severs the tube (vas deferens) that connects the place where sperm is made with the place where sperm is stored. Since no sperm can reach the storage place, no sperm can be released. Most of the time, vasectomy completely blocks sperm from being released in the seminal fluid. However, occasionally the cut ends of the vas can find each other and a connection can be formed that again allows sperm to pass into the seminal fluid. Since vasectomy affects only the supply of sperm and does not affect anything in the woman's reproductive tract, there is no known harm to embryos conceived when the vasectomy fails.

2C. Permanent Barrier Methods: Tubal Occlusion Procedures

The fallopian tubes in a woman can be closed in a number of different ways, including surgically removing a piece of tube, burning the tubes, applying clips from the outside, or applying occlusive material to the inside of the tube. All of these procedures close off the tube completely (most of the time) and prevent sperm from penetrating past the point of obstruction. However, occasionally sperm do penetrate past the occlusion and fertilization can happen. When an embryo is formed in a woman who has had tubal sterilization procedure, the embryo often has great difficulty traveling through the tube, past the area of occlusion. When the embryo is still in the tube at the time he or she is ready to implant, then implantation happens in the tube instead of in the womb.

> MOST BARRIER METHODS HAVE NOT BEEN SHOWN TO INTERFERE WITH EMBRYOS AFTER FERTILIZATION, NOR DO THEY PREVENT IMPLANTATION IN THE ENDOMETRIAL LINING.

Pregnancies diagnosed in women with previous tubal sterilization procedures are rare (5/1000) but when pregnancies do occur, the embryo is frequently implanted in the tubes (ectopic pregnancy). An ectopic pregnancy in the fallopian tube is a life-threatening problem for women because, as the pregnancy grows, the tube cannot stretch enough so, at some point, the tube ruptures and the woman can easily bleed to death. To date, there is no accepted procedure to replace the ectopic pregnancy into the womb.[16] So embryos implanted ectopically will die, and sometimes the mother will also die from internal hemorrhage unless the ectopic pregnancy is surgically removed. When ectopic pregnancies are diagnosed, the treatment is to surgically remove the embryo or part or all of the tube.

Summary

Barrier methods work primarily by preventing sperm transport to the egg. Most barrier methods have not been shown to interfere with embryos after fertilization, nor do they prevent implantation in the endometrial lining. The exception is permanent sterilization procedures that involve the woman's fallopian tubes. Fallopian tube sterilizations carry an increased risk that any embryos created will implant in the damaged portion of the tube (ectopic pregnancy), a life-threatening condition requiring surgery.

3. HORMONE-BASED CONTRACEPTIVES (ARTIFICIAL HORMONES AND HORMONE BLOCKERS)

Hormone-based contraceptives include those drugs and devices that interfere with the ability of the woman to release eggs and prepare her body to nurture an embryo. This broad group includes two major categories: artificial hormones and hormone blockers/antihormones.

Artificial Hormone Contraceptives: The artificial hormone category includes common birth control pills, mini pills, shots, vaginal rings, patches, and any other way of getting artificial hormones into a woman's circulatory system in sufficient quantities to interfere with the natural cyclic release of her own hormones.

Antihormone/Progesterone Blocker Contraceptives: The antihormone/progesterone-blocker category includes two drugs—the abortion pill mifepristone (RU-486, Mifeprex), used commonly overseas as an emergency contraceptive, and the second generation abortion drug ulipristal (Ella, Ella-One) approved in the US as an emergency contraceptive.

All hormone-based contraceptive drugs and devices, whether they are artificial hormones or progesterone blockers, work by disrupting the

16 There are three case reports of successful attempts at transfer of an ectopic pregnancy: (1) C. J. Wallace, "Transplantation of Ectopic Pregnancy from Fallopian Tube in Cavity of Uterus," *Surgery, Gynecology & Obstetrics* 24 (1917): 578–79; (2) Landrum B. Shettles, "Tubal Embryo Successfully Transferred in Utero," *American Journal of Obstetrics and Gynecology* 163 (1990): 2026–27; and (3) J. M. Pearce, "Term Delivery after Intrauterine Relocation of an Ectopic Pregnancy," *British Journal of Obstetrics and Gynaecology* 101 (1994): 717–18. (However, the Pearce article was retracted in 1995.) Two case reports do not in themselves provide enough information about the risks, and attempts at tubal transfer to date must be considered experimental. The Watson Bowes Research Institute (http://watsonbowesresearchinstitute.org) is seeking funding for research in ectopic transplantation.

symphony of natural hormone release and response that causes egg release and also prepares a woman's body to receive and nurture an embryo. This disruption occurs by targeting the release and function of two natural hormones in a woman's body: the hormone LH and the hormone natural progesterone.

Recall from the earlier section about normal physiological processes of reproduction that the "LH surge" is the trigger that causes the egg to be released from the ovary. Recall also that the amount of LH in the LH surge determines the number of cells in the follicle that will later go on to produce progesterone. So the amount of LH in the LH surge and the amount of progesterone produced later in the luteal phase of the cycle are directly related.

The hormone progesterone is responsible for causing the embryo to travel down the tube into the womb, and for preparing the lining of the womb to receive and continue to nourish the embryo through the first part of pregnancy. So, both LH and progesterone in perfectly timed amounts are necessary for normal embryo survival. Blocking or decreasing either of these hormones has significant ramifications for the embryo.

All hormone-based contraceptives work primarily by interfering with the release of LH from the brain.[17] The various artificial hormone combinations and the progesterone blockers cause one of three things to happen with LH:

1. Hormone-based contraceptives can cause very little LH to be released. If there is very little LH released, then no egg release will happen. If the egg is not released, then it cannot be fertilized, and no embryo would be formed. If hormone-based contraceptives always prevented the release of an egg, then there would be no concern about harm to embryos. But since we know for certain that women can become pregnant while taking hormonal contraception, we know for certain that some eggs are released and we know for certain that some embryos are formed.

17 ESHRE Capri Workshop Group, "Ovarian and Endometrial Function during Hormonal Contraception," *Human Reproduction* 16, no. 7 (2001): 1527–35. See also Rachel Steward et al., "Comparison of Cervical Mucus of 24/4 vs. 21/7 Combined Oral Contraceptives," *Contraception* 86 (2012): 710–15. Quoted here: *"The main contraceptive effect of combined oral contraceptives (COCs) is inhibition of the midcycle lutenizing hormone (LH) surge to prevent ovulation. However, several studies have shown that the percentage of ovulatory cycles in women using low-dose COCs ranges between 1.5% and 16.8%. With this high rate of ovulatory cycles in women taking COCs, we would expect the pregnancy rate with COC use to be much higher than the perfect use failure rate of 0.3% were there not other effective mechanisms of contraceptive action in addition to ovulation inhibition. Another potential mechanism of contraceptive action is the suppression of follicle-stimulating hormone secretion during the follicular phase of the cycle, thereby preventing follicular maturation; however, follicular development has been shown to occur in 23%–90% of cycles in women using COCs. There are also many progestin-related mechanisms that likely contribute to the overall efficacy of the combined contraceptives, such as thickening of cervical mucus, impairment of tubal mobility and peristalsis, and effects on the endometrial lining, making it less suitable for implantation."*

2. Hormone-based contraceptives can allow enough LH surge to allow the egg to be released, but not enough LH surge to change very many cells in the corpus luteum to be able to later produce progesterone. (This situation of insufficient LH surge happens naturally in a disease called "luteal phase deficiency," which is a cause of recurrent miscarriage. Treatment of LPD involves giving natural progesterone as a supplement throughout the luteal phase of the woman's cycle, and throughout the first few months of her pregnancy.)

THERE ARE SIGNIFICANT CONCERNS ABOUT HOW HORMONE-BASED CONTRACEPTION WORKS.

   Hormone-based contraceptives can allow eggs to be released, but in this situation of "break through ovulation," the LH level is most often abnormally low, mimicking LPD.[18] If an embryo is created under these circumstances, the corpus luteum will not make enough progesterone to allow for the correct travel time through the tube, or allow for correct preparation of the mother's womb for implantation, or allow for the lining of the womb to nurture the growing embryo through the first part of his or her life. This action of the hormone-based contraceptive causes embryos to die. An abnormally low LH is a common occurrence for the 3 percent to 40 percent of women who release eggs on the birth control pill, and in women who release eggs after taking progesterone blockers.

3. In some women who take artificial hormone contraceptives, the LH surge may not be affected much at all. In this case, an egg will be released normally, and the corpus luteum of the ovary will make normal amounts of progesterone. If an embryo is formed under these circumstances, the ovary will form a normal corpus luteum and produce a normal amount of progesterone. This is the situation for most women who become recognizably pregnant using artificial hormone contraceptives, and then go on to carry that pregnancy to term.

18 L. B. Zapata et al., "Effect of Missed Combined Hormonal Contraceptives on Contraceptive Effectiveness: A Systematic Review," *Contraception* 87, no. 5 (2013): 685–700, www.ncbi.nlm.nih.gov/pmc/articles/PMC4322904/pdf/nihms653707.pdf. Quoted here: ". . . among women who did ovulate, cycles were usually abnormal (i.e., low progesterone levels, small follicles and/or poor cervical mucus)."

However, progesterone-blockers kill embryos after implantation. Both RU-486 and Ella directly destroy both the corpus luteum and the place where the embryo implants. Thus it is very rare for an embryo to survive[19] during use of progesterone blockers such as RU-486 or Ella because of direct actions on the corpus luteum and the lining of the womb.[20] That is why both RU-486 and Ella are so "effective" as contraceptives.

How often are eggs released during the use of hormone-based contraceptives?

The answer depends on a host of different factors, including when in her cycle the woman takes the drug, how much she weighs, whether or not she has taken any drugs that interfere with the hormone-based contraceptive, exactly what kind of hormone-based contraceptive she is taking, and more. But in general, when researchers study one hundred women who are using birth control pills as hormonal contraception, somewhere between 2 percent and 40 percent of those women will have follicle rupture (ovulation) each cycle.[21] Compared to the rate of follicle rupture in women not using contraception (60 percent) a 2–40 percent rate of rupture predicts that there should be around three to fifty-seven pregnancies each year in that one hundred women using hormonal contraception. But in one hundred women who use birth control pills as hormonal contraceptives there are one to four pregnancies each year. That fact has led researchers to conclude that hormonal contraceptives likely work in some ways other than just preventing egg release.

What other ways could hormonal contraception work?[22] In addition to interfering with the LH surge, artificial hormone-based contraceptives can affect the ability of the tube to transport the embryo. Some hormonal contraceptives that use only progestins (the "mini-pill") can slow down the tube, increasing the likelihood that the embryo will implant in the tube instead of in the womb. Antihormones such as RU-486 and Ella can speed up the tubal transport, causing embryos to reach the womb before the embryo is capable of implanting.

19 Donna Harrison and James Mitroka, "Defining Reality: The Potential Role of Pharmacists in Assessing the Impact of Progesterone Receptor Modulators and Misoprostol in Reproductive Health," *Annals of Pharmacotherapy* 45, no. 1 (2011): 115–19.

20 Reel, Hild-Petito, and Blye, "Antiovulatory and Postcoital Antifertility Activity of the Antiprogestin CDB-2914 When Administered as Single, Multiple, or Continuous Doses to Rats," 129–36. (During development of the drug ulipristal, the original experimental names for ulipristal were CBD-2914, VA2914, HRP2000, or RTI 3021-012.)

21 See footnote 18. Reisman, *Sexual Sabotage*, 45.

22 See footnote 18.

Hormone-based contraceptives can also directly interfere with the growth and development of the lining of the womb, which can hinder or prevent an embryo from implanting in the lining. Both tubal interference and direct interference with the growth and development of the lining of the womb can cause embryos to die. These mechanisms of action have been called euphemistically "interception," "endometrial contraception," and "contra-gestation."

Once the embryo has implanted, artificial hormone-based contraceptives do not dislodge the embryo or lead directly to embryo death. In contrast, progesterone blockers—RU-486 (mifeprex) and ulipristal (Ella)—can directly destroy the embryo by directly blocking the action of progesterone in the womb. So, both RU-486 and ulipristal can both prevent implantation and can cause abortion after implantation. Both RU-486 and Ella can also directly destroy the corpus luteum of the ovary,[23] so that it cannot make progesterone to support the early pregnancy.

In summary, there are significant concerns about how hormone-based contraception works. Although frequently these drugs can prevent egg release, when egg release does happen and embryos are formed, the additional effects of the hormone-based contraceptives make implantation and embryo survival much less likely. For couples who care about never causing harm or death to their embryonic children, hormone-based methods are not a safe option.

4. IUDS: INTRAUTERINE DEVICES

It has been known for hundreds of years in the veterinary world that inserting something into the womb of an animal will prevent that animal from being able to carry a pregnancy to term. The IUD is a piece of metal or plastic of various different shapes placed inside a woman's womb that sets up a chronic inflammation inside the womb. The 2008 international working group on IUDs published this remarkably honest comment: "There is sufficient evidence to suggest that IUDs can prevent and disrupt implantation. The extent to which this interference contributes to its contraceptive action is unknown. The data are scanty and the political consequences of resolving this issue interfere with comprehensive research."[24] An embryo created during the use of an IUD would have very little chance

23 Yuval Yung et al. "Progesterone Antagonist, RU486 Represses LHCGR Expression and LH/hCG Signaling in Cultured Luteinized Human Mural Granulosa Cells," *Gynecological Endocrinology* 30, no. 1 (2014): 42–47.

24 ESHRE Capri Workshop Group, "Intrauterine Devices and Intrauterine Systems," *Human Reproduction Update* 14, no. 3 (2008): 197–208.

of implanting in the inflamed endometrial lining,[25] and embryos who do not implant die.

But inflamed wombs bleed easily. So, to improve the bleeding problem, IUD manufacturers started adding artificial hormones to the IUD, hoping to shrink the lining of the womb so that it would not bleed constantly. These artificial hormones also thicken the mucus of the cervix and slow down the movement of the woman's fallopian tube.

It has been claimed recently by those marketing IUDs that the hormonal IUD (Mirena) prevents the egg from being released from the ovary. While there is some slight decrease in egg release for women in the first year on Mirena, after a year of Mirena use, follicular rupture rates are similar to the follicular rupture rates of women who are not using any contraception, which are similar to the rates of copper IUD users.[26] So preventing egg release cannot possibly be the major mechanism of preventing a recognizable pregnancy in Mirena IUD users.

ANY COUPLE WHO CARES ABOUT SURVIVAL OF THEIR EMBRYONIC CHILDREN SHOULD AVOID THE USE OF AN IUD.

Those marketing Mirena IUDs also claim that the progesterone component prevents sperm from coming into the womb by thickening cervical mucus. There may be some cervical mucus thickening with progesterone IUD use, but, after a few years, cervical changes disappear. "The presence of good cervical mucus was observed in 69% of the ovulatory cycles studied in the LNG-IUD users. This indicates that effects on cervical mucus cannot be the main mechanism of action of the LNG-IUDs"[27] In fact, both sperm and embryos have been found in the tubes of Mirena and other IUD users, providing direct evidence that sperm can be and are present when eggs are released and that embryos[28] can be and are formed during the use of IUDs. In addition, about 1 in 125 IUD users become pregnant with the IUD in place. For these women, the pregnancy is most often ectopic (where the embryo implants in the tubes) because embryos who make it to the uterus cannot implant. If the embryo

25 ESHRE Capri Workshop Group, "Intrauterine Devices and Intrauterine Systems," *Human Reproduction Update* 14, no. 3 (2008): 197–208.

26 I. Barbosa et al., "Ovarian Function after Seven Years' Use of a Levonorgestrel IUD," *Advances in Contraception* 11, no. 2 (1995): 85–95. *"In the regularly menstruating LNg-IUD users, according to progesterone levels, 93% of the cycles were ovulatory but just 58% of these 'ovulatory' cycles showed normal follicular growth and rupture."*

27 I. Barbosa et al,, "Ovarian Function after Seven Years' Use of a Levonorgestrel IUD," 85–95.

28 Maria Ortiz and Horacio Croxatto, "Copper-T Intrauterine Device and Levonorgestrel Intrauterine System: Biological Bases of Their Mechanism of Action," *Contraception* 75 (2007): S16–S30.

does somehow manage to get through the tube and manages to implant in the womb, the trouble is not over. Intrauterine pregnancies that happen with an IUD in place frequently miscarry, become infected, and die, or deliver very prematurely.[29] The chronic inflammation from the IUD disrupts the entire course of a pregnancy for those embryos who do manage to implant in the womb.

In summary, the IUD is designed to work by killing embryos. Any couple who cares about survival of their embryonic children should avoid the use of an IUD.

5. EMERGENCY CONTRACEPTION

Emergency contraceptives are all capable of killing embryos; the more effective the emergency contraceptive, the more likely it is to kill embryos. Any emergency contraceptive that works *after* egg release must be capable of killing embryos. There are four methods commonly used for emergency contraception:

A. Single-dose progestins (Plan B and Next Choice)
B. Single-dose progesterone-blockers RU-486 (mifepristone, Mifeprex) and ulipristal (Ella, Ella-One)
C. IUDs placed during the luteal phase
D. "Menstrual regulation/menstrual extraction" (i.e., early abortion)

A. Single-Dose Progestins (Plan B, Next Choice)

Progestins are artificial hormones that resemble natural progesterone but do not have all the actions of natural progesterone. Plan B works poorly as an emergency contraceptive because it does not have much effect after fertilization. Plan B can delay the release of an egg if taken several days before the LH surge. However, if Plan B is taken immediately before the LH surge, egg release will still happen but the LH surge will be decreased, causing a luteal phase defect as discussed above.

If a woman has already released an egg and takes Plan B, there seems to be little if any effect on her embryo. Single-dose Plan B after egg release probably does not affect either progesterone production or implantation.

B. Antihormones/Progesterone Blockers

29 American College of Obstetricians and Gynecologists, *Practice Bulletin* 121 (July 2011), reaffirmed 2015, www.acog.org/~/media/Practice%20Bulletins/Committee%20on%20Practice%20Bulletins%20--%20Gynecology/Public/pb121.pdf?dmc=1.

As discussed previously, Ella (ulipristal, Ella-One) is a second generation abortion drug identical in action to the abortion drug RU-486. Ella can prevent the egg from being released, if taken several days before the egg is about to be released. However, if taken on the day of egg release or after, Ella directly kills the embryo by blocking the action of progesterone to prepare the lining of the womb for implantation, by directly destroying the tissues in the womb that respond to progesterone and nourish the implanted embryo, and also by destroying the corpus luteum of the ovary that makes progesterone to sustain the early pregnancy.

C. The IUD

The IUD is also very effective as an "emergency contraceptive" because the IUD destroys the ability of the womb to allow for implantation by setting up a chronic inflammation inside the womb. If the embryo has already implanted, the IUD will dislodge the embryo, causing an induced abortion.

D. "Menstrual Extraction"

This term is a euphemism for surgically removing the lining of the womb. If the embryo has not yet implanted, then removing the lining will prevent the embryo from implanting. If the embryo has already implanted, then this procedure is an early elective abortion.

In summary, any emergency contraceptive that is effective after egg release must work by killing embryos. This includes Ella, the IUD, and "menstrual extraction." Plan B is a very ineffective emergency contraceptive that can delay egg release if taken several days before the release of an egg. But if Plan B is taken immediately before the release of an egg, Plan B can lead to the death of the embryo by decreasing the LH surge and inducing a luteal phase defect.

Conclusion

Each one of the five different contraceptive approaches outlined above results in a particular environment inside the woman's womb. Since embryos can be and are created during the use of each of these methods, it is important for couples to understand the basics of each approach in order to make informed decisions about the risks that their embryonic children will face when created during contraceptive use. For couples who care about never doing harm to their embryonic children, this article will serve as the beginning of a discussion about available methods of spacing children.

However, for Christian couples many questions remain—questions about the integrity of the body, the meaning and purpose of the one-flesh relationship, and radical trust in God's promises of sufficiency and provision. These deeper theological issues will remain at the heart of any discussion about the procreation and care of children in a faithful marriage.

CHAPTER 5

PASTORAL CONSIDERATIONS OF CONTRACEPTION

D. Richard Stuckwisch

Matters pertaining to marriage, procreation, and contraception are most properly addressed with personal pastoral care. Every particular situation is different, and in this fallen world there are no pat and easy answers for all the questions and challenges confronting husbands, wives, and families in their life together. Yet, the Word of God does speak to these various vocations and stations in life, which are established and given by Him. And by the wisdom of His Word and Spirit, we offer here some basic underlying principles to be considered and taken into account, especially as Christian couples contemplate using contraception.

The question of contraception has been made much more difficult by rampant confusion over marriage itself. At the same time, developments in contraception and birth control have, for their part, contributed to this confusion, especially by serving and supporting the separation of marriage, sex, and procreation in societal thinking and practice.

For our purposes, let us briefly define marriage as the exclusive and lifelong union of one man and one woman.[1] It is consummated and centrally defined by the conjugal union of the male and the female, dependent upon the bodily distinction and complementarity of the sexes. It is ordered especially for the procreation and rearing of children in the fear and faith of God, but also for the care and cultivation of the earth under the authority of God. It is personal and private, on the one hand, involving the naked intimacy of husband and wife. But marriage is also public, societal, and communal, establishing generations, family circles, and social connections.

Marriage is an objective calling and office, and spouses have duties and responsibilities toward each other, God, and their other neighbors in the world. It is undertaken with mutual and parental consent and with a public commitment of enduring faithfulness. It is appropriate and desirable for

1 For several excellent discussions of marriage from a variety of perspectives, cf. Sherif Girgis, Ryan T. Anderson, and Robert P. George, *What Is Marriage?* (New York: Encounter Books, 2012); Edward Sri, *Men, Women, and the Mystery of Love* (Cincinnati: Servant, 2015); and Christopher Ash, *Marriage: Sex in the Service of God* (Vancouver: Regent College Publishing, 2003).

emotions of friendship and romance to develop and grow within marriage, but these emotions are not its basis or its purpose.

Created in the image of God, the man and the woman are given to each other in the mutual love of self-sacrifice and personal commitment to what is good and right and true. They are given to delight in each other in the fear and faith of God. And they are blessed by His Word and Spirit to be fruitful and multiply, to fill the earth and have dominion over it (Genesis 1:26–28; 9:1–7). Within this holy office and by this good work, the man and his wife are given to share and to confess the life and love of the Holy Trinity. In their union of love, in heart and mind, body and soul, they signify the marriage of Christ and His Bride, the Church (Ephesians 5:22–33). Likewise, in their fruitfulness, that is, in their bearing and rearing of children, there is an image of, a participation in, and a contribution to the Church's fruitfulness in bearing the children of God by the Gospel of Christ.

> TO SAY IT BLUNTLY, MEN AND WOMEN DO NOT MAKE BABIES. GOD MAKES BABIES.

In some ways, it is simply a basic fact that, if there are no children being conceived and born, then the Church will not grow as she otherwise would. But there is also the sense in which the children born to a Christian husband and wife, baptized and catechized in the name of Christ, not only belong to the fruitfulness of the Church but also signify the fruitfulness of the Church, who by the Word and Spirit of Christ conceives and gives birth to the children of God. Thus, when considering questions of contraception or "family planning," we should first of all ask this: What does this confess concerning the Church and her fruitfulness in making disciples of the Lord Jesus Christ, in giving birth to the children of God?

Also belonging to the image of God is the dominion that man is given over the earth. That dominion, properly speaking, is a stewardship of faith and love, carried out in the name of the Lord and belonging to the beauty and good order of His creation. It is not an absolute or open-ended lordship, but a God-given authority over and responsibility for the particular garden where God, the Lord, has placed a man and his wife.[2] It is required of them, as stewards of God's good creation and good gifts, to be faithful in their care for and administration of that garden.

Practically speaking, in view of the topic at hand, this dominion and stewardship means, first of all, that husband and wife will normally en-

2 Cf. Luther's helpful comments on Adam's work in the garden in his *Lectures on Genesis* (2:15) in AE 1:101–3.

gage in marital relations (conjugal union) as a matter of course in their life together. Indeed, they should not withhold themselves from each other except by mutual agreement for a time for the sake of prayer (1 Corinthians 7:5). The one-flesh union is integral to marriage and a basic good of marriage. What is more, the bodies of the husband and wife are not simply their own, respectively, but they belong to each other, and they owe each other the mutual affection of sexual intimacy, also for the sake of protecting each other against the temptations of the flesh. After the fall into sin, there is this additional benefit and purpose of marriage. It is the one place and relationship wherein sex is sanctified by God's Word and therefore righteous and holy, and by which husbands and wives are guarded against the lusts and enticements of the flesh outside of holy matrimony.

It is also in this conjugal union of the man and his wife that the Lord our God, who is alone the author and giver of life, conceives children where and when it pleases Him. It is much the same as the way that God obtains the saving faith where and when it pleases Him in those who hear the Gospel. Men and women are not given the decision, really, whether or when to have children. To say it bluntly, men and women do not make babies. God makes babies. Men and women are not able to create new life; nor is it within their power and prerogative to choose conception. What men and women are given to do is to love each other, also bodily, in conjugal union within their marriage, and to leave the creation of new life to God.

Husbands and wives are called to cleave to each other in faith before God and in faithfulness to each other. They do so in the confidence that God is the one who will bless them with fertility (or not) according to His grace and wisdom. It is in His mercy that He multiplies their love for each other with sons and daughters, whether by nature or adoption, and/or by faith and love within the household and family of His Church.

GOD IS THE ONE WHO WILL BLESS THEM WITH FERTILITY (OR NOT) ACCORDING TO HIS GRACE AND WISDOM.

Granted, though men and women cannot create new life, it is within their power and ability to destroy the temporal life that God has entrusted to their care. They are able, tragically, to hurt and kill the bodies of their children. But such destruction, harm, and violence, even when it is done quietly and covertly in the secret place of the womb, is forbidden and prohibited by God. It is murder, contrary to the Fifth Commandment. It is sinful.

In a quite distinct and different way, because the Creator and Preserver of all things has established an orderly creation, and because He is most faithful in upholding His creation in its natural order, it is also possible for men and women to avoid the likelihood of conception. As this potential course of action rests upon the faithfulness of God, it is especially ironic when conception is thus avoided due to a lack of trust and confidence in the providential care of the same Lord God!

In any event, the actual avoidance of conception does not involve the destruction or murder of an unborn human being. Hence, it is a most significant distinction and a decisive point, to begin with, whether one is avoiding the likelihood of conception or harming an already conceived child.

The Distinction between Contraception and Birth Control

One also has to be cautious and circumspect at precisely this point. In recent decades, the term *conception* has been craftily defined to mean the *implantation* in the womb of a fertilized egg (an embryo, which is to say, a human being in the earliest stage of life). So everything up until that point of implantation is considered "preconception" in this kind of legalese. Here, though, by "conception" we refer to the union of the sperm and the egg, the beginning of the embryo, even prior to implantation in the womb. This means that a "fertilized egg" is actually a human being, created in the image of God for life with Him in Christ. To avoid conception, properly speaking, requires intervention prior to fertilization.[3]

To be clear and precise, therefore, let us distinguish between "contraception" and "birth control." Although these terms are typically used in a broad and comprehensive manner as synonyms, there needs to be some way of differentiating between the avoidance of conception on the one hand and the actual destruction of human life on the other hand. Notwithstanding the common usage, the terms at hand already imply this fundamental distinction. Thus, we use them here as follows:

1. "Contraception" avoids the likelihood of conception by seeking to prevent the union of the man's sperm with the woman's egg. "Birth control," by way of contrast, aims to prevent the actual birth of a child. It does so, whether in whole or in part, by hindering, inhibiting, and preventing

3 See chapter 4 for detailed information on contraception and its effect on the embryo.

the normal growth and development of an already fertilized egg—that is, an embryo—by doing harm and violence to a newly conceived human life.

2. "Birth control," thus defined, is sinful and immoral because it violates the Fifth Commandment. It is that simple. Various forms of "birth control," even though they may typically be described as "contraceptives," are actually abortifacients to a greater or lesser extent. While they may work to reduce the frequency of conception, they also work in part by ensuring that any children who are conceived will not be able to implant in the womb and grow and live.

CHRISTIANS SHOULD CERTAINLY OPT FOR CAUTION AND NOT ENGAGE IN WHAT AMOUNTS TO A KIND OF "RUSSIAN ROULETTE" WITH THEIR UNBORN CHILDREN.

Along these lines and for these reasons, birth control pills are not a morally acceptable option because they inhibit and prevent the implantation and survival of the human embryos who are conceived while the pills are being used. They also do short-term and long-term violence to the woman's body in the process, a serious concern that has not been given the attention it requires.

It is true that there are different kinds of birth control pills, some of which are more or less harmful and egregious than others. But even at best, there are serious concerns and significant uncertainties, which ought not to be ignored. Christians should certainly opt for caution and not engage in what amounts to a kind of "Russian roulette" with their unborn children.

Regrettably, many well-meaning Christians have in the past been misled into using birth control without being given the facts. When years have been invested in this decision and practice, when incomes are at stake, and when consciences are weighted down and under attack, there is a resistance, often a refusal, to receive and accept the truth. Yet, as painful and difficult as it may be, there needs to be a willingness to acknowledge past mistakes and sins, to bear the fruits of repentance in newness of life, and to proceed in faith and love in the confidence of the Lord's mercy, in the forgiveness of His cross and the righteousness of His resurrection.

The Use of Contraception

In contrast to birth control, the use of contraception in itself is neither sinful nor immoral, but neutral and free. The conjugal union and the fruitfulness of holy marriage are gifts and blessings of God, which should not be despised but received in faith and with thanksgiving. But there is no word of God commanding marital relations or forbidding the avoidance of conception at any given time or under every and all circumstances. The Lord has left the specific arrangements and activities of husbands and wives to be worked out in mutual love and in the freedom of faith before Him, as the counsel of St. Paul to the Church at Corinth also demonstrates (1 Corinthians 7).

This is not to say that using contraception is of no consequence or significance. Rather, it is subject to the contextual criteria and moral considerations of faith and love in relation to God and neighbor. With these very criteria and considerations in mind, there is also a significant difference to be noted between the temporary or intermittent use of contraception and a permanent "sterilization" or long-term ongoing avoidance of conception.

It may well be that avoiding the likelihood of conception is at times a godly exercise of dominion over the creation. We might compare it to Adam restraining the animals and preventing them from coming into the Garden of Eden, and to his ordering and organizing of the garden, choosing what to plant and what not to plant, cultivating and pruning, and so forth, as a stewardship of that which God entrusted to his care and oversight (Genesis 2:5–20). To be sure, the avoidance of conception is not always called for, nor is it always undertaken as an exercise of godly dominion over and good stewardship of creation. It is not always done responsibly, with virtue, in the fear and faith of God. But it may be so. And where and when contraception is used, it ought to be in faith, for the purpose of glorifying God, caring for His creation in peace, and serving the neighbor in love.

Although circumstances may sometimes suggest that it would be wise to avoid the likelihood of conception, contraception is not the rule but the exception. This point absolutely needs to be made and emphasized clearly because the mindset over the past fifty years or more has been turned utterly and completely around. Even in the thinking and conversation of many Christians, the basic idea is that couples are going to use contraception, that they are going to avoid children until such and such a time, or else deliberately space their children apart, as though this sort of choice and control were the norm, the standard. Hence, if a couple is not using contraception, it is supposed that they have made a conscious choice and are actively "trying" to have children. It should be obvious that this language of "trying," when it comes to having children, is nothing else than the flip side of the pro-choice rhetoric so prevalent in the ideology of abortion activists.

For husbands and wives with a larger than average number of children, there are likely to be questions and comments from others (both friends and strangers alike) as to why they are seeking and trying to have so many. It would be better to assume that the man and his wife are simply living in love for each other, cleaving to each other faithfully within their marriage, engaging in normal marital relations, and welcoming whatever children the Lord entrusts to their care within their vocations and stations of life. They may well be nervous and afraid, hard-pressed and weary within and without, yet persisting in the joyful confidence of faith and in love for God, for each other, and for each and all of their children. By the same token, one should not assume that couples with few or no children have deliberately avoided conception or engaged in birth control. Barrenness and infertility, miscarriage and stillbirths, are grievous crosses to bear in their own right, often in silence and plagued by feelings of guilt, inadequacy, or shame. The assumptions of our contraceptive culture do not help but only add to the weight of these burdens.

Again, it needs to be stated clearly and unequivocally: contraception is not the rule but the exception. It should not be regarded as the norm or the standard. The true norm, the starting point, the baseline and default position—where faith and love reside to begin with—is that a husband and wife will be open and receptive to children as they go about their normal marital relations. That perspective and priority has been the Church's teaching, in opposition to contraception and birth control, for almost her entire history.[4] We should not burden consciences with laws beyond those of faith and love, but such longstanding tradition calls us to be circumspect and cautious in considering contraception. Christians should certainly not be bullied, coerced, or enticed into adopting the world's contraceptive mindset, but should be encouraged by the blessing of marriage and of human life by God, the Creator and Preserver of all things, by His Word and by His own incarnation, cross, and bodily resurrection.

It is well known that the Roman Catholic Church, while opposed to contraception and birth control, has permitted the use of "Natural Family Planning" (NFP). By this approach, a couple avoids the likelihood of conception by refraining from marital relations at those times when the woman is fertile. The Roman Church has allowed for the practice of NFP on the

4 For a helpful overview and summary discussion of this history, cf. David S. Hasselbrook, *Contraception and Christendom* (Missoula, MT: Neofita Eleon Publishing, 2014).

grounds that it does not misuse or violate the conjugal act.[5] In this view, it is more "natural" and less intrusive than barrier methods of contraception, which allow for sexual intercourse while blocking the man's sperm from uniting with the woman's egg.

Nevertheless, deliberately refraining from marital relations on a particular occasion, or at any given time, for the purpose of avoiding conception is itself another method of "contraception." While NFP differs from other methods in significant ways, it does entail its own kind of interference and intrusion upon the marriage, and it is no less subject to the same considerations of faith and love. Withholding and abstaining from the natural affections and intimacy of marriage, especially at those very times when the woman is most fertile and, by God's design, most interested in sexual intimacy, is hardly "natural." This is not to say that NFP is necessarily wrong or inappropriate, but only to qualify its use in much the same way that contraception in general must be qualified.

The differences between NFP and typical (temporary) barrier methods of contraception do not appear to be ethically decisive. Husbands and wives may agree to refrain from marital relations for a time, for the sake of prayer, which is an exercise of faith and self-discipline. Otherwise, they are not to withhold themselves from each other, but are to render the conjugal duty that belongs to their marriage, not only because of its inherent goodness, but for the sake of love, in order to guard against sexual immorality (1 Corinthians 7:5). So, in considering whether to avoid the likelihood of conception, the criteria of faith and love may in some cases suggest NFP, and in other cases a barrier method. Either way, deliberately taking an action (or deliberately avoiding an action) for the purpose of avoiding what is the natural outcome of married life and marital relations is an intrusion and to that extent "unnatural." The question is whether this or that kind of intrusion is warranted and permissible in a given case—a godly exercise of dominion over the creation, an act of faith and love—or whether it is prompted by sin, by idolatry or unbelief.

CHRISTIANS SHOULD UNDERSTAND THAT THEIR CHOICES, DECISIONS, AND ACTIONS ARE A CONFESSION OF THEIR FAITH AND A TESTIMONY TO AND FOR THEIR NEIGHBORS.

5 For a brief but helpful discussion of Roman Catholic perspectives on contraception and the periodic continence of NFP, cf. Edward Sri, "How Contraception Harms Love," in his *Men, Women, and the Mystery of Love* (Cincinnati: Servant, 2015), 116–27.

Contraception as an Exercise of Faith and Love

When decisions to avoid the likelihood of conception are driven by ungodly fear instead of the fear of God—by doubt and despair, laziness, selfishness and greed, personal ambition, and so on—then such decisions and actions are sinful violations of faith and love, irrespective of the method of contraception that is used. These are the points at which husbands and wives must examine their hearts and minds and consciences, and discipline themselves in repentance. These are the sins of idolatry and unbelief that often undergird and drive the avoidance of children. Motivations of this kind hardly differ at all from those underlying abortion, notwithstanding the difference between contraception per se and abortion or birth control.

Christians should understand that their choices, decisions, and actions are a confession of their faith and a testimony to and for their neighbors. One might insist that these matters are personal and private and nobody else's business, and that is true to some extent. Yet, marriage and family are public matters, of public interest and concern. And the example of Christians is instructive. Couples should therefore be circumspect and take care in all their words and actions. Where there may be confusion or misunderstanding, they might consider providing clarity and explanation, rather than leaving people to make their false assumptions and draw their erroneous conclusions. Christians are called to live by faith in the Word of God, as citizens of the kingdom of God, and that is a deeply countercultural way of life. As the pressures of the world's way of thinking and acting increase, Christians stand fast and boldly confess their faith and love in Christ by their speaking and their way of living.

Before the Lord our God (*coram Deo*), we are bound in our conscience not to sin. Although we do in fact sin every day in our thoughts, words, and deeds, we are called daily to repentance, to faith in the forgiveness of sins, and to newness of life. Wherever we have done wrong, even if it has been ongoing for a very long time, we are called to begin doing what is good and right henceforth. In being called to repentance, we are not called to wallow in guilt and shame and regret, nor to remain in our sins, but to rejoice in the forgiveness and righteousness of Christ, and to rise up with Him to a new life in heart and mind, soul and body. This fundamental pattern of repentant faith is rooted in our Baptism into the cross and resurrection of Christ Jesus. We live no longer for ourselves, but for Him who for our sake died and was raised (2 Corinthians 5:14–15), who gave Himself for us that He might sanctify us by the washing of water with His Word and adorn us with His beautiful righteousness (Ephesians 5:25–27). It is in that faith, hope, and confidence that we go about our lives in the world. And the fact is that marital relations and the use (or non-use) of contraception both belong to that realm of life, in which we do have freedom and ability to make choices and decisions, to discipline ourselves, to do what is right, and to flee what is wrong.

The Providence of God

The first duty and good work of faith is to receive and trust the forgiveness of sins, the free and clear redemption of the Gospel, and the life and salvation that are established and given in Christ. On that basis, faith also trusts and confesses, in thought, word, and deed, that the Lord our God will surely provide all that is needed for each and every child that He conceives.

We must confess this confidence in the providence of God, even when external evidence and experience appear to contradict it. The Maker of the heavens and the earth will provide all that is needed for this body and life that He has created for the sake of His holy love. This hope belongs to our most basic confession of the faith. For He who did not spare His own Son but delivered Him up for us all will freely give us all things in and with Christ Jesus (Romans 8:32). He does not accuse or condemn us, nor count our trespasses against us, but with His forgiveness of all our sins He also gives us daily bread for body and soul. He opens His hand to provide all that we need for this temporal life on earth, and by the Gospel He grants to us the kingdom of heaven forever.

> HIS GOOD AND GRACIOUS WILL IS NOT THWARTED OR UNDONE BY OUR SIN.

To be sure, the Lord's gracious providence in this fallen world is granted in, with, and under the cross, finally to be realized and fully received in the resurrection of the body. Such is the theology of the cross, which is a hidden, mysterious, difficult, and painful theology. And yet, we know it to be true and good and right, because God Himself has taken the cross upon Himself, and by the cross He has revealed Himself and His glory and accomplished our redemption and salvation. Hence, the certainty of the Lord's divine providence does not negate, nor is it contradicted by, the present frailty of our mortal flesh. For His power is perfected in weakness.

Christians die. Sometimes they die in the womb or in early childhood. Sometimes they die when they are parents, and they leave behind widows and orphans. Christians do sometimes go hungry, naked, and homeless, as did that poor man, Lazarus, before he was carried to Abraham's bosom (Luke 16:19–31). Yet, none of these conditions is able to undo the promise of God, that He will provide all that is needed for this body and life and for the life everlasting of body and soul. Nor does the promise of His providence mean that Christians will not suffer these things. We live by faith in the hope and promise of the resurrection, because we know that the Crucified One is also risen from the dead and lives and reigns to all eternity. This testimony is everywhere the preaching of the apostles: God raised Jesus from the dead. Therefore, even in the face of suffering, sickness, and death, Christians can say, "God is good, He is faithful, and His steadfast loving-kindness does not end." He is the author and giver of life even in the midst of death.

Behind the fact that His providence is not denied even by death is the fact that His good and gracious will is not thwarted or undone by our sin. Not by our doubts and fears and weaknesses. Not by our greed and selfishness. Not by our laziness and lust. Not by depression or despair. Not even abortion or any other birth control; neither contraception, nor infertility, nor miscarriage; nor the brokenness of heart, mind, or body, shall be able to separate us from the love of God, which is in Christ Jesus our Lord (Romans 8:35–39). For He was crucified for our transgressions, and God the Father raised this same Jesus from the dead for our justification (Romans 4:25; Acts 2:22–36). He is our righteousness, who ever lives to make intercession for us (Romans 8:34; Hebrews 7:25). For His sake, our dear Father in heaven does not cast us away from His presence, nor does He withdraw His gracious hand from us. He continues to love us, to care for us, and to provide for all our needs, even as He calls us daily to repentance by the preaching of the cross and resurrection of His Son, until by His grace He shall call us also from the grave to the life everlasting.

To the point at hand, then, Christians receive and welcome children from the hand of the Lord in the hope and confidence of the resurrection and the life everlasting. At the same time, they do not suppose that life and salvation depend on having children. Nor do they suppose that bearing and rearing children will be a painless and trouble-free undertaking. There is pain and sorrow, infirmity, and sometimes death in pregnancy, childbirth, childhood, and parenting, as in both marriage and celibacy.

Christians, therefore, take seriously both the cross and the resurrection as they approach, consider, and live within their vocations and stations in life.

It is likewise the case that in, with, and under the cross, even in this fallen and perishing world, the Lord's gracious providence is granted through various masks and means, including such things as the medical care of physicians and the loving care of husbands and fathers for their families. These earthly means should not be despised or ignored in preference for some "miraculous divine intervention," but should be recognized and received in confidence as the Lord's ordinary divine work. They are the instruments by which God does His own work in the world.

So, for example, if a husband determines, perhaps on the advice of a doctor, that it is in the best interests of his wife and family to avoid the likelihood of conception, this decision should not be approached or understood as a thwarting or avoidance of God's purpose, but may be undertaken and received as precisely the way that God acts to preserve and protect the woman and the family. What that means, of course, as for parents with their children and pastors with their congregations, is that husbands must proceed in the fear and faith of God, since they are accountable to Him. Office and vocation are not a blank check with which a man may do as he pleases, but a sacred trust and stewardship of God's grace for the sake of the neighbor he is given to serve in love.

Wherever there is sin at work in thought, word, or deed, husbands and fathers, wives and mothers, and all of us alike are called to repentance. The fact that God works everything together for the good of those who love Him, who are called by His Word and Spirit according to His purposes (Romans 8:28–30), does not mean that it is ever permissible to sin. It is simply that Christians proceed within their callings in the confidence of His Gospel, knowing that He is faithful in calling them to repentance, and that He does not permit sin to persist, but in love He disciplines His children in the way of life (Hebrews 12:5–13).

It is a great mystery that God unfailingly accomplishes His purposes, while yet allowing man a freedom of choice and decision in his life on earth. How that can be is hidden from us, but such is the testimony of the Holy Scriptures (Ecclesiastes 3:9–15). His Christians are not called to second-guess God, but to trust Him precisely within their own vocations and stations in life, and to carry out their duties and responsibilities in the confidence that He will accomplish His purposes in them and through them and for them, and for their neighbors, even when it all seems confusing, chaotic, and unclear. We exercise the knowledge and the wisdom He provides, and we employ the skills and the resources He has given to do our jobs, to care for our neighbors, and to live in faith and love under the cross in the hope of the resurrection.

These same points and principles pertain not only to Christian individuals and couples, but to the Church collectively as the Body of Christ. For we belong to one another in Christ and none of us lives or dies to himself alone. The Church should not leave the married or the unmarried to face or bear the difficult challenges of life in isolation. Rather, in calling her members (and the world) to repentance and encouraging faithfulness in vocation, the Church should seek to provide tangible assistance and support in the name of the Lord. Let there be no case in which children are avoided, despised, neglected, or put to death (within or outside of the womb) because the Church on earth failed to do or say what she could have done to help by the grace of God. Instead, let us learn together how better to serve and support couples and families, especially where illness and infirmity might otherwise undermine or overwhelm holy marriage and its fruitfulness.

LET THERE BE NO CASE IN WHICH CHILDREN ARE AVOIDED, DESPISED, NEGLECTED, OR PUT TO DEATH (WITHIN OR OUTSIDE OF THE WOMB) BECAUSE THE CHURCH ON EARTH FAILED TO DO OR SAY WHAT SHE COULD HAVE DONE TO HELP BY THE GRACE OF GOD.

Faith, Love, and Vocation

Now, then, living by faith in the Lord's divine providence does not mean that Christians ignore, dismiss, or reject His mediated gifts and guidance. Neither does faith put the Lord God to the test by proceeding recklessly or foolishly into harm's way without cause, that is, where love does not require it. On a mundane level, it is not a lack of faith but appropriate caution and discretion to look both ways before crossing the street. Along the same lines, it is not a lack of faith but an appropriate use of reason for a husband and wife to consider the conditions and circumstances of their context before engaging in marital relations or using contraception of any kind.

A Christian's faith in Christ is to be active in love for the neighbor. And such love will surely exercise the knowledge and wisdom of experience, while also giving thoughtful consideration to the neighbor's burdens, finitude, frailties of the flesh, mortality, and any other weaknesses of heart, mind, body, and soul. An honest recognition of sin and death, and of the cross, will temper ideology with compassion and gentleness, patience and forgiveness. The theology of the cross is really both the starting point and the decisive bottom line in approaching our life in this world.

The key to parsing these things and discerning where faith and love are to be found, in contrast to the sin that dwells in our fallen flesh, is rooted in vocation. To be more specific and precise, in considering contraception, the key to living in faith and love is for the husband and his wife to live within their respective vocations in relation to each other. In love for his wife, the husband considers her welfare, listens carefully to her concerns, and finally exercises his headship and authority to care for her, to bear her burdens, to strengthen and support her in every weakness, to shelter and protect her from the assaults and accusations of the devil, and to cover all her sins and shame with his own honor. He takes into account not only her bodily health and well-being but also her heart and mind, her soul and spirit.

IN A FALLEN AND PERISHING WORLD, IT IS NOT IDEOLOGY BUT LOVE THAT RULES AND CARRIES THE DAY.

THE VOCATION OF HUSBAND

A husband will certainly care for his wife by catechizing her, strengthening and encouraging her with the Word and promises of God. Yet, recognizing her frailties and weaknesses, not only of the body and mind but of faith, he will not simply insist that his wife must buck up and bear the burdens of this life, come what may. He provides instead a thoughtful accommodation and tender care for her shortcomings and struggles of body and soul, in order to sustain her in peace. He does not address her frailties, faults, and failures with the crushing condemnation of the Law, but with the life-giving balm and free forgiveness of the Gospel. He does not try to make her righteous by compulsion, by demands or expectations, but he justifies her in this life by loving her and giving himself for her in the faith and love of Christ. He exemplifies the way of faith and love, which is the good and acceptable will of God. He admonishes and corrects, as needs may be, in opposition to the temptations of the devil, the world, and the sinful flesh (as Adam should have done for Eve), but even this he does in the gentleness and tenderness of love for his bride.

This care and concern for his wife, this calling to serve and support her and give attention to her needs, is what turns a husband away from himself and his own interests, so that he is not wrapped up in thinking about his own fears, his own doubts and trepidations, or his own ego and ambitions, but is guided by love. His thinking is rightly directed to caring for the woman who has been given to him. This outward turning of the heart and mind to the neighbor is absolutely fundamental and key to considering these questions and challenges of marriage and family and learning to respond to them, practically and concretely, in faith and love.

Not only as a husband to his wife, but as a father to his family, a man must also consider the needs (including the special or extraordinary needs) of those children the Lord has already entrusted to his care and to his wife. The reality is that one child with extraordinary health and developmental needs can present a more demanding, more exhausting, and more time-consuming challenge than even ten healthy children without such needs. Where that is the case, should a man insist that he and his wife must continue as per usual, without taking any steps to avoid or limit the likelihood of conceiving more children, even though his wife and family are already taxed to the limits of their abilities and resources? Perhaps not. It is not that God would ever fail to provide, but, again, that God normally provides and cares for each family especially by the way and means of a husband and father who actively exercises wisdom and love for his own wife and children. In a fallen and perishing world, it is not ideology but love that rules and carries the day. In this way, the conscience is freed from legalism and from guilt, and the Christian is able with joy to serve and care for his neighbor, the husband for his wife, the father for his children.

THE VOCATION OF WIFE

The wife is also given to live within her vocation. Therefore, in faith before God, she speaks to her husband in love. Instead of bottling up her hurts and fears, her weariness and pain, and hiding them inside, she freely opens up her heart and mind to the man God has given her, allowing him the opportunity to love and care for her. She also speaks to him as an advocate on behalf of those children the Lord has already entrusted to her. Though she is not the head of the family, she does have this vocation from the Lord to care for her children as their mother. She needs to be able to do that, and she ought to represent their needs in conversation with her husband, especially where and when he may not be aware or paying attention or prioritizing their needs as he should. There ought to be this kind of open communication, on the part of a wife with her husband, concerning both herself and the family. And then, with steady faith, she submits to her husband's headship and authority, as unto Christ her Lord (Ephesians 5:22–24). For she is confident that the God and Father of our Lord Jesus Christ, who gave her to this man in holy marriage, will also continue to love and serve and care for her through this man, even in spite of his own shortcomings and weaknesses.

Here we are not talking about situations involving abuse or neglect. But neither are we talking about that hypothetical husband who listens well, always makes good choices, and has all wisdom and savvy. The principles at hand are not so much offered for some kind of idealistic circumstance, where discernment and decisions are likely to be clear and straightforward. No, the reality is that both husbands and wives alike are fallen, sinful creatures, flawed and fallible. They do make mistakes. They miss the mark. They do things they should not and fail to do as they should (Romans 7:14–25). Yet, they are to exercise confidence in the forgiveness of the Gospel and know that the Lord is with them in their callings, in their stations in life. He is faithful, and He will protect and provide for them. He will strengthen and support them in their life together, in their duties to each other and their children. He will indeed, by His grace and mercy, and according to His divine wisdom, accomplish His purposes through them, in spite of their frailties and failings.

Godly Decisions

Normally within marriage, faith and love will remain open and receptive to the likelihood of conception, notwithstanding personal fears and trepidations. Husbands and wives go about their life together in love for each other, children are conceived and born in due season, according to the grace of God; they are baptized, catechized, nurtured, and fed within the Church, and God as the author and giver of life is glorified in them. That pattern is and remains the norm, albeit always where and when it pleases God, in, with, and under the cross in this body and life on earth.

There may be times, however, when faith and love will choose to avoid the likelihood of conception, even in spite of personal desires or "ambitions" for more children. Circumstances that might suggest a short-term avoidance of conception could possibly include an injury, illness, or infirmity of the wife, a period of unemployment, or the husband's completion of a necessary degree for the sake of his job, in order to provide for his family's basic needs of shelter, food, and clothing. In some cases, a woman's body may need time to recover from a previous pregnancy and childbirth or miscarriage. An ongoing long-term avoidance of conception would be comparatively quite rare, and might only be called for in situations where the woman's life or sanity would be seriously threatened by future pregnancies. Certainly great caution should be taken, at the very least, before a couple would ever seek the permanent "sterilization" of either spouse. It is difficult to envision the circumstances that might commend such a drastic course of action. And of course, in all of these examples, whenever a child is conceived, a husband and wife will receive and care for that child in love.

THE COMFORT, CONFIDENCE, AND COURAGE OF A MAN'S CONSCIENCE BEFORE GOD IN ALL THINGS, AT ALL TIMES, IS NOT FOUND IN HIMSELF, NOR IN HIS CHOICES, DECISIONS, AND ACTIONS, NOR EVEN IN HIS FAITHFULNESS AND LOVE, BUT SOLELY IN CHRIST JESUS, OUR SAVIOR AND OUR GOD.

In determining whether or not to use contraception, as a servant of God and the head of his family, a husband does not always do what he prefers or feels like. He makes decisions in godly fear, in wisdom, and in faith. Sometimes a decision will be in agreement with his wife's preferences, and sometimes it will not. And sometimes it will agree with his own personal preferences, sometimes not. He guards himself against the temptations of his flesh on all sides, within and without, by considering and serving the needs of his wife and family.

Even caring for their wives in love, husbands do not justify themselves. The comfort, confidence, and courage of a man's conscience before God in all things, at all times, is not found in himself, nor in his choices, decisions, and actions, nor even in his faithfulness and love, but solely in Christ Jesus, our Savior and our God. At the end of every day, at the end of this life, and in the hour of judgment, we are all unworthy servants. At best we have done no more than our duty. Yet, Christ the Lord enters in, seats His servants at His table, and girds Himself to serve us by His divine grace. For

He has redeemed us from death and the grave, atoned for all our sins, justified us with His righteousness, and reconciled us to His God and Father. So, too, He grants us life and health and strength by His Holy Spirit, and He sanctifies us with His own divine holiness, with His pure and perfect innocence, and with His eternal blessedness.

The same Lord Jesus Christ is the incarnate Son, the image of God in the flesh, who is alone the perfect man, the perfect Bridegroom, the perfect husband. He has given Himself for His own Bride, the Church, in order to cleanse her and sanctify her by the washing of water with His Word, to clothe her with Himself in all His glory, to feed her with Himself and cleave to her in love, and to unite her to Himself as one flesh and blood with Him. Only in this holy matrimony of Christ and His Bride is there at last, finally and forever, the perfect marriage of the man and the woman, which no man nor even death shall be able to sever or put asunder. In this marriage, alone above all others, there is no doubt or fear, no greed or selfishness or lust; there is no frailty or weakness; there is no sickness or death; there is no contraception, no birth control, no miscarriage or stillbirth; no heartbreak or despair. In this marriage, by the cross and in the resurrection of Christ Jesus, our Lord, there is and remains forever the fruitfulness of His perfect faith and the dominion of His perfect love. So do we live, as dear members of His Holy Bride, by His grace alone.

CHAPTER 6

CHRISTIAN SEX EDUCATION: THE GREAT COVER-UP

Matthew Rueger

Until recently, Christians have enjoyed the tacit social approval of biblical values with regard to sex. Open sexual hedonism was relegated to the counterculture. It was the immoral minority that cast aside monogamy and fidelity. Now, however, hedonism, pornography, and sexual perversity have become mainstream. Sex has become so open that *Playboy* recently changed its format and did away with fully nude centerfolds because pornography is so commonplace and so available that nudity fails to sell copies. Within a very short time, society has relegated Christian morals to the lunatic fringe and made pagan hedonism the norm.

It is to the gurus of this cultural shift that we send our children for education. And not surprisingly, sex features prominently in their instruction. Parents who are concerned about what schools might teach their children may try to exempt their children from certain sex education classes, but due to the pervasiveness of sex education throughout the curriculum, it is all but impossible to shield children from it. As a father of seven, I thought I had dismissed my children from the grosser sex education classes, only to find out later that they got the mother lode of graphic sex education in other classes, such as physical education and health. They were shown how to put condoms on cucumbers and made to listen to teachers give answers to anonymous student questions about sex acts and techniques.

Christian children are thrust into this sexually charged culture whether they want to be or not. It is essential that Christian parents prepare their children for it. Many parents think this means having to beat the schools to the punch and be first to have that "sex talk" with their kids. They may even purchase Christian sex education materials to help them explain the facts better. Most parents seem to have bought into the premise that children need to be taught about sex because if they are not, something bad will happen.

Sex Education through the Years

Educating the young to deal with a sexualized world has a long history in America. The American Social Hygiene Association (ASHA) began in 1913 as an effort to confront the problems of prostitution and venereal diseases. Early sex education lectures exposed the public to the medical reality of venereal disease and stressed the importance of abstinence before marriage. Their basic message was that a moral life was a hygienic life.[1] Chastity and monogamy were discussed as ethical imperatives.

Yet, the 1920s suggested that the methods were not having the desired effect on culture. A new openness with sexual expression manifested itself in dress, dance, and social conversation. Victorian modesty gave way to the brash behavior of the roaring twenties. The possibility presented itself that sex education may have even played a role in the sexual revolution of the 1920s. Sex education changed perceptions of what one could say or print as part of the public conversation about sexual conduct.[2] It did not stop the problems it set out to address; it may have even exacerbated them.

Sex educators sought to adjust their methods in answer to the apparent failure of older curricula. In the mid-1940s, ASHA unveiled a plan to shift emphasis to family life classes. These classes included instruction on financial management, child rearing, parental responsibility, and sexual conduct.[3] A conscious effort was made to paint the traditional family as the bedrock of a healthy society. The baby boom took hold in this pro-family atmosphere. Society at large had a positive view of family life and generally accepted the Christian ethic of monogamy and sexual fidelity.

Then, in 1948, the atomic bomb of sexual perception exploded with the publication of *Sexual Behavior in the Human Male* by Alfred Kinsey. Kinsey destroyed traditional views of sex and morality by making the claim that the actual sexual practices of Americans were much more "diverse" than the general public admitted. The publisher of this volume claimed that it represented an "objective factual study of sexual behavior."[4] Kinsey bolstered the validity of his research by thanking a long list of contributors and supporters. He thanked the 12,000 contributing subjects to his study, the President and Dean of Indiana University, the Rockefeller Foundation,

1 Jeffrey P. Moan, *Teaching Sex* (Cambridge, MA: Harvard University Press, 2000), 49.

2 Moan, *Teaching Sex*, 80–81.

3 Moan, *Teaching Sex*, 124, 128, 131. It should be noted that these were not the first such classes. Examples of similar classes can be found decades earlier.

4 Alfred Kinsey, Wardell Pomeroy, Clyde Martin, *Sexual Behavior in the Human Male* (Philadelphia, PA: W. B. Saunders Co., 1948), ix.

the National Research Council's Committee for Research on Problems of Sex, and people with connections to Yale, Johns Hopkins, Princeton, and Harvard.[5] One is left with the impression that his work carried the full support of respected academia.

Utilizing what Kinsey claimed were scientific methods, he came to such conclusions as these: 37 percent of the total white male population had at least some homosexual experience to the point of orgasm, 10 percent of the white male population was exclusively homosexual,[6] 26–28 percent of college-age rural males had achieved sexual climax with animals,[7] 69 percent of the total white male population had gone to a prostitute for sex at least once,[8] and babies as young as five months old can have orgasms (four months old for a baby girl).[9] Kinsey claimed his research was purely academic and his methods scientific. It was not his intent to shock or scandalize the American public. He was simply the messenger of reality.

> NOTHING IS OFF LIMITS FOR DISCUSSION IN MOST CLASSROOMS BECAUSE NOTHING IS SEEN AS OBJECTIVELY WRONG WHEN IT COMES TO SEX.

Judith Reisman, who made it her life's work to study Kinsey and his methods, would disagree. What Kinsey claimed was normal sexual behavior in the human male was in reality based on abnormal subjects. Reisman examined Kinsey's sample base of 12,000 American males.

> From 1938 through 1940, his subjects were largely the homosexual demi monde ("450 homosexual and 110 inmates"). From 1941–1945 at least 8,327, or 68 percent of his total sample, would be draft dodgers, violent felons, homosexuals and other aberrants, available to answer Kinsey's 350 intimate questions. Post World War II, by 1946 Kinsey added "1,400 convicted sex offenders in penal institutions" "two hundred sexual psychopath patients" and well over 600 sexually abused boys. In sum, 86 percent of deviant "subjects" defined the Libido of The Greatest Generation![10]

5 Kinsey, *Sexual Behavior*, vii–viii.

6 Kinsey, *Sexual Behavior*, 650, 651.

7 Kinsey, *Sexual Behavior*, 671.

8 Kinsey, *Sexual Behavior*, 597.

9 Kinsey, *Sexual Behavior*, 177.

10 Judith Reisman, *Sexual Sabotage* (Washington DC: WND Books, 2010), 56.

Reisman demonstrated that Kinsey was not the unbiased scientific mind he claimed to be. He was a practicing bisexual and sexual masochist who regularly hosted orgies in his attic.[11] She further pointed out that Kinsey's research methods, especially with babies and toddlers, amounted to sexual child abuse that was at the time (and still is) illegal. Through interviews with Kinsey's co-workers, Reisman discovered Kinsey's intent of eliminating traditional concepts of marriage and normalizing his own sexual behavior.[12]

But the damage was done to the American psyche. The public, not knowing Kinsey's ulterior motives or flawed methods, read his conclusions with shock. Mainstream sex educators concluded that older, morals-based approaches to sex education had obviously failed, so they sought new models. In 1964, Mary Calderone, former medical director of Planned Parenthood, founded SIECUS (the Sex Information and Education Council of the United States). Following Kinsey's beliefs, she helped construct a more "values-free" form of sex education; one that began with the idea that individuals are sexual beings from birth. She pushed for sex education beginning in kindergarten.[13] Calderone's approach differed from other sex educators in that she emphasized sexual pleasure for all ages and decried traditional moralistic teaching because of the guilt she believed it produced.[14] Calderone held that people are moral when they live up to their own standards (regardless of whether those standards are divine in origin or self-defined).[15]

EVEN WHEN THE OVERALL MESSAGE IS ABSTINENCE, THE METHOD OF OPEN PUBLIC DISCUSSION OF SEX IN AUDIENCES OF MIXED GENDERS TEACHES A DIFFERENT LESSON.

Sex education began expanding its scope beyond the mere act of sex. With the research and development of "the pill," which Planned Parenthood claims to have helped finance,[16] sex educators used birth control to

---

11 Reisman, *Sexual Sabotage*, 40–41, 65–67.

12 Reisman, *Sexual Sabotage*, 45.

13 Jane E. Brody, "Mary S. Calderone, Advocate of Sexual Education, Dies at 94," *New York Times*, October 25, 1998, accessed November 11, 2015, www.nytimes.com/1998/10/25/us/mary-s-calderone-advocate-of-sexual-education-dies-at-94.html?pagewanted=all.

14 Janice Irvine, *Talk about Sex: The Battles over Sex Education in the United States* (Berkeley and Los Angeles, CA: University of California Press, 2002), 24–25.

15 Irvine, *Talk about Sex*, 28. Referencing an oral history taken by Tolman, July 22, 1987, Schlessinger Library, Radcliffe College.

16 Planned Parenthood, "History and Successes: The 1960s," accessed November 12, 2015, www.plannedparenthood.org/about-us/who-we-are/history-successes.

press gender equality issues. *Roe v. Wade* in 1973 allowed the new "values-free" approach to include abortion as a valid choice for ending pregnancies. The homosexual revolution added another dimension to sex education, giving secular educators impetus to pursue sexual orientation sensitivity training in their curricula. Gender identity is now included in discussions with children. All these forces reshaped the direction and methods of secular sex education.

For the first fifty years of sex education in America, its stated goals were the strengthening of the family, elimination of aberrant sexual behavior, and the prevention of venereal diseases. Today's goals have little in common with the past. The ultimate goal of today's sex educators is the indoctrination of youth into a "values-free" ideology that includes (among other things) these beliefs: people are sexual beings from birth, sexual orientation and gender identity are morally neutral issues subject only to one's individual determination, masturbation is normal and harmless, personal rights and choice are more important than human life, and premarital sex is expected and permissible, provided it is governed by safe sex practices and mutual agreement. It is a crassly humanistic ideology that places the self as the sole arbiter of morality. This ideology both shapes and explains the methods of sex education.

In past decades, Christians have raised objections to specific teachings within sex education curricula that are at odds with Christian morality. The "what" of sex education has received the most attention. In recent years, however, criticisms have arisen over the methods used in the classroom. The "how" of sex education can be just as damaging to the young as what is actually discussed. In particular, the graphic discussions of the most intimate details about sex acts, held in mixed gender classrooms, is a method purposely employed to desensitize individuals and destroy traditional moral taboos. Nothing is off limits for discussion in most classrooms because nothing is seen as objectively wrong when it comes to sex. The method becomes as problematic as the amoral material taught.

The Method Is the Message

Well-intentioned Christians have tried to "baptize" secular sex education materials by substituting Christian morals for the values-free morality of secular curricula. Christian sex education materials cite biblical prohibitions with regard to premarital sex and homosexual practices. They acknowledge that sex education is properly the duty of parents. Some of these programs try to describe the sex act in gentler terms than secular material in order to demystify sex for curious young minds. They may highlight the dangers of STDs and early pregnancy, acknowledge the existence of birth control methods, but reiterate the fact that God prohibits intercourse between unmarried people.

While one can applaud the intent of Christian sex educators to counter the hedonistic message of secular humanists, the vast majority of them fail to recognize the danger of the method they employ, namely, the method of open discussion about sex acts that is sometimes graphic and highly descriptive. In paging through one such Christian text I found pictures of both the female and male genitalia. There were little arrows with labels pointing to the different parts and naming them. I am sure the reason for it was to answer a natural curiosity children may have and give them opportunity to discuss it in a Christian environment. But is satisfying a natural human curiosity a valid biblical goal? And is the method consistent with the goals and aims of Holy Scripture? I would argue "no" on both counts.

The method of bringing sex into the open for public discussion is itself a message. What God's Word takes great care to cover, contemporary sex education unashamedly exposes. Within the classroom, old-fashioned modesty that blushes when sex acts are discussed is seen as problematic and prohibitive to "healthy conversations." Immodesty, in the form of a willingness to put any sexual question into the open, is championed as positive for children because it allows for freer discussion. By eliminating boundaries and allowing any and every aspect of sex into the public discussion, sex educators believe that children's curiosity can be satisfied in a controlled environment. There is no consideration given to the fact that the more graphic and immodest the message is within the controlled environment of the classroom, the more it legitimizes being graphic and crass about sex outside the classroom. The approach of discouraging modesty and promoting immodesty in conversation affects a broad range of human interactions. It affects what people consider appropriate to discuss with one another, what clothing they wear, and how they act around the opposite sex. Even when the overall message is abstinence, the method of open public discussion of sex in audiences of mixed genders teaches a different lesson.

Immodesty as a Method

It should be obvious that when immodesty is employed as a method, it teaches children to be immodest. My own experience with sex education in high school health class in the early 1980s showed me how sex education curricula encouraged immodesty. We were asked to draw male and female genitals as an assignment. While I refused to do the assignment, other boys in the class completed it by photocopying their private parts and handing the pictures in to the female teacher.

MODESTY IS ONE OF THE FIRST EXPRESSIONS OF THE SINFUL SELF.

Open discussions, where no questions are out of bounds and assignments require having to learn about the sexual organs of both sexes, purposely aim at breaking down inhibitions. In the world of values-free sex education, inhibitions are harmful because they limit sexual expressiveness and repress the free flow of sex information. The same method is used to train sex educators. Sex education teachers are encouraged to undergo a Sexuality Attitudes Reassessment (SAR), wherein they are shown sexually explicit images and encouraged to discuss them openly with one another. The goal of this exercise is twofold: (1) to make sex educators comfortable with discussing sexual matters publicly, and (2) to break down latent moral objections within their consciences. It is a method advertised by the Institute for the Advanced Study of Human Sexuality. This "institute," the first dean of which was Kinsey researcher Wardell Pomeroy, is one such training ground for sex educators. They offer SAR courses that provide immersion in explicit images and discussion of all forms of sexual behavior culminating in participation in the San Francisco gay pride parade.[17] These educators understand the power of explicit images and discussions in changing moral judgments.[18]

Talking about Sin

The way Scripture speaks about sex stands in stark contrast to the method of open graphic discussion described above; yet, the world in which St. Paul's epistles were written may have been just as sexualized as ours. The sexual exploits of senators and politicians with women, boys, and other men were part of the public discourse in the Roman senate.[19] The

17 Institute for the Advanced Study of Human Sexuality, "Summer SAR Program," accessed November 24, 2015, www.humansexuality education.com/summer-sar.html.

18 One should note here the relationship between the pornography industry and sex education. Calderone, as the head of SIECUS, was invited by *Hustler* magazine to write a regular column. Cf. Janice Irvine, *Talk about Sex*, 30–31. Why would *Hustler* have a vested interest in a sex education column if not because both pursued the same ends, namely, to remove the bounds of what is forbidden and encourage sexual hedonism?

19 Louis Crompton, *Homosexuality and Civilization* (Cambridge, MA: Harvard University Press, 2006), 82–83. While the example from Cicero's speeches predates St. Paul by some one hundred years, it does demonstrate that the practice of discussing such things in the Senate had a long history prior to Paul.

heterosexual and homosexual activities of the Caesars were well-known.[20] Prostitution was legal, taxed, and at times featured as an element of the worship of certain gods. Greek culture made popular the gymnasium and the institution of pedophilia associated with it; Roman culture gladly adopted it. Sexual hedonism and deviancy were normalized in the culture of St. Paul's Gentile ministry. The way Paul speaks to the topic of sex in that context provides us with a counter model to that of the secular classroom.

MODESTY BESPEAKS REVERENCE AND RESPECT TOWARD GOD.

Though Paul warned against "speaking of the things that they do in secret," he did not shy away from addressing sexual sin. Paul reiterated many of the Old Testament prohibitions to impress upon the followers of Christ that sexual chastity was an expectation of God's Law. He condemned homosexuality using terms that were both colloquial and blunt.[21] He renounced immoral behaviors such as fornication, adultery, and "unclean" activities.[22] He labeled the sins in order to condemn them, but did not engage in graphic descriptions of the sins.

In some respects, the Old Testament is more graphic in detailing forbidden sexual practices. In Genesis 38:9, Onan is condemned for "emitting" on the ground.[23] Leviticus 18 and 20 expressly condemn incest, bestiality, and homosexuality. They prohibit having intercourse with, or exposing the nakedness of, in-laws and relatives. They mandate that hus-

20 Suetonius, *Lives of the Twelve Caesars*, trans. H. M. Bird (Hertfordshire: Wordsworth, 1997), 33–34, 101–2, 150–51, 185, 194, 259.

21 For example, in 1 Corinthians 6:9 Paul uses the term *malakoi* (μαλακοὶ, sing. μαλακός), which carries the primary meaning of "soft." "Soft" was a colloquial term used by Romans for "homosexual." See Craig A. Williams, *Roman Homosexuality: Ideologies of Masculinity in Classical Antiquity* (New York: Oxford University Press, 1999), 128f. As Williams explains it, the Latin word *mollis* ("soft") was a general term for men who conducted themselves like women sexually. The second term for "homosexual" used by Paul in this passage is *arsenokoitai* (ἀρσενοκοῖται), a compound word meaning "male coitus." It directs attention to the male who plays the dominant role in the homosexual encounter. Cf. Gregory Lockwood, *1 Corinthians*. Concordia Commentary (St. Louis: Concordia, 2000), 199.

22 *Pornos* (πόρνος) noun or *porneuō* (πορνεύω) verb, trans. *immorality* or *fornication*, a word that originally had to do with prostitution but eventually took on the general meaning of any unchaste or unlawful sexual intercourse. Cf. Gerhard Kittle, *Theological Dictionary of the New Testament*, vol. 6, trans. Geoffrey W. Bromiley (Grand Rapids: Eerdmans, 1988), 587, 593. Used by Paul in 1 Corinthians 5:9, 10, 11; 6:9, 18; 10:8; 2 Corinthians 12:21; Galatians 5:19; Ephesians 5:5; 1 Timothy 1:10. *Moicheia*, trans. *adultery*, has primarily to do with sexual sins with one who is not one's spouse. Cf. Bauer, Danker, Arndt, and Gingrich, *A Greek-English Lexicon of the New Testament and Other Early Christian Literature*, 3rd ed. (Chicago: University of Chicago Press, 2000), s.v. "μοιχεία." Various forms of the word used by Paul in Galatians 5:19 (variant); Romans 2:22; 13:9; and 1 Corinthians 6:9. *Akatharsia*, trans. "1. any substance that is filthy or dirty, *refuse*. 2. a state of moral corruption." BDAG, s.v. "ἀκαθαρσία." This word is mirrored in English when calling immoral things "dirty." Used by Paul in Romans 1:24; 6:19; 2 Corinthians 12:21; Galatians 5:19; Ephesians 4:19; 5:3; Colossians 3:5; 1 Thessalonians 2:3; 4:7. *Aselgeia*, trans. as sexual excess, licentiousness, debauchery, or lacking moral restraint. BDAG s.v. "ἀσέλγεια." Used by Paul in Romans 13:13; 2 Corinthians 12:21; Galatians 5:19; Ephesians 4:19.

23 ESV has "waste the semen on the ground." The Hebrew is more modest and reads: *weshicheth 'artsah* (וְשִׁחֵת אַרְצָה lit. a "corrupt act on the ground"). Brown-Driver-Briggs, *Hebrew and English Lexicon*, s.v. "שָׁחַת." BDB renders *shachath* שָׁחַת as corrupt act, injure, violate, destroy, spoil, ruin, or pervert.

bands and wives not engage in intercourse during the time of the woman's period. Deuteronomy 22:5 also lists cross-dressing as a forbidden practice. The language of Scripture demonstrates that the piety of faith does not preclude publicly recognizing and labeling certain activities as sin. Yet, it is not insignificant that the details of these sexual sins are not discussed at length. Modesty is maintained even while discussing the "grosser" sexual sins.

Modesty as a Method

Modesty is one of the first expressions of the sinful self. Immediately after Adam and Eve fell into sin, they covered their nakedness with makeshift garments made of vegetation. The Hebrew text uses the word *chagoroth* (חֲגֹרֹת), which the ESV translates as "loincloths."[24] The word means something that wraps around the body, a sash, or belt.[25] It seems to have been a simple wrapping around the waist. Though their sin seemingly had nothing to do with sex, they instinctively felt the need to cover their genitals.[26] As Leupold wrote in his commentary, ". . . man instinctively feels that the very fountain and source of human life is contaminated by sin."[27] Sin had somehow exposed something broken in their humanity that would be passed down to their progeny, and that exposure needed to be covered. When God asked them why they hid from Him, Adam cited his nakedness as the reason.

God did not try to overcome their shame by teaching them to accept their nakedness, nor did He chastise them for covering up what He had created to be good. Just the opposite—God agreed to their need to cover up and made them clothing that covered their bodies more completely. In Genesis 3:21, the garment made by God out of animal skin is described as a *kathenoth* כָּתְנוֹת). Most standard versions of the Bible translated this as "garments."[28] KJV seems closest to the meaning with the translation "coats."[29] The word implies a longer type of garment that had sleeves and

---

24 NKJV and NIV translate the word as "coverings." RSV and KJV have "aprons."

25 Cf. William L. Holladay, *A Concise Hebrew and Aramaic Lexicon of the Old Testament* (Grand Rapids: Eerdmans 1971), 95.

26 Genesis 3:7.

27 H. C. Leupold, *Exposition of Genesis* (Grand Rapids: Baker Book House, 1976), 1:151.

28 So ESV, NIV, RSV. NKJV has "tunics."

29 Holladay, *A Concise Hebrew and Aramaic Lexicon of the Old Testament*, 167. Holladay offers the translation, "long shirt-like (under-) garment."

covered the whole of the body from neck to ankles.[30] Whereas Adam and Eve covered only their naked midsections, God covered the whole of the bodies. Further, God's use of animal skins represents the first time blood is shed for mankind. God sheds it in order to cover the shame of Adam and Eve. Luther saw in the use of animal skins a symbol of death pointing to the consequences of sin: "A pelt was his daily garb as a daily reminder of his lost bliss."[31] Others have seen in this a prefiguring of Christ's redemptive act wherein blood was shed to cover sin and shame. Regardless, it seems clear that the covering made by God was more than merely practical. It expressed a modesty meant to teach and protect mankind. The act of covering the body held didactic power; it said something beyond, "I'm ashamed of my private parts." It made a statement about the pervasive nature of sin and God's desire to shed blood to cover the consequence of sin.

Modesty as Worship

Curiously, modesty is not limited to humanity, nor is it always tied to sin or shame. In Isaiah's description of the seraphim, he pictures them as having six wings, four of which are used to cover their face and feet (Isaiah 6:2). What would be the purpose of covering up if not as an expression of heavenly modesty? Such an expression, divorced from sin or shame, is an element of the seraphim's worship of God. The very act of covering up some part of the body represents respect and fealty.

As angels appeared to mankind, they likewise showed modesty in dress. The "young man" (angel) who appeared to the women in the tomb to announce Jesus' resurrection is pictured in Mark's Gospel as being dressed in a white robe (Mark 16:5). Though admittedly the biblical evidence is scarce, it seems safe to assume this single description is representative of all angelic appearances to mankind. The lack of passages expressing shock at people seeing naked angels is itself suggestive that they were clothed. Instead of simply seeing this as a capitulation to the weakness of humanity, it seems more likely that their act of covering is an expression of their relation to God, as servants and creatures. In 1 Corinthians 11, when St. Paul discusses head coverings within the church, he links a woman's head covering

30 Cf. Genesis 37:3, 23, 32 with reference to Joseph's coat given to him by Jacob. The construction in v. 3 is *kethoneth passim* (כְּתֹנֶת פַּסִּים), which is translated in many versions as a "coat of many colors." According to Brown Driver Briggs, the root word *pas* (פַּס) means "flat of hand or foot (palm, sole)." Cf. BDB, s.v. "פַּס." So a better translation of this garment is a coat that reaches from the palm of the hand to the sole of the foot. The argument could be made that the length of this particular *kethoneth* (כְּתֹנֶת) was its distinguishing factor and what set it apart from the *kethoneth* (כְּתֹנֶת) worn by Joseph's brothers. Even if this is so, it seems undeniable that the design of this garment necessitated sleeves that covered the arms to some degree and a length that extended down the legs.

31 AE 1:222.

with angelic modesty saying, "That is why a wife ought to have a symbol of authority on her head, because of the angels."[32] Modesty bespeaks reverence and respect toward God.

Modesty as an Image of Grace

Modesty is used in the New Testament as an image of grace. Eschatological redemption is not pictured as an uncovering of the purity God originally created but as the bestowal of a new covering given by Christ. Thus Paul's statement in 2 Corinthians 5:2–4:

> For in this tent we groan, longing to put on our heavenly dwelling, if indeed by putting it on we may not be found naked. For while we are still in this tent, we groan, being burdened—not that we would be unclothed, but that we would be further clothed, so that what is mortal may be swallowed up by life.

In Revelation, St. John describes salvation as being covered in robes made white by the blood of the Lamb.[33] Jesus describes His kingdom of grace as a wedding reception where the guests are clothed with special wedding garments (Matthew 22:11–22). All these eschatological images of redemption involve covering up with new Christological garments. While it might seem reasonable to expect grace portrayed as a stripping away of the old clothing of sin and a restoration of Adam's original unashamed innocence, there are instead these images of covering up with more perfect garments. Ironically, Christ's redemptive work involved His being stripped naked and held up to public shame, but the goal of His humiliation was to cover us with grace to prevent our shame.

Modesty as Sex Education

The language of covering up, then, informs faith in several ways. It does speak of sin and of Christ's salvific work to cover sin. It bespeaks worship, reverence, and humility before God, and it shows respect to other

32 1 Corinthians 11:10. Cf. Lockwood, *1 Corinthians*, 374–75. Lockwood explores various interpretations of this phrase and concludes that it is probably a call to remember that their conduct in worship is in the presence of angels. But as Lockwood stated earlier, the importance of Paul's discussion about head coverings is in "establishing the universal and permanent principle that men and women at worship should conduct themselves modestly and sensibly . . ." (p. 362). If modesty is the point of the discussion, then the injunction that a wife covers her head "because of the angels," would seem most logically to be pointing to angelic modesty. She should cover her head in worship because even the angels cover themselves in modesty before the throne of God in heaven.

33 Revelation 6:11; 7:13–14. One may also note the practice of being dressed in a white robe after Baptism as a symbol of Christ's purity covering the individual, or the use of the funeral pall as the image of Christological covering.

human beings. The very form of biblical language used in reference to sex suggests a purposeful attempt to cover up in order to show respect to both God and man. Adam and the early patriarchs "knew" their wives.[34] They "went in" to be with them[35] or "laid with" them.[36] Some have suggested that Ruth's "uncovering the feet" of Boaz is a euphemism for exposing his sexual organs.[37] When St. Paul speaks to married couples about their sexual responsibilities to each other, he speaks of it as "rendering affection" or "having authority over the body" of the other (1 Corinthians 7:3–4). There is obvious and consistent care exercised to avoid graphic descriptions of sexual acts or sexual organs. This is something more than just old-fashioned shyness. It is part of a method of instruction designed to promote respect and honor.

Modern sex education methods uncover sexual activity and speak in crass terms in order to destroy modesty.[38] When children giggle or squirm over explicit discussions, teachers tell them that "there is nothing to be embarrassed about." But when Adam and Eve showed embarrassment with their nakedness, God helped them cover up more. In her book *A Return to Modesty*, Wendy Shalit makes a convincing case for modesty as a God-given protection for children. When modesty is destroyed and children are no longer shy about sexual exploration and expression, they are more vulnerable and at risk.[39] Embarrassment is the shield of an active conscience protecting individuals from harm. To force someone to violate his or her conscience is to transgress the law of love.[40] To force conversations about sex on children whose conscience is telling them that they should be embarrassed and turn away is to sin against them. As Jesus stated, it would be better to have a millstone fastened around one's neck and be drowned in the sea, rather than cause one of His little ones to sin (Matthew 18:6). Inasmuch as modesty is a method pointing to greater truths about faith, grace, and self, Christians ought to understand the immodesty of modern sex education as a method working toward the destruction of faith, grace, and self.

---

34 Genesis 4:1, 17, 38:26; 1 Samuel 1:9.

35 Genesis 16:4; 29:23, 30; 38:2, 9, 18; Ruth 4:13.

36 Genesis 19:33–35; 30:16; 34:2; 2 Samuel 12:24.

37 Ruth 3:7. Cf. T. J. Wray, *Good Girls, Bad Girls: The Enduring Lessons of Twelve Women of the Old Testament* (Lanham, MD: Rowman and Littlefield Publishers, Inc., 2008), 73.

38 Cf. Kristin Luker, *When Sex Goes to School* (New York: W. W. Norton and Co., 2006), 165.

39 Wendy Shalit, *A Return to Modesty* (New York: Touchstone, 2000), 22.

40 Cf. Acts 24:16; 1 Corinthians 8:7–13; 10:23–33.

Women, more than men, seem to be sensitive to the damage immodesty is doing to children. A majority of books cited in this article are written by women. In addition to those already cited, readers should reference Linda Bartlett's *The Failure of Sex Education in the Church* (2014), and Miriam Grossman's *Unprotected* (2007), *You're Teaching My Child What?* (2009), and *The Black and White Puppy* (2015). These women are sounding the warning bell that the secular attack on modesty is harming children.[41]

Family as Sex Education

One does not need graphic and embarrassing discussions to educate children about sex. Christian parents teach their children about sexual matters in the normal mundane examples of modesty and fidelity in the home. Coach John Wooden once wrote that the best thing a father can do for his children is to love their mother. When husbands and wives model mutual respect and love within the home, children do learn how to interact with the opposite sex, how to respect differences, and how to be polite to and patient with the other. They learn to see the opposite sex as someone to be cherished, nurtured, and cared for—not exploited for personal pleasure. They also see something of what it means to live as Christ to a member of the opposite sex, and to see Christ in one's spouse.[42] Most sex education does not involve any formalized teaching about sex. It involves spouses working to fulfill their marriage vows to each other and exemplifying modesty and Christological love.

> MAINTAINING A SOUND CHRISTIAN MARRIAGE, MARKED BY MUTUAL RESPECT, LOVE, MODESTY, AND FAITH, IS PERHAPS THE MOST POWERFUL FORM OF SEX EDUCATION ANY CHRISTIAN PARENT CAN PRACTICE.

Here Luther's treatment of the Sixth Commandment fits perfectly. Instead of focusing on descriptions of adultery or discussions about sex acts, he simply directs readers to the nature of Christian marriage. Luther says:

> Let me now say in conclusion that this commandment demands not only that everyone live chastely in thought, word, and deed in his condition, that is, especially in the estate

41 Cf. Linda Bartlett, *The Failure of Sex Education in the Church* (Iowa Falls: Titus 2 for Life, 2014), 138; and Miriam Grossman, *You're Teaching My Child What?* (Washington DC: Regnery, 2009), 30, 76, 184.

42 Consider Ephesians 5:22–33.

> of matrimony, but also that every one love and esteem the spouse given him by God. For where conjugal chastity is to be maintained, man and wife must by all means live together in love and harmony, that one may cherish the other from the heart and with entire fidelity. For that is one of the principal points which enkindle love and desire of chastity, so that, where this is found, chastity will follow as a matter of course and without any command.[43]

Maintaining a sound Christian marriage, marked by mutual respect, love, modesty, and faith, is perhaps the most powerful form of sex education any Christian parent can practice.

Living in modesty and love does not preclude having to address difficult sexual issues at times. As children grow, they ask innocent questions about the world around them that demand straightforward and thoughtful answers. Small children will ask about differences between boys and girls or about where babies come from. When asked, parents must give honest answers and not make up stories about storks or cabbage patches. But honesty does not necessitate graphic sexual imagery or language. There are some issues that simply must be discussed in preparing children for adulthood. I remember as a child finding a bloody napkin in the bathroom wastebasket and asking my father if someone had gotten hurt. He told me that it is nothing to be concerned about, and that women naturally go through a period of bleeding each month as part of being able to have babies. I didn't need or want to know any more than that. Again, there is a need for mothers to explain to daughters what ovulation involves and how it will affect them so they do not panic at their first period. Innocent discussions of such a nature should not be embarrassing discussions in front of fellow classmates but private conversations between loving parents and their children, preserving the modesty of the child.

Sex and Being

One thing both Christian and secular sex educators can agree upon is that the heart of the matter really is not about sex; it is about being. In fact, the term *sex education* is no longer the standard term en vogue to describe what sex educators are trying to do. Educators prefer the term *sexual education*. The term *sexual* is meant to convey the idea that any and every

---

43 *Concordia Triglotta* (St. Louis: Concordia, 1921), 643.

aspect of how sex impacts the individual is the essence of what defines the individual.[44] The idea that "people are sexual beings from birth" is a given foundational starting point in today's curricula. "Sexuality" is said to define individuals throughout their lives. The effect of this doctrine is to move the topic of sex into the realm of ontology. Sex is not what one does; it is who one is.

St. Paul also tied sexuality to ontology, but he did it in order to contrast it with true identity in Christ and to call the immoral to repentance. In 1 Corinthians 6, as Paul addresses Christians, he connects their former identity with their previous immoral actions.

> Or do you not know that the unrighteous will not inherit the kingdom of God? Do not be deceived: neither the sexually immoral, nor idolaters, nor adulterers, nor men who practice homosexuality, nor thieves, nor the greedy, nor drunkards, nor revilers, nor swindlers will inherit the kingdom of God. And such were some of you. But you were washed, you were sanctified, you were justified in the name of the Lord Jesus Christ and by the Spirit of our God.[45]

Immorality, as Paul discusses it, is more than mere act; it goes to the core of one's being.[46] Individuals were adulterers. They were immoral and idolaters. But his purpose in defining individuals by their sins is ultimately to lead the Corinthians to understand the nature of grace. "*But* you were washed, *but* you were sanctified, *but* you were justified." The ESV loses the force of the threefold *alla* (ἀλλὰ) with its single "but" at the beginning of the phrase, but Paul's phrasing is more powerful. ἀλλὰ marks a threefold negation of their former selves. The profound nature of Christ's salvific

---

44 Consider the Position Statement of SIECUS: "Human sexuality encompasses the sexual knowledge, beliefs, attitudes, values, and behaviors of individuals. Its various dimensions involve the anatomy, physiology, and biochemistry of the sexual response system; identity, orientation, roles, and personality; and thoughts, feelings, and relationships. Sexuality is influenced by ethical, spiritual, cultural, and moral concerns. All persons are sexual, in the broadest sense of the word." SIECUS, Position Statements, "Human Sexuality," accessed December 2, 2015, www.siecus.org/index.cfm?fuseaction=Page.viewPage&pageId=494&parentID=472.

45 1 Corinthians 6:9–11. The ESV translation of "men who practice homosexuality" is poor inasmuch as it is unclear and somewhat confusing to what Paul is saying. The emphasis in the ESV seems to be on homosexual acts ("practice") not necessarily on homosexuals. "Men who practice homosexuality" is a translation of two distinct words; *malakoi* (μαλακοὶ), which literally means "soft," and was a general term for men who played the woman sexually or who were sexually "effeminate." *Arsenokoitai* (ἀρσενοκοῖται) is a compound word involving *arsēn* (ἄρσην = male) and *koitē* (κοίτη), the word for "bed," which euphemistically meant "intercourse" (taking someone to bed). The compound word literally means "male-sex" and addresses the other side of homosexual intercourse, describing the one who is actively doing the sodomizing. Paul is not simply identifying certain acts as wrong. He is tying people's identity to those acts, so that act becomes one's identity; it is who one is. He is not condemning just those who *practice* homosexual acts but those who are sexually effeminate and those who are "sodomizers."

46 Cf. Matthew 15:19.

work marked a change in their identity. Their acts have not been merely pardoned; they as individuals have substantially been changed and redefined by Christ's actions.

Changed identity is an essential element in Paul's instruction about sexual matters. In speaking to the case of incest within the Corinthian congregation, Paul directs them to their new identity: "Cleanse out the old leaven that you may be a new lump, as you really are unleavened" (1 Corinthians 5:7). Then he tells them, "Do you not know that your body is a temple of the Holy Spirit within you, whom you have from God? You are not your own, for you were bought with a price. So glorify God in your body" (6:18–20). To the Ephesians Paul says, "Put off your old self, which belongs to your former manner of life and is corrupt through deceitful desires, and to be renewed in the spirit of your minds, and to put on the new self, created after the likeness of God in true righteousness and holiness."[47]

Each of these speaks to a change in identity as the answer to sexual immorality. He does not tell them what new thing they need to do. He reminds them who they are: "a new lump," "unleavened," "the temple of the Holy Spirit," "bought with a price," "the new self, created after the likeness of God." This Christological change at the core of one's being, a change so profound it alters who we are, is the foundation of St. Paul's sex education. Instead of focusing on the act of sex, he focuses on the new identity Christ has created within us. This new identity defined by Christ shapes what we do with our bodies.

The Ultimate Goal

The goal of Christian sex education actually has less to do with sex than it does with salvation in Christ. The primary concern of Holy Scripture is with the eternal life of the individual. To that end, it adopts a method of modesty, a divine "covering up" in terms of how sex is discussed, how God's people are clothed, and how husband and wife are to love each other. Covering up matters of sex does not mean that Scripture or Christianity considers sex as bad or as something to be avoided.[48] Instead, it recognizes that the souls of God's children need protecting. It is a sad fact of human nature that people are attracted to forbidden fruit. The more sex is dangled

---

47 Ephesians 4:22–24. "Through deceitful desires," trans. of "*kata tas epithumias tēs apatēs*" ("κατὰ τὰς ἐπιθυμίας τῆς ἀπάτης"). *Epithumias* (ἐπιθυμίας, desires) does carry sexual overtones. It is the same word used by Christ in Matthew 5:28, which is normally translated "lust."

48 Paul's instruction in 1 Corinthians 7:5 that husbands and wives should not "deprive one another" is evidence that he understands sex as good and beneficial between husbands and wives.

before the eyes of human beings, the more their sinful nature urges them to seize the forbidden fruit.

Sexual modesty recognizes the biblical reality of fallen human nature and seeks to protect souls weakened by sin. It serves God's ends, which are to lead His sheep past temptations and guide them to eternal life. The "values-free" morality taught in sex education curricula is, in reality, a soul-destroying model that sets individuals against God's Word. It seeks to enslave people to passions and lusts and rob them of the purer life Christ has placed within them. As God exemplified in Eden when He covered Adam and Eve, modesty is an expression of love intended to protect the redeemed life God has given His people in His Son.

CHAPTER 7

SELF-POLLUTION: ITS DEFINITION AND CURE

Benjamin T. G. Mayes

INTRODUCTION

A frog dropped into a boiling pan of water will jump right out of it. But place him in a cool pan of water, turn up the heat gradually, and he will not notice the change in temperature. Eventually he will boil to death without saving himself from the heat. The same thing has happened to Christians regarding sexual ethics in general and regarding one sexual practice in particular: masturbation, or auto-eroticism. Norms, attitudes, and teachings have changed gradually. The sexual revolution in Western society in the 1960s brought to the mainstream new sexual permissiveness that had been held by elites for decades. As the new attitudes regarding masturbation, premarital sex, erotic fantasies, pornography use, and sexuality took hold in Western culture, churches were not left unaffected. Historical theology, however, can serve as a thermometer to show how much Christian thinking has changed regarding sexual ethics, to uncover areas in our own thinking that are unsound, and to challenge us to repent.

> THIS ITALIAN SEXUAL REVOLUTION INCLUDED NOT JUST FORNICATION AND ADULTERY, BUT ALSO UNASHAMEDLY HOMOSEXUAL BEHAVIOR.

SEXUAL REVOLUTIONS

The sexual revolution in the 1960s in North America, Europe, and elsewhere was not the first time that people had argued for sexual permissiveness. Martin Luther (1483–1546) was aware of a sexual revolution that had occurred in the Italian Renaissance and that had thoroughly corrupted the morals of the Italian church. In his commentary on Psalm 101 (1534), Luther wrote:

> Such Epicureans and scorners of God are now spreading publicly in Germany, too, as they spread previously in Italy. Unfortunately this may lead to Italian domination both in temporal and in spiritual affairs. This was brought in by the courtesans and mercenaries, as they saw and learned it in Rome and in the Latin land. With such Italian domination the Italian plagues and misfortune will also come. And that will be the end of Germany; it will be called "done for."[1]
>
> This terrible and thoroughly papal, that is, epicurean and Italian, way of life is on the increase. Therefore let anyone help who is able to help. And pity the poor youth, those dear descendants of ours, as well as all the elect children of God still to be added, some of them yet unborn. . . . The prophecy I have cited will certainly be fulfilled. God grant that before it is fulfilled, we may prove to be men who have acted and taught against it, and that together with all those who are dear to us we may depart in a good hour and be rescued with Lot from condemned Sodom and Gomorrah (Genesis 19:16). Amen.[2]

This Italian sexual revolution included not just fornication and adultery, but also unashamedly homosexual behavior. Luther writes in *War Against the Turk* (1529):

> God visits them with the same plague, too, and smites them with blindness so that it happens to them as St. Paul says in Romans 1[:28] about the shameful vice of the dumb sins,[3] that God gives them up to a perverse mind because they pervert the word of God. Both the pope and the Turk are so blind and senseless that they commit the dumb sins shamelessly, as an honorable and praiseworthy thing. Since they think lightly of marriage, it serves them right that there are dog-marriages (and would to God they were dog-marriag-

---

1 AE 13:191.

2 AE 13:192–93.

3 Luther translated γενέσεως ἐναλλαγή in Wisdom 14:26 (in a list of sexual sins) as *stummen Sünden*, "mute sins" (WA DB 12:90–91). Johann Gerhard defines the "mute sins" as pederasty (i.e., homosexual intercourse), bestiality, and self-pollution (including masturbation). Gerhard, *Loci Theologici*, locus "De conjugio," § 487. These sins were called "mute," because if Christians describe these sins in detail, they may give the impression that these sins, though sinful, are not "shameful"; and detailed descriptions of these sins cause the reader or hearer to imagine them, and thus may lead him into shameful thoughts.

> es), indeed, also "Italian marriages" and "Florentine brides" among them; and they think these things good. I hear one horrible thing after another about what an open and glorious Sodom Turkey is, and everybody who has looked around a little in Rome and Italy knows very well how God revenges and punishes the forbidden marriage, [fn: I.e., homosexuality] so that Sodom and Gomorrah, which God overwhelmed in days of old with fire and brimstone [Genesis 19:24], must seem a mere jest and prelude compared with these abominations.[4]

The same report and complaint was given by Martin Chemnitz (1522–86) a generation later:

> Now particularly in Italy and even at Rome, right under the eyes . . . of the most holy father, brothels, that is, public workshops of shameful deeds, function openly and are farmed out for revenue. Let me not speak of the fact that in recent years the legate of the pope himself, as Sleidanus writes, gave out a public writing in which he was not prevented by any shame, if not Christian then at least human, from, for his own part, defending and commending to others, in public contempt of 2 Peter 2, that horrible vice on account of which Sodom together with the neighboring cities was burnt by the fire of divine wrath.[5]

Moreover, from the writings of ancient Greek and Roman authors, which the reformers read in both Greek and Latin, the reformers knew about the ancient sexual revolutions that had occurred in Greek and Roman societies.[6] Thus it is clear that the reformers were quite aware of the wide variety of sexual practices and sins that had been practiced in the past and at their own time. There was no naïveté. They vigorously opposed the sexual revolution that they had seen happening in Italy and did all they could to prevent it from taking hold in Germany.

About 400 years later in 1961, a remarkable book was issued by the Family Life Committee of The Lutheran Church—Missouri Synod and published by Concordia Publishing House. The book was entitled *Sex*

---

4 AE 46:198.

5 Martin Chemnitz, *Examination of the Council of Trent*, trans. Fred Kramer (St. Louis: Concordia, 1986, 2007), 3:22.

6 See the discussion of Priapus in Luther, *Against the Spiritual Estate* (1522), AE 39:261.

and the Church: A Sociological, Historical, and Theological Investigation of Sex Attitudes, under the general editorship of Oscar E. Feucht.[7] The book was remarkable because of its aims. The second premise of the book is that it attempted to unite "modern knowledge and insight" with traditional Christian doctrine on sexual attitudes and practice.[8] A source for this "modern knowledge and insight" was the father of the sexual revolution himself, Alfred Kinsey, though the authors of *Sex and the Church* admitted that Kinsey's findings may not always be valid.[9] Nevertheless, in a discussion of masturbation, the authors directed readers to Kinsey's book *Sexual Behavior in the Human Male*.[10] In trying to unite modern sexual attitudes with traditional Christian doctrine, Feucht and his fellow authors examined the teaching of Luther and Lutheran Orthodoxy (the period after the Reformation from ca. 1580–1700), yet all of this examination was based on secondary sources; the authors did not engage with the primary texts, the writings of Luther and other Lutheran theologians, directly.

IN THE LCMS, THE SEXUAL REVOLUTION WAS NEVER ADOPTED IN WHOLE.

What is even more remarkable about this book is its timing. It was published in 1961, as the sexual revolution was coming into general acceptance in America. Moreover, it was a time when Lutherans had recently ceased speaking German. After the two world wars, American Lutherans generally ceased teaching German, and at the same time very few classic Lutheran writings had been translated into English. Only a few volumes of the American Edition of Luther's Works had been published. The previous English translation of Luther contained only about a dozen volumes. Nothing of Martin Chemnitz, Johann Gerhard, or the vast Lutheran Bible commentary tradition had been translated from German and Latin. Therefore, Feucht's *Sex and the Church* appeared at a time when few people were in a position to evaluate its claims on the basis of the primary texts, and at a time when few people were inclined to do so.

A major thesis of *Sex and the Church* is that Luther freed Christian sexual ethics from the moralistic shackles of Roman Catholicism. A second major thesis is that the sexual ethics of Lutheran Orthodoxy do not need to

7 Feucht is well-known for authoring *Everyone a Minister: A Guide to Churchmanship for Laity and Clergy* (St. Louis: Concordia, 1974).

8 Oscar E. Feucht et al., eds., *Sex and the Church: A Sociological, Historical, and Theological Investigation of Sex Attitudes* (St. Louis: Concordia, 1961), 9–10.

9 Feucht et al., *Sex and the Church*, 7.

10 Feucht et al., *Sex and the Church*, 99.

be taken seriously since, according to the authors of *Sex and the Church,* the dogmaticians of the period were "on the road back to the asceticism of the Middle Ages."[11] As we shall see, the first of these theses is a half-truth, and the second thesis is simply false. *Sex and the Church* overlooked the fact that an Italian sexual revolution was taking place at the time, and Luther and Lutheran Orthodoxy vigorously opposed this sexual revolution on the basis of Holy Scripture. Thus the aims of *Sex and the Church,* to unite modern insights with traditional doctrine, turns out actually to be an attempt to set aside large portions of traditional Lutheran sexual ethics in favor of the very practices and attitudes that Luther and Lutheran Orthodoxy rejected.

In the LCMS, the sexual revolution was never adopted in whole. The LCMS never adopted free love and the acceptance of homosexual behavior, for example. Instead of wholesale adoption, the LCMS unwittingly accepted only parts of the sexual revolution's agenda, among which was the view that masturbation is permissible for Christians. This chapter will not deal with the crass errors of the sexual revolution, but only with the question of whether masturbation is permissible.

Mollities, the Voluntary Emission of Semen

Masturbation is a thoroughly unpleasant word and topic. The nineteenth-century German word for it was *Selbstbefleckung,* "self-pollution," which will be used here. The word especially applies to male sexual self-stimulation, but the same principles that are being discussed here will also apply to females. Here the term *self-pollution* means not the involuntary emission of semen as can happen in adolescent boys and in men while sleeping, but auto-erotic behavior, and specifically the voluntary emission of semen outside of intercourse.

In The Lutheran Church—Missouri Synod's openness to some aspects of the sexual revolution, typified by the book *Sex and the Church,* self-pollution was considered not sinful in and of itself, but something that may have negative consequences. *Sex and the Church* states that self-pollution is not discussed in either the Old Testament or the New Testament; Thomas Aquinas and the Medieval Church considered it a grievous sin and so did Lutheran Orthodoxy.[12] Luther's views on the subject are passed over in silence. In this way, the strong implication is made that the Lutheran Orthodox theologians departed from Luther and were regressing to the overly

11 Feucht et al., *Sex and the Church,* 101.

12 Feucht et al., *Sex and the Church,* 24, 34, 69, 99, 225–26.

strict moralism (asceticism) of the Middle Ages.[13] A number of contemporary Lutherans are cited, with whom the LCMS was not in fellowship, some of which reject self-pollution and some of which claim it is sometimes permissible. Alfred Kinsey's research is cited to show how prevalent self-pollution is.[14] As a result, *Sex and the Church* leaves self-pollution, i.e., auto-erotic behavior, open as a non-sinful sexual expression for Christians. Perhaps as a result of this book, or else as a result of the same general attitude, Missouri Synod publications beginning in the 1960s stated that self-pollution is an acceptable practice for Christians in many situations.[15] However, continuous Lutheran teaching from the Reformation until the sexual revolution of the 1960s has identified self-pollution as sin on the basis of several passages of Scripture (such as Genesis 38:9 and 1 Corinthians 6:9) as well as on the basis of the created purposes of marriage and the sinfulness of lust.

A contributing factor to the LCMS's moderate sexual revolution may have been mistranslations of key vocabulary within Luther's Works: American Edition. The standard Latin word for auto-erotic behavior, used since the classical Latin era through the eighteenth century, was *mollities.* In Latin-English dictionaries of classical Latin, this is defined usually as "softness." From the usage and definitions given by Martin Luther and Johann Gerhard, however, it is clear that the term means any voluntary ejaculation outside of intercourse, no matter how this is caused. Thus it includes auto-erotic behavior (for example, masturbation), together with *coitus interruptus,* and (if it is possible) any other voluntary ejaculation, even if not caused by touching genitalia. (One could imagine a drug having this effect.) *Mollities* ("softness"), however, does not include involuntary ejaculation. The word was used in this sense by classical authors,[16] but Latin-English dictionaries cover over the specific meaning by giving very general definitions such as "effeminacy, voluptuousness, wantonness," which, of course, say nothing specific.[17]

In the ESV, 1 Corinthians 6:9–10 is translated as: "Do you not know that the unrighteous will not inherit the kingdom of God? Do not be deceived: neither the sexually immoral, nor idolaters, nor adulterers, nor men

---

13 Chemnitz's and Gerhard's views on the topic are likewise omitted.

14 Feucht et al., *Sex and the Church,* 142–43, 170, 225.

15 For example, Roger Sonnenberg, *Human Sexuality: A Christian Perspective* (St. Louis: Concordia, 1998), 90–94.

16 See Heinrich Georges, *Ausführliches Lateinische-Deutsches Handwörterbuch,* 8th ed., 2 vols. (Hannover: Hahnsche Buchhandlung, 2003), s.v. "mollitia" II.B.

17 Charlton Thomas Lewis and Charles Short, eds., *A Latin Dictionary, Founded on Andrews' Edition of Freund's Latin Dictionary* (Oxford: Clarendon Press, 1962), s.v. "mollitia" II.

who practice homosexuality, . . . will inherit the kingdom of God."[18] Luther translates it somewhat differently. Instead of "men who practice homosexuality," he translates it as "*noch die Weichlingen, noch die Knabenschender*" (that is, "nor the soft, nor the boy-violators").[19] Luther sees "the soft" as meaning those who practice *mollities*, "softness," voluntary, individual seminal emission. Here one must ask what is meant by "the soft" in the Greek of 1 Corinthians 6:9. The words μαλακός, μαλακίζομαι, μαλακία (*malakos, malakizomai, malakia*) have an interesting history of usage among Christians. In classical Greek, the adjective μαλακός meant either "soft" or "sensual, unable to resist sensual enticements and pleasures."[20] Likewise, the noun μαλακία meant "softness" or "moral weakness." More specifically this noun could mean "unnatural lust."[21] In the Greek translation of the Old Testament, the noun μαλακία normally meant "illness" (e.g., Exodus 23:25) and the adjective μαλακός meant simply "soft" (Proverbs 25:15). By the New Testament era, however, the adjective μαλακός had come to be used in a specific sense, related to "sensual." As a noun, it sometimes meant a "catamite." This is the sense in which scholars think it is being used in 1 Corinthians 6:9,[22] though the broader meaning of "sensual" should not be ruled out. By the late patristic era, we have another use of the noun μαλακία, of the adjective μαλακός, and of the verb μαλακίζομαι. Here it has to do with Onanism, self-pollution.[23] This use is a specific example, perhaps the foremost example, of the broader meaning of the μαλακός words, having to do with a sensual lifestyle. So when Luther and the entire Christian tradition from the late patristic era onward understood μαλακοί in 1 Corinthians 6:9 as those who practice self-pollution, they un-

LUTHER CONNECTED THE SIN OF SELF-POLLUTION WITH ONAN'S SIN IN GENESIS 38:9–10.

18 Greek: οὔτε μαλακοὶ οὔτε ἀρσενοκοῖται. Following the definitions of Frederick W. Danker, *A Greek-English Lexicon of the New Testament and Other Early Christian Literature*, 3rd ed. (Chicago: University of Chicago Press, 2000); ESV understands μαλακοὶ as "catamites," the passive homosexual partner, and ἀρσενοκοῖται as the active homosexual partner, but harmonizing both elements into the general phrase "men who practice homosexuality."

19 WA DB 7:100–101. Luther understood the word μαλακοὶ as people who practice *mollities*, voluntary individual seminal emission.

20 Franz Passow, *Handwörterbuch der Griechischen Sprache*, 5th ed. (Leipzig, 1852), s.v. "μαλακός." Cf. Henry George Liddell, Robert Scott, and Henry Stuart Jones, eds., *A Greek-English Lexicon* (Oxford: Clarendon Press, 1958), s.v. "μαλακός" III.c. (hereafter "LSJ").

21 LSJ s.v. μαλακία 1., 2.

22 Danker, *A Greek-English Lexicon of the New Testament*, s.v. "μαλακός" 2.

23 See Evangelinus Apostolides Sophocles and Joseph Henry Thayer, *Greek Lexicon of the Roman and Byzantine Periods* (Boston: Little, Brown, and Co., 1870), s.v. "μαλακός" 3. Sophocles' testimonies for this meaning of the Greek words dates back to the late 300s AD. See also Henricus Stephanus, Carolus Benedictus Hase, et al., *Thesaurus Graecae Linguae*, nova editio (Parisiis: Ambrosius Firmin Didot, [1830]), s.v. "μαλακία."

derstood this word as a species of its genus, an instantiation of how a sensually minded person behaves. That is, even if μαλακοί in 1 Corinthians 6:9 meant "catamites" specifically, the term itself was used commonly in the Greek language for a sensual person, and an extreme example of a sensual life is self-pollution.

Yet, Luther's thoughts on self-pollution were not drawn just from the meaning of a word in 1 Corinthians 6:9. In his comments on Romans 1:24, he writes:

> The uncleanness, or [softness],[24] is every intentional and individual pollution that can be brought about in various ways: through excessive passion from shameful thoughts, through rubbing with hands, through fondling of another's body, especially a woman's, through indecent movements, etc. I have called it "intentional" in order to differentiate it from the pollution that takes place during the night and sometimes during the day and the waking hours, but which happens to many people involuntarily. Such things are not intended. I have called it "individual," for when it becomes heterosexual or homosexual intercourse, it has a different name.[25]

Here the translator mistranslated *mollities* as "effeminacy," even though Luther himself gives the definition. *Mollities* does not mean "effeminacy." It means, according to Luther, voluntary individual emission of semen, however this might occur. The same mistranslation occurs in his commentary on Genesis 19:4–5 (the story of the destruction of Sodom and Gomorrah). Luther says:

> But what shall we suppose was in the mind of godly Lot, toward whose house everybody was going during this uproar in the whole city? He alone feared God, and in his house he maintained discipline and chastity to the utmost of his ability, while the others indulged freely and without shame in adultery, fornication, [softness],[26] and even incest to such an extent that these were not regarded as sins but as some pastime, just as today among the nobility and the lower

24 *mollities*, "individual voluntary ejaculation." This is mistranslated "effeminacy" in AE 25:166.

25 AE 25:166.

26 *molliciei* (WA 43:56), "individual voluntary ejaculation." This is mistranslated "effeminacy" in AE 3:254.

> classes of Germany fornication is regarded as a pastime, not as a sin, and for this reason is also entirely unpunished.[27]

Here once again, the word *mollities* was translated as "effeminacy," but should have been translated as "softness" with a footnote explaining that this means self-pollution.

Luther connected the sin of self-pollution with Onan's sin in Genesis 38:9–10. In Genesis 38, Onan's sin was not auto-eroticism, but *coitus interruptus*, a form of birth control that enabled him still to enjoy sexual intercourse with Tamar while avoiding the natural effect of the conjugal act (her pregnancy). In the ESV, Genesis 38:9–10 reads:

> But Onan knew that the offspring would not be his. So whenever he went in to his brother's wife he would waste the semen on the ground, so as not to give offspring to his brother. And what he did was wicked in the sight of the Lord, and He put him to death also.

Luther comments on these verses as follows:

> Onan must have been a malicious and incorrigible scoundrel. This is a most disgraceful sin. It is far more atrocious than incest and adultery. We call it [softness],[28] yes, a Sodomitic sin. For Onan goes in to her; that is, he lies with her and copulates, and when it comes to the point of insemination, spills the semen, lest the woman conceive. Surely at such a time the order of nature established by God in procreation should be followed. Accordingly, it was a most disgraceful crime to produce semen and excite the woman, and to frustrate her at that very moment. He was inflamed with the basest spite and hatred. Therefore he did not allow himself to be compelled to bear that intolerable slavery. Consequently, he deserved to be killed by God. He committed an evil deed. Therefore God punished him.[29] . . . He preferred polluting himself with a most disgraceful sin to raising up offspring for his brother.[30]

---

27 AE 3:254.

28 *molliciem* (WA 44:317). This is mistranslated "unchastity" in AE 7:20–21.

29 AE 7:20–21.

30 AE 7:21.

Notice here also that Luther considers Onan's sin a sodomitic sin, a variety of sodomy, and as worthy of death. Since normal fornication is seen by him as a sin that casts out faith and the Holy Spirit,[31] it is certain that he regards this sin as doing the same. He also classifies Onan's sin as *mollities.* Here once again the English translation published in Luther's Works disguises the fact that Luther was using a specific Latin term with a technical meaning. *Mollities* was mistranslated here as "unchastity," but "unchastity" is far too broad a term. Instead, it should have been "softness" with a footnote explaining that this means "voluntary seminal discharge outside of a woman's body." From this Bible passage, another technical Latin term arose, *onania,* that is, "Onan's sin."[32] By this, Lutheran theologians meant both *coitus interruptus* and self-pollution; what joined these two concepts together was the voluntary spilling of seed outside of intercourse. It should be recognized that *coitus interruptus* and self-pollution are essentially the same in how they end, even though the method to arrive at the sexual climax may differ. As long as Lutherans used Latin for theology, *onania* and *mollities* meant both of these—*coitus interruptus* and self-pollution—but not the general term *unchastity* or the unrelated term *effeminacy*.

Not only does Luther use this definition early in his career, but late as well. In a sermon for the Fourteenth Sunday after Trinity in 1545, he stated that the word *impurity* in Galatians 5:19 refers to "defiling oneself, the sin of 'softness'" (footnote: "*mollities,* i.e., masturbation").[33]

In summary, Luther sees self-pollution as a species of the slightly broader phenomenon *mollities,* which we can best call "voluntary individual seminal discharge." He considers it a counter-natural sin more serious even than adultery, in the same category as sodomy; one for which Onan was rightly put to death by God. It was one that he knew was prevalent in Italy, and was one of the reasons he was convinced that so few people could live chastely outside of marriage. In the Holy Scriptures, he saw it as being discussed in Genesis 38:9–10 ("spilling seed"); Romans 1:24 ("dis-

---

31 "It is, accordingly, necessary to know and to teach that when holy men, still having and feeling original sin, also daily repenting of and striving with it, happen to fall into manifest sins, as David into adultery, murder, and blasphemy, that then faith and the Holy Ghost has departed from them [they cast out faith and the Holy Ghost]. For the Holy Ghost does not permit sin to have dominion, to gain the upper hand so as to be accomplished, but represses and restrains it so that it must not do what it wishes. But if it does what it wishes, the Holy Ghost and faith are [certainly] not present. For St. John says, 1 John 3, 9: *Whosoever is born of God doth not commit sin, . . . and he cannot sin.* And yet it is also the truth when the same St. John says, 1, 8: *If we say that we have no sin, we deceive ourselves and the truth is not in us*" (SA III III 43–44). W. H. T. Dau and F. Bente, eds., *Triglot Concordia: The Symbolical Books of the Ev. Lutheran Church, German-Latin-English* (St. Louis: Concordia, 1921), 491.

32 See E. Eckhardt, *Homiletisches Reallexikon* (St. Louis: Success Printing Co., 1907), s.v. "Ehebrechen" 6., *Onanie*.

33 AE 58:289. See also *1 Corinthians 7* (1523), AE 28:28; *Against the Spiritual Estate* (1522), AE 39:298.

honoring their bodies"); 1 Corinthians 6:9 ("soft"); and Galatians 5:19 ("uncleanness").

Writing almost one hundred years later, Johann Gerhard had exactly the same views. In his *Theological Commonplaces,* "On Marriage," he gives a definition:

> Sodomy is the counter-natural mixing together either with males or with brutes (Leviticus 18:22–23; Romans 1:26). It is named differently with respect to the former kind "pederasty"; with respect to the latter, "bestiality," and in general "mute sins," which should not even be named among Christians. Here one should place the crime of Onan, the voluntary profusion of semen, called *mollities* ["softness"], about which the scholastics correctly argue, saying that it is a sin more serious even than adultery. (*On Marriage,* § 487; Preuss ed., 7:298)

In a listing of sins against the Sixth Commandment, Gerhard says:

> In our deeds we sin in various ways against this commandment: through fornication among unwed persons; through adultery among spouses; through rape when shame is brought on a woman by force; through incest when there is a union of blood kin and relatives in prohibited grades; through sodomy, bestiality, pederasty, softness [*mollities*]—or, the voluntary emission of semen, which Thomas [Aquinas] declares "is a sin worse than going to a prostitute"—[and] through prostitutional concubinage. (*On the Law,* § 161; Preuss ed., 3:73)

> We are forbidden by our sense of decency to speak in the presence of chaste ears about the sin of onanism. (*On the Law,* § 165; 3:75)

Gerhard's list of sins against the Sixth Commandment is explained in more detail in his German work *The School of Piety* (*Schola Pietatis*).[34] With regard to self-pollution, he reiterates what was stated in the *Theological Commonplaces.*

Here let us summarize what we have learned. The difference between the sexual revolutions of the sixteenth century in Italy and of the twentieth century in Europe and America is that Luther and the reformers knew Latin and Greek well, and they were in close contact with the foregoing Christian teaching on sexual morality, most of which they accepted as agreeing with Scripture. The moderate LCMS sexual revolution, on the other hand, took place when Lutherans had, with only a few exceptions, lost contact with their Latin theological heritage (which happened in the nineteenth century) and with their German theological heritage (which happened in the twentieth century), due to a decline in education and the transition from German to English among American Lutherans. Luther's statements on self-pollution do not usually go into detail and do not explain why self-pollution is a sodomitic sin, worse than adultery. Also, he does not explain in what respect it is worse (e.g., with regard to eternal condemnation, with regard to damage to the life of faith and the Spirit among believers, or with regard to practical consequences in this life). It is clear, however, that Luther thinks it is a sin abominable to the Lord and worthy of death. His lack of explanation, moreover, makes it clear that he does not mean to introduce anything new or different from what was taught previously about this sin. That is, he does not ever correct his medieval forebears for teaching that self-pollution is a sin. What he rejects about the foregoing medieval tradition is its prohibition of clerical marriage, precisely because this prohibition often leads to the sin of self-pollution, along with fornication, adultery, and sodomy, not to mention impure thoughts.

What, then, shall we say to the 1961 book *Sex and the Church*? First, did Luther really free Christian ethics from the moralistic shackles of Roman Catholicism? As we have seen, this is a half-truth. It is true according as Luther advocated clerical marriage and taught more clearly that marriage is God's good creation. It is false if it is thought that Luther saw lust as a

34 Johann Gerhard, *Schola Pietatis, Oder Ubung der Gottseeligkeit, Worinnen Die vornehmsten Haupt- und Kern-Sprüche Heil. Schrifft, welche zur Theologia Morali und Christlichen Sitten-Lehr gehörig, gründlich eröffnet, und zur Beförderung eines rechtschaffenen und thätigen Christen-Wandels erkläret werden. Bey dieser neuen und fünfften Auflage is nunmehro beygefüget worden des seel. Herrn Authoris Evangelischer Wegweiser, wie solche Ubungen zu Vermehrung gottseliger Andacht recht zu gebrauchen sind, ed. Johann Georg Walch* (Nürnberg: in Verlegung W. M. Endters seel. Töchter und J. A. Engelbrechts seel. Wittib., 1736) 4.3.26, 896–912. Three books have appeared in English translation so far: *Schola Pietatis* (1623), trans. Elmer Hohle, vol. 1 (Malone, TX: Repristination Press, 2006); vol. 2, ed. Rachel Melvin (2013); vol. 3, ed. Rachel Melvin (2015).

created good or that he allowed self-pollution or other auto-erotic practices as permissible. In fact, as we have seen, Luther castigated the moral laxity of the Italian church in its renaissance sexual revolution. Instead of freeing Christian ethics from moralistic Roman Catholic shackles, Luther wanted to correct Italian license and bring about obedience to God's Word.

> HOW CAN CHRISTIANS, HAVING BEEN FORGIVEN, NOW FIGHT AGAINST SEXUAL TEMPTATIONS AND BEGIN TO HEAL FROM SEXUAL SINS?

Second, were the dogmaticians of Lutheran Orthodoxy really on a road back to the overly strict moralism (asceticism) of the Middle Ages? No. Rather, there is no discernible difference between the sexual morality set forth by Luther and what was taught by Johann Gerhard, the foremost representative of Lutheran Orthodoxy. Instead of viewing the Reformation as a time of sexual freedom, we should see it, with Lutheran Orthodoxy, as a time when pious churchmen strove to defend their people from the Italian sexual revolution and to bring them to a flourishing of traditional Christian chastity.

Resistance to and Healing from Sexual Sins

Fornication, adultery, self-pollution, and other kinds of unchastity are spiritual maladies, not merely problems with consequences in this world. St. Paul makes clear that sins of these sorts have special seriousness and consequences (1 Corinthians 6:18–20). One may not compare fornication and unchastity to other sins in an attempt to minimize the seriousness of these sexual sins. Among the classic Lutheran theologians, Johann Gerhard dealt with sexual sins and healing from them in perhaps the most detail. His five books entitled *The School of Piety* have immense value because in them he not only diagnoses sexual illness but also prescribes a cure.

Gerhard first makes clear that there are terrible punishments and consequences for fornication and unchastity, consequences that affect one's possessions, body, reputation, life, spouse, and children. But not only this—there are punishments and consequences for one's mind and soul as well. Many passages of Scripture speak to the bad effects on the mind. These would be understood as natural, physical effects. Hosea 4:11: "whoredom, wine, and new wine enslave the heart" (cf. also Sirach 19:2).[35] The example

35 Gerhard often quotes books of the Apocrypha alongside the canonical Old Testament and New Testament. For the text of the Apocrypha and how it compares with the Old Testament and New Testament, see Edward A. Engelbrecht, ed., *The Apocrypha: The Lutheran Edition* (St. Louis: Concordia, 2012).

of Samson (Judges 14–16) also shows that after engaging in sexual sins one's reason and intellect are weakened or taken away. "Therefore the heathen, who give themselves over to lewdness, have their understanding darkened, are ignorant, have a blinded heart, and are alienated from the life of God" (Ephesians 4:18–19).[36] Anecdotes testify that addiction to pornography or other unchastity can indeed lead to a complete change of personality, interests, desires, and understanding. Gerhard also describes the effects of unchastity on the soul: hellfire and damnation (Job 24:15, 18–19; 31:9–12; Proverbs 5:5; 7:27; 9:18; 22:14; 23:27). In Romans 1:12, those who do such things are worthy of death—not only temporal death but also and especially eternal death. In 1 Corinthians 6:9, fornicators, adulterers, the soft, and pederasts will not inherit the kingdom of God. In Galatians 5:21, the works of the flesh include adultery, fornication, impurity, and unchastity; those who do such things will not inherit the kingdom of God. (See also Ephesians 5:5; Colossians 3:6; Hebrews 12:14; Revelation 21:8; 22:15.)[37]

ANECDOTES TESTIFY THAT ADDICTION TO PORNOGRAPHY OR OTHER UNCHASTITY CAN INDEED LEAD TO A COMPLETE CHANGE OF PERSONALITY, INTERESTS, DESIRES, AND UNDERSTANDING.

Gerhard brings up the seriousness of these sins not to exclude such people from salvation, but to do precisely the opposite: to call them to healing and salvation. This brings up the question: How does one heal from self-pollution and sexual sins in general? Medical specialists may be able to give advice regarding treatments that affect the body. Here, Johann Gerhard instructs us from God's Word on healing that affects the whole human person in body and soul. In general, the answer will be the same as to the question, "How is the old man put to death and how does the new man grow and gain strength?" (cf. Romans 6:6; 8:1–13; Ephesians 4:20–24; Colossians 3:9–10). Luther discussed this in terms of living in one's Baptism.[38] Gerhard puts this healing process in terms of the pursuit of godliness (1 Timothy 4:8; 6:11).[39] And the Augsburg Confession (1530), Article XII, puts it in terms of the life of repentance. For Gerhard and the Augsburg Confession, the parts of this healing are the same:

36 *Schola Pietatis* (German), 888–93.

37 *Schola Pietatis* (German), 891–92.

38 SC IV 11–14.

39 *Schola Pietatis* (German), 6; (English), 1:11.

(1) contrition, (2) faith, (3) good works as the fruit of repentance.[40] That is to say, healing from sexual sins, similar to healing from other sins, is a matter of growth and struggle—the part of Christian life that classic Lutheran theology calls "sanctification." Here Adolf Köberle reminds us that according to Scripture there is more than one motivation for sanctification and the healing of a Christian's moral and spiritual life. Besides *thankfulness* for the free forgiveness of sins through faith for Christ's sake, there is also the power of Christ's example, with the sternness of obedience and of the fear of God. This last motivation is especially important in the struggle to overcome sexual sins. A Christian who does not fear God's wrath and the faith-destroying, enslaving power of sin will easily be overcome by the power of sin, especially sexual sin.[41]

If the life of repentance is the pursuit of godliness, as Gerhard says it is, then the God-given means to promote repentance will be the same things that aid a person toward healing from sexual sin. For contrition (i.e., pain and regret concerning sin), what is needed is the Law and commanding will of God, along with the fear of God. The fear of worldly consequences plays a role here too. Being fallen creatures at the same time as we are believers, the fear of worldly penalties works together with the fear of God and even with love for God. This fear of worldly consequences can include shame, loss of family, loss of employment, or even criminal punishment in certain cases. As noted above, Gerhard sets forth these things to Christians for consideration in avoiding sexual sins.[42] Next, the means to faith and grace are discussed very often in our confessions, hymns, and theology. Here let the sin-sick, repentant person come to the Means of Grace, finding absolution, consolation in Gospel preaching, Holy Baptism (if not yet a Christian), and the Holy Supper. Along with these things, Gerhard adds the hearing or reading of God's Word, devotional contemplation, praying zealously and diligently, and disciplining the body.[43]

How can Christians, having been forgiven, now fight against sexual temptations and begin to heal from sexual sins? Gerhard gives his pastoral advice. First, meditate on God's Word. That is, diligently hear, read, and exercise yourself in the Scriptures, especially in passages that give the rea-

40 See the detailed description of these parts in *Schola Pietatis* (German), 298–383; (English), 2:145–284.

41 Adolf Köberle, *The Quest for Holiness* (Minneapolis: Augsburg, 1938), 168. On the fear of God in sanctification, see pp. 164–68.

42 *Schola Pietatis* (German), 888–93.

43 *Schola Pietatis* (German), 226–98; (English), 2:29–143.

sons for avoiding fornication.[44] These reasons include God's serious command, God's good will for His human creatures, the dignity of chastity, the ugliness of fornication, the necessity of chastity, our calling by God to be Christians, the characteristics of godliness, the rewards of chastity, and the disadvantages of fornication.[45] The way to defend oneself from the fiery arrows of the devil is with the shield of faith (Ephesians 6:6). This faith comes from the Word of God, and it is maintained, strengthened, and increased through the Word (Romans 10:18). Gerhard remarks, "Love the knowledge of Scripture, and you will not love the vices of the flesh."[46]

Second, think about divine omniscience. God the Lord sees and hears all that we do and say. As Scripture says, "And no creature is hidden from His sight, but all are naked and exposed to the eyes of Him to whom we must give account" (Hebrews 4:13). Gerhard remarks, "Let divine fear pierce your flesh, lest fleshly love deceive you."[47] And, "How brief is the pleasure of an hour, for which eternal life is lost!"[48]

Third, mortify (or put to death) the corrupt lust. Smother the sparks of lust before they flare up. Just as one can put out a spark before it catches flame far more easily than after it has begun to flame and rage, so also lusts can be extinguished much more easily when they first start to occur than if they are pondered, thought about, and explored. Gerhard says, "When the harmful, evil lust is still smoldering, one can easily smother it through the power of the Spirit. But if one is negligent in this, it can easily become a harmful lust that consumes the man in body and soul."[49] As Christ says in Matthew 5:29; 18:8; Mark 9:47, "If your right eye offends you, pluck it out," etc. Here Christ is speaking not of external body parts but of the inner parts of the old man, that is, about the evil lusts of the flesh, which can be felt in all parts. He also is not speaking of physical plucking and chopping, but inward, spiritual plucking and chopping off,

THERE IS NO FOOL-PROOF PROCEDURE TO CONQUER SIN.

44 *Schola Pietatis* (German), 904. These include Exodus 16:6; 20:14; 22:31; Deuteronomy 5:18; 23:17; Matthew 5:27; 19:18; Mark 20:9; Luke 18:20; Romans 13:9; James 2:11; Leviticus 11:45; 19:2, 29; 20:6; Acts 15:20, 29; 21:25; Romans 13:13–14; 1 Corinthians 5:11; 6:13, 20; 10:8; Ephesians 5:3; Colossians 3:5; 1 Thessalonians 4:3–5; 1 Peter 3:7; 1 Timothy 1:10; 2 Corinthians 6:6; Philippians 4:8; Titus 2:5; Hebrews 12:14, 16; 13:4. See *Schola Pietatis* (German), 867–96 for much more.

45 *Schola Pietatis* (German), 876–96.

46 *Schola Pietatis* (German), 904–5.

47 *Schola Pietatis* (German), 904–5.

48 *Schola Pietatis* (German), 906.

49 *Schola Pietatis* (German), 906.

when the evil lust in the heart is put to death and put away.[50] How does one "mortify" or "put to death" a feeling or desire? Gerhard does not explain this explicitly, but here advice can be given, nevertheless. Pray for the Holy Spirit to come to you and fill you with desires only for good, chaste things. Pray against the temptation. Pray that the evil act and those who tempt would be brought to shame and confusion. Psalm 83:16: "Fill their faces with shame, that they may seek Your name, O LORD." Pray for the swift rebuke and destruction of Satan and his angels, who are the ones promoting this temptation. Pray for freedom from Satan's bonds. Next, stir up hatred in your heart against the images you have seen or imagined. As Luther says, imagine them from the inside out, full of all vile excrement, urine, blood, and pus, just like everyone else.[51]

Fourth, avoid enticements to lust. Here Gerhard gives many examples of temptations, taking some of his examples from Holy Scripture. They can be summarized with the motto, "Flee temptation."[52] You will know individually what tempts you toward lust. Flee and avoid these things.

Fifth, pursue modesty and shame. He says, "Shame is the guardian of chastity."[53]

Sixth, view marriage in a pious and godly manner. Marriage is a medicine against the forbidden, evil lusts. It is the duty of parents to help find a spouse for their sons and daughters, if they see that their sons or daughters cannot live chastely outside of marriage.[54]

Seventh, and finally, make diligent and constant prayer. Luther's words on the importance of prayer match Gerhard's exactly:

> Take for yourself your Creed and the Ten Commandments, and they will tell you. Direct your life according to them, and find assistance in the Our Father. Beginning with yourself, pray for yourself and for the Church, that God's name be kept holy everywhere, etc., and also that your life go on according to His will. If you do this diligently, then you will certainly be walking wisely, avoiding sin, and doing good. This attentiveness and understanding will not allow you the opportunity to do evil. God's Word will soon tell you to keep

50 *Schola Pietatis* (German), 906.

51 Cf. Luther, preface to Urbanus Rhegius, *Refutation* (1535), AE 60:88.

52 *Schola Pietatis* (German), 906–11.

53 *Schola Pietatis* (German), 911.

54 *Schola Pietatis* (German), 911.

> His name holy, increase His kingdom, and not cause your neighbor pain or harm.[55]

This advice reflects the command of the Lord Jesus Himself, whose model prayer includes a petition against temptation (Matthew 6:13; Luke 11:4), and who instructed His disciples to watch and pray that they may not enter into temptation (Matthew 26:41; Mark 14:38).

In addition to Gerhard's seven counsels on fighting sexual temptation, the practice of private confession and individual absolution recommends itself. The experience of those who practice it shows that private confession to one's pastor has many benefits. It leads to a more serious consideration of one's sins, which leads a person to strive seriously to overcome them. Moreover, most people feel a psychological need to unburden their consciences by revealing their transgressions. Also, private confession makes the penitent person open to the specific words of counsel that one's pastor can provide to the individual struggles that the penitent faces. The benefit, then, of individual absolution is the great comfort that comes when the Gospel is applied specifically to the individual. Here the general proclamation of the Gospel and forgiveness for Christ's sake is made specific. In this respect, it is similar to the sacraments of Baptism and the Lord's Supper, both of which are always applied specifically to individuals.[56]

There is no fool-proof procedure to conquer sin. Christ died for all sins, including sexual sins. He offers forgiveness to those who repent of their sins and want to do better, and He calls all people to live a life of repentance and healing from whatever sins particularly tempt them.

Let us conclude, then, with the model prayer that Gerhard provides, a prayer for chastity:

> O almighty, eternal God, merciful Father! You are a holy, pure, and chaste God, and You abhor all impurity. I confess and lament to you from my heart that I have sometimes felt evil, shameful lusts, which have arisen from my heart and made me impure in Your sight (Matthew 15:19–20); that in thoughts, words, and deeds I have not always been as holy, pure, and chaste as I should rightly be. O dear heavenly Fa-

55 Luther, *Church Postil* (1540–44), Epistle for Trinity 20, AE 79:208.

56 See also Luther's admonition to confession, an appendix to the LC (*Concordia*, pp. 649–53): "When I urge you to go to Confession, I am doing nothing else than urging you to be a Christian. If I have brought you to the point of being a Christian, I have thereby also brought you to Confession. For those who really desire to be true Christians, to be rid of their sins, and to have a cheerful conscience already possess the true hunger and thirst."

ther, forgive me for this by grace for the sake of Christ and His precious merit, and henceforth sanctify my body and soul through Your Holy Spirit, that I may live in chastity and purity. Lord God, Father, and Lord of my life, protect me from immodest sights (Sirach 23:4) and turn away from me all evil lusts (v. 5). Let me not fall into debauchery and unchastity, and protect me from shameless hearts (v. 6). O Lord Jesus Christ! You are the pure and chaste bridegroom of my soul, and have seriously commanded me to pluck out the eye that causes me to sin, and to chop off the hand and foot that cause me to sin (Matthew 5:29; 18:18). Give me grace and power to become strong through the Spirit in the inward man (Ephesians 3:16), that I may suppress and kill the evil desire of the flesh. O heavenly Gardener of Paradise, bring to me from the Paradise of God the beautiful, sweet-smelling lilies of chastity. Plant them in my heart, water them through the dew of the Spirit, that they may ever grow and increase within me, and give a sweet aroma before God and men. O Holy Spirit! You are a spirit of chastity and of sanctification (Romans 1:4), whose fruit is chastity (Galatians 5:22). Wash me from all unrighteousness, and give me Your divine grace, that I may cleanse myself of all pollution of flesh and of spirit, and may continue with sanctification in the fear of God (1 Corinthians 7:1). O precious and worthy Spirit of my soul, purify and sanctify Your own temple, that I may be holy, pure, and chaste both in body and soul (1 Corinthians 7:34). Lead me finally into the heavenly Jerusalem, into which nothing common and unclean will enter (Revelation 21:26), but only those whose spirit with soul and body is kept without reproach for the coming of our Lord Jesus Christ (1 Thessalonians 5:23). Be pleased to work this in me by grace, O Holy Spirit, You who live and reign with the Father and the Son, one true God, highly praised forever. Amen![57]

57 *Schola Pietatis* (German), 912.

CHAPTER 8

A BIBLICAL RESPONSE TO HOMOSEXUALITY

Tom Eckstein

As we strive to speak God's truth in love regarding the issue of homosexuality,[1] we must be sure to distinguish between *having* same-sex attraction[2] versus *affirming* same-sex attraction and acting on it. A person may have a homosexual orientation and yet be a repentant Christian who does not celebrate this desire but grieves over it, trusts in Christ for forgiveness, and strives to resist the temptation to act on it or repents if he or she does act on it during a moment of weakness. This is different from one who celebrates same-sex attraction and acts on it without remorse or seeing any need to be forgiven for this sin. In other words, we must make the distinction between *repentant* Christians and those who are *unrepentant*.

For example, consider Paul's words in 1 Corinthians 6:9–11:

> Or do you not know that the unrighteous will not inherit the kingdom of God? Do not be deceived: neither the sexually immoral, nor idolaters, nor adulterers, nor men who practice homosexuality, nor thieves, nor the greedy, nor drunkards, nor revilers, nor swindlers will inherit the kingdom of God. And such were some of you. But you were washed, you were sanctified, you were justified in the name of the Lord Jesus Christ and by the Spirit of our God.

1 The word *homosexuality* describes the erotic desire a person has for a member of the same sex. Some argue that the word was first coined by Karoly Maria Kertbeny in 1869 in an attempt to create a non-pejorative term to describe same-sex erotic desire and behavior. See Gary Greenberg, "Gay by Choice? The Science of Sexual Identity," *MotherJones.com*, August 2007, www.motherjones.com/politics/2007/08/gay-choice-science-sexual-identity?page=2.

2 What is the cause of homosexuality in some people? The scientific consensus today is that the "gay gene" has not been discovered. Most agree that homosexuality is the result of a complex interaction between nature and nurture that is different for every individual. For example, in 2010 the American Psychological Association (APA) stated that the scientific evidence for a gene that is the exclusive cause of homosexual orientation is not conclusive. In their brochure *Answers to Your Questions for a Better Understanding of Sexual Orientation & Homosexuality*, we read the following: "There is no consensus among scientists about the exact reasons that an individual develops a heterosexual, bisexual, gay or lesbian orientation. Although much research has examined the possible genetic, hormonal, developmental, social, and cultural influences on sexual orientation, no findings have emerged that permit scientists to conclude that sexual orientation is determined by any particular factor or factors. Many think that nature and nurture both play complex roles." For more information about this, see Tom Eckstein, *Bearing Their Burden* (Lulu, 2010), 184–97; Stanton Jones and Mark Yarhouse, *Homosexuality: The Use of Scientific Research in the Church's Moral Debate* (Downers Grove, IL: InterVarsity Press, 2000).

When Paul says "such were some of you" (v. 11), he does not mean that all the repentant Christians in Corinth who used to practice homosexuality no longer had a homosexual orientation. Of course, it is possible that some repentant Christians may experience some level of change from a homosexual orientation to a heterosexual orientation, but this is not the experience for many repentant Christians today who continue to have a homosexual orientation. Therefore when Paul says "such were some of you," he means that those Corinthian Christians who used to engage in homosexual behavior but still have a homosexual orientation are now moved by the Holy Spirit to grieve over their past homosexual behavior as well as their current desires for it and trust in Christ for forgiveness and the strength to live a sexually pure life. In the same way, many repentant Christians with a heterosexual orientation continue to struggle with heterosexual desires that are contrary to God's will, and yet they can rejoice in the fact that there is "no condemnation for those who are in Christ Jesus" (Romans 8:1). The same wonderful Gospel promise applies to repentant Christians who continue to struggle with the challenges of having a homosexual orientation.

However, as we attempt to witness to those who practice same-sex behavior, we will discover that some of them claim to be faithful Christians who do not consider their same-sex behavior to be against God's will for their lives. A primary reason for this view is that there are some who attempt to argue that Holy Scripture does not condemn same-sex behavior within adult, consensual, committed relationships. Many people have been deceived by books that teach this very thing.[3] How do we respond to those who suggest that Scripture does not condemn same-sex behavior within an adult, consensual, committed relationship?

Old Testament Teachings on Sexual Behavior

To understand what Scripture teaches about same-sex desire and behavior, we must begin with the first two chapters of the Book of Genesis, where we read about God's creation of the universe and all life. The whole of Scripture is clear that the creation account found in Genesis 1–2 is to be

3 For example, see such books as Matthew Vines, *God and the Gay Christian* (New York: Convergent Books, 2014); John Boswell, *Christianity, Social Tolerance, and Homosexuality* (University of Chicago Press, 1980); Herbert Chilstrom and Lowell Erdahl, *Sexual Fulfillment* (Minneapolis: Augsburg, 2001); William Countryman, *Dirt, Greed & Sex* (Minneapolis: Fortress Press, 1988); Daniel Helminiak, *What the Bible Really Says about Homosexuality* (Tajique, NM: Alamo Square Press, 2000); Tom Horner, *Jonathan Loved David: Homosexuality in Biblical Times* (Philadelphia: Westminster Press, 1978); John Tyler Connonley and Jeff Miner, *The Children Are Free* (Indianapolis: Jesus Metropolitan Community Church, 2002); Jack Rogers, *Jesus, the Bible, and Homosexuality* (Louisville: Westminster John Knox Press, 2009); Robin Scroggs, *The New Testament and Homosexuality* (Minneapolis: Fortress, 1983); Walter Wink, *Homosexuality and Christian Faith* (Minneapolis: Fortress Press, 1999).

viewed as literal history.[4] For example, the genealogies in both the Old and New Testaments view Adam as a historical person. Also, Jesus' quotation from Genesis in Matthew 19 and many other biblical texts confirm that Scripture views the creation account in Genesis 1–2 as historical.

In Genesis 1:27–28, we are told that humans were created in God's image as male and female, and that they were to "be fruitful and increase in number." In 2:21–24, we see that the finishing touch of God's creation takes place when He gives the first man and first woman to each other in marriage. Genesis teaches that marriage is a unique human relationship that is between one man and one woman, and that God's gift of sex is "very good" only within His gift of marriage. The purpose of sex within marriage is (1) to produce new human life and (2) to celebrate the promise of unconditional love made by the man and woman who commit themselves to each other in marriage (we especially see this second aspect of the purpose of sex in the Song of Songs).

HOW DO WE RESPOND TO THOSE WHO SUGGEST THAT SCRIPTURE DOES NOT CONDEMN SAME-SEX BEHAVIOR WITHIN AN ADULT, CONSENSUAL, COMMITTED RELATIONSHIP?

Scripture teaches that marriage—especially the husband's sacrificial love for his wife—is a reflection or picture of God's unconditional love for His "Bride," that is, His redeemed people. Throughout the Old Testament, we see God using marriage to speak about His relationship with His people. In Ephesians 5, Paul teaches that Christian marriage is patterned after the relationship between Christ and His "Bride," the Church.

Sadly, after sin entered the world via the rebellion of Adam and Eve, God's plan for marriage and the purpose for His gift of sex has been twisted and rejected in many ways. Some people point out that the following examples of sexual sin can all be found in Holy Scripture: fornication (that is, sex outside of marriage), prostitution, incest, adultery, polygamy, homosexuality, and even bestiality. But wherever such behaviors are found in Scripture, it is clear that these texts are not *prescriptive*, as though God were

4 Some suggest that there are two contradictory creation stories found in Genesis 1 and 2, respectively. However, Horace Hummel writes: "There is no compelling reason why Gen. 1 and 2 need be read as two disparate creation accounts, as the critical dogma goes. One of its major supporting arguments is that Gen. 1 ends and climaxes with man (male and female) while chap. 2 begins with man (male only). But the two dovetail perfectly if we understand Gen. 1 as a 'wide-angle' introduction to all of creation, while Gen. 2 zooms in for a 'close-up' of the Bible's primary interest." See Horace Hummel, *The Word Becoming Flesh* (St. Louis: Concordia, 1979), 65. Also, for a more thorough response to the suggestion that Genesis 1 and 2 are two contradictory creation stories, see Tom Eckstein, *Bearing Their Burden* (Lulu, 2010), 41–45.

commanding and condoning such things. Instead, such texts are *descriptive* in nature in that they give accounts of people's rebellion against God's plan for our sexual lives as revealed in Genesis 1–2.

Using the creation account in Genesis as a foundation, the Old Testament teaches that sexual behavior is "very good" only within the context of marriage between one man and one woman. All sexual behavior outside of this context is rebellion against God's purpose for sex, which is meant to be the celebration of the marriage commitment between one man and one woman. Outside of the marriage commitment, sex becomes meaningless and the sinful using of another human being for one's own pleasure (see 1 Thessalonians 4:1–8).

The New Testament agrees with the Old by using the creation account in Genesis as the foundation for teaching that the only godly context for sexual behavior is between one man and one woman in marriage. In Matthew 19, Jesus quotes from Genesis 1–2 in order to condemn divorce and establish that marriage between one man and one woman is God's institution. Paul does the same thing in 1 Corinthians 6:12–17, where he quotes Genesis 2:24 in order to condemn the sin of prostitution as well as other sexual sins listed in 1 Corinthians 6:9–10. In Ephesians 5:21–33, Paul quotes Genesis 2:24 as the basis for his teaching about godly, monogamous, Christian marriage.

IN NO PLACE DOES SCRIPTURE EVER SPEAK OF HOMOSEXUAL BEHAVIOR IN A POSITIVE WAY NOR DOES SCRIPTURE EVER SPEAK OF GOD'S RELATIONSHIP TO HIS PEOPLE IN TERMS OF A HOMOSEXUAL RELATIONSHIP.

At this point we must understand that in no place does Scripture ever speak of homosexual behavior in a positive way nor does Scripture ever speak of God's relationship to His people in terms of a homosexual relationship. Therefore, Christians who wish to speak of marriage as a relationship between "any two people who love each other and are committed to each other" in order to affirm homosexual behavior fail to see how this nonbiblical definition of marriage could be used to affirm a "marriage" between an adult parent and an adult child (of the opposite sex or same sex) or between a brother and sister (or brother and brother or sister and sister) or between multiple individuals.

In fact, if one ignores the biblical teaching that marriage is between one man and one woman, then one has no good reason to limit marriage as a relationship between *two* people. Most Christians who wish to affirm gay marriage will insist that marriage is between *two* people. But why do they insist on this if they deny that Scripture limits marriage to one man and one woman? In other words, why has marriage always been understood as a relationship between *two* people? The reason is that there are *two* sexes: male and female. If one denies that marriage is limited to one man and one woman, then one is being completely arbitrary when one limits marriage to a relationship between *two* people. Therefore, those Christians who wish to affirm homosexual "marriage" should be consistent and also affirm polygamy as well as polyamory.

Simply put, Scripture's teaching about heterosexual sex within marriage is enough to help us understand that God does not condone but condemns homosexual behavior regardless of the context or the motivation of the individuals involved. However, Scripture has even more to say about homosexual behavior outside of Genesis 1–2.[5]

MORAL AND CEREMONIAL LAWS

In Leviticus 18–20, we find a list of sexual sins and other nonsexual sins that God condemns. In this section, we also read of God's clear condemnation of homosexual behavior. "You shall not lie with a male as with a woman; it is an abomination" (18:22). "If a man lies with a male as with a woman, both of them have committed an abomination; they shall surely be put to death; their blood is upon them" (20:13). Here we see that it is not merely violent, homosexual rape that is condemned. God also condemns consensual homosexual behavior between two men because Leviticus 20:13 condemns them both, and Scripture teaches that a rape victim would never be condemned.

The moral laws in Leviticus 18 and 20 apply to all people of all times and places. These moral laws must be distinguished from the civil and ceremonial laws found in Leviticus that were given only to the people of Israel and only for a temporary period of history.

For example, some Christians dismiss what Leviticus says about homosexual behavior because Leviticus also condemns the eating of shrimp (see

5 I will not be examining the event that led to the destruction of Sodom (see Genesis 19:1ff). The reason is that this event describes homosexual gang rape and does not directly address the modern issue of whether same-sex behavior can be affirmed if it takes place between adults within a consensual, loving, committed relationship. For readers who wish to know how to respond to those who attempt to use the Sodom event as way to affirm same-sex behavior within loving, committed relationships, see Eckstein, *Bearing Their Burden*, 52–56.

11:10). This is what I call the "Red Lobster fans who think homosexuality is a sin are inconsistent" argument. But such Christians fail to distinguish between the food laws given only to Israel and only for a temporary period of history versus the moral laws that apply to all people of all times and places. God never condemns the *Gentile* nations for eating shrimp. But in Leviticus 18 and 20, God clearly condemns the *Gentile* nations (see 18:1–3) for their sexual sin—including homosexuality.

In his commentary on the Book of Ezekiel, Horace Hummel writes:

> The OT places moral and ceremonial laws beside each other without the sharp distinction between them later made by Christians. Christ fulfilled the entirety of the OT for our sakes. The ceremonial law has been rendered obsolete, and indeed since the destruction of the temple in A.D. 70 much of it is impossible to perform, but God's moral law remains normative for Christians and for all peoples. To the best of my knowledge, no Christians prohibit intimacy during menstruation. However, even most secular societies regard mother-son incest as heinous, and this is also an excellent example of 'natural law' (cf. Oedipus).[6]

Simply put, we would be foolish to ignore the universal moral laws (including the various *sexual* laws) in Leviticus 18–20 simply because there are also civil and ceremonial laws in Leviticus that no longer apply to us.[7]

Of course, some Christians who want to affirm same-sex behavior within adult, consensual, committed relationships will then say: "Since Leviticus commands the death penalty for homosexuality, do you believe that we should execute homosexuals today?" No, I do not. Am I then being inconsistent? No. The fact is that Leviticus and other Old Testament texts command the death penalty in Israel for various other sins as well—includ-

6 See Horace *Hummel, Ezekiel 21–48* (St. Louis: Concordia, 2007), 684–85.

7 Leviticus 18:19 and 20:18 prohibit a man from having sexual relations with his wife during her period. This is an example of a ceremonial law for Israel found in the midst of various moral laws intended for all people of all times and places. For example, even though Leviticus condemns consensual homosexual behavior for both Jew and Gentile with the penalty being death for those in Israel who engage in this behavior (and never allows for a lesser penalty), Leviticus 15 shows that the law prohibiting a man from having sex with his menstruating wife belongs to the purity regulations given only to the people of Israel and the penalties for such behavior were not very severe if the action took place by accident. In addition, the New Testament says nothing about the law in Leviticus prohibiting sex during menstruation whereas the New Testament clearly condemns all forms of same-sex behavior. Simply put, the law in Leviticus prohibiting an Israelite man from having sex with his menstruating wife does not apply to Christians today. Of course, this does not mean that a husband and wife should not avoid such behavior for other reasons. Also, obviously, a husband should never force himself on his wife during such a time if she is not willing. For more information about this particular law in Leviticus prohibiting sex during menstruation, see Eckstein, *Bearing Their Burden*, 67–70.

ing adultery, incest, and bestiality! Yet, most Christians I know—including those who want to affirm same-sex behavior within committed relationships—agree with Leviticus that adultery, incest, and bestiality are sinful, but they do not suggest we should execute people for these behaviors. Are they being inconsistent?

What we must understand is that Old Testament Israel functioned as a theocracy, and this arrangement ceased when God's Son fulfilled the Old Testament and finished His work. The Christian Church does not impose civil penalties for sins but leaves decisions about such penalties up to the government, whose job it is to promote good and punish evil (see Romans 13:1–7). Nevertheless, Christians still warn people that various sins against God can lead to a fate far worse than physical death if we refuse to repent. The fact that God required the death penalty in the Old Testament for homosexual behavior, adultery, bestiality, murder, etc., shows that God was very serious about His hatred of such things. In fact in Romans 1:28–32 and 6:23, the apostle Paul clearly states that all sin is worthy of death. Even though Jesus did not encourage the death penalty for such sins, He still clearly taught that we must repent of such sins and trust in Him for salvation or face something far worse than physical death. (See Luke 13:1–5; Matthew 5:27–30; 7:13–21; 10:26–39; 11:20–24; 18:6–7; also 1 Thessalonians 4:1–10). This is why Jesus could rescue the woman caught in adultery from being stoned to death and yet say to her: "Neither do I condemn you; go, and from now on sin no more" (see John 8:1–11).

CHRISTIANS STILL WARN PEOPLE THAT VARIOUS SINS AGAINST GOD CAN LEAD TO A FATE FAR WORSE THAN PHYSICAL DEATH IF WE REFUSE TO REPENT.

In addition, some point out that Leviticus condemns only *male* homosexuality. They thereby suggest that at least *female* homosexual behavior can be affirmed. What they fail to note is that Leviticus condemns mother/son incest but says nothing about father/daughter incest. Does this mean we can affirm father/daughter incest? Not at all. The point is that the latter is understood to be condemned by the example of the former. We see the same thing in Matthew 5 when Jesus says that a man who lusts after a woman in his heart is guilty of adultery. Jesus says nothing about a *woman* lusting after a *man*. Does this mean that Jesus affirms women who lust after men in their hearts? Of course not. Jesus' example of male lust assumes that it is sinful for women as well. In other words, what's bad for the gander is bad for the goose. Paul makes this obvious point when he condemns *female* homosexual behavior in Romans 1.

New Testament Teachings on Sexual Behavior

We are now ready to examine the New Testament Gospels and note what Jesus has to say about homosexuality. Christians who wish to affirm homosexual behavior within committed relationships are quick to point out that Jesus never condemns homosexual behavior. In fact, Jesus never mentions homosexual behavior at all. They thereby conclude that Jesus is indifferent regarding homosexual behavior or that He maybe even affirmed it. But the problems with this are obvious when one considers the witness of Scripture as a whole. Below are the following reasons why Jesus condemns homosexual behavior:

1. Jesus' silence on homosexuality does not mean that He affirmed it. Jesus never mentions bestiality (Leviticus 20:15–16), incest (18:6–18), or the abuse of people with physical disabilities (19:14). Does this mean that Jesus would tolerate or even affirm such behaviors?
2. The Jewish culture of Jesus' day condemned even consensual homosexual behavior between adults.[8] Therefore, Jesus did not need to address that sin issue within the Jewish culture. In addition, if Jesus had affirmed homosexual behavior, we should find evidence of Him condemning the views of His own people since He never hesitated rebuking and correcting them on other issues where He disagreed with them.
3. Jesus' use of Genesis 1–2 in Matthew 19:1–12 shows He viewed the creation account as a commentary on God's will for human sexuality. In Matthew, Jesus teaches that the only alternative to sex between one man and one woman in marriage is celibacy! (Some suggest that Jesus' mention of eunuchs in these verses is an affirmation of homosexual behavior. But the Greek term *eunouchoi* refers to those who are celibate for various reasons and not to those who engage in homosexual behavior.)

8 For a thorough treatment of the Jewish view of homosexual behavior in Jesus' day, see Robert Gagnon, *The Bible and Homosexual Practice* (Nashville: Abingdon Press, 2001), 159–92.

4. In Mark 7:21, Jesus speaks negatively of "sexual immorality" (the Greek word translated as "sexual immorality" is *porneiai*) along with adultery. The Greek term *porneiai* was used among the Jews of Jesus' day to speak of all the sexual prohibitions listed in Leviticus 18 and 20—and this included consensual homosexual behavior. So, when Jesus condemns *porneiai,* He is condemning all forms of homosexual behavior.
5. If Jesus had openly affirmed consensual homosexual behavior between committed adults, we would have expected His Jewish enemies to use this to discredit Him. But the Jews say nothing about Jesus' affirmation of homosexual behavior.
6. Jesus' love for sinners does not mean that He tolerated or affirmed their sin. Jesus calls us to turn away from the sins He has forgiven. There is no reason to believe that Jesus would make an exception for homosexual behavior when He clearly expected people to repent of all other sexual sins.
7. Jesus entrusted His teaching to His chosen apostles (see John 17:16–20; Acts 26:15–18). When Paul shares Jesus' teaching with the Gentiles (whose culture had many who *did* affirm homosexual behavior), he clearly addresses the issue and condemns even consensual homosexual behavior between adults. Since the apostle Paul speaks for Jesus, we see that Jesus would have condemned homosexual behavior even between committed adults.[9]

Next, we consider the teaching of the apostle Paul on the issue of homosexual behavior. Romans 1:26–27 clearly condemns all forms of male or female homosexual behavior regardless of the type of relationship between the people involved. Paul, who in Romans 1 alludes to the creation account in Genesis 1–2, bases his argument on the fact that God is the Creator and that His creation is intended to function according to His design. In other words, when Paul says that homosexual behavior is "contrary to nature," he means that it goes against God's plan for His gift of sexuality between

9 Some who are desperate to find a way to argue that Jesus would have affirmed homosexual behavior between committed adults have used Matthew 8:5–13 and Luke 7:1–10 to suggest that Jesus may have affirmed a committed homosexual relationship when He healed a Roman centurion's servant because some Roman masters of that time did have sex with their male slaves. Since Jesus did not condemn their possible homosexual relationship (in fact, He doesn't mention it at all!), some use this as evidence that Jesus at least tolerated such behavior. RESPONSE: First, not all pagan Roman masters had sex with their slaves. Second, the pagan Roman masters who did have sex with their slaves usually did this in order to abuse and demean their slaves. Do people want to argue that Jesus would have affirmed an abusive relationship? Finally, the context shows that the Roman centurion was not a pagan but was likely a "God-fearer" (Greek = *phoboumenos*), which means he would have submitted to the Jewish moral laws—including their sexual laws (which condemned even consensual homosexual behavior). The Jews would not have honored this man if he had been involved in homosexual behavior with his slave. For a more thorough response, see Tom Eckstein, *Bearing Their Burden* (Lulu, 2010), 80–84.

one man and one woman within marriage. Of course, some have attempted to find ways to reinterpret what Paul clearly says about homosexual behavior.

In his book *Christianity, Social Tolerance, and Homosexuality*, John Boswell argued that God was only condemning heterosexuals who acted contrary to their sexual orientation and engaged in homosexual behavior.[10] But there is nothing in Romans 1 to support such an interpretation! When Paul condemns men and women for sexual behavior that is "contrary to nature," he means that men and women were created to function in a heterosexual manner and that homosexual behavior is obviously contrary to this.

In fact, even many Bible scholars who affirm homosexual behavior within committed relationships now dismiss Boswell's argument. For example, in his book *Homoeroticism in the Biblical World*, Martti Nissinen writes:

> The distinction between sexual orientations is clearly an anachronism that does not help to understand Paul's line of argumentation. Paul does not mention *tribades* or *kinaidoi*, that is, female and male persons who were habitually involved in homoerotic relationships; but if he knew about them (and there is every reason to believe that he did), it is difficult to think that, because of their apparent "orientation," he would not have included them in Romans 1:26–27. . . . It is essential to notice that Paul speaks of homoeroticism precisely as a practice . . . for him, there is no individual inversion or inclination that would make this conduct less culpable . . . nothing would have made Paul approve homoerotic behavior. Clearly, Paul, to whom marriage was the only acceptable venue for sexual life, could not have approved of any same-sex interaction that even resembled sex between a man and a woman.[11]

In addition, in his book *Homosexuality and Civilization*, Louis Crompton responds to Boswell's argument with these words: "Some interpreters, seeking to mitigate Paul's harshness, have read the passage as condemn-

---

10 See John Boswell, *Christianity, Social Tolerance, and Homosexuality* (University of Chicago Press, 1980), 108–17; 303–32.

11 See Martti Nissinen, *Homoeroticism in the Biblical World* (Minneapolis: Fortress Press, 1998), 109 and 111–12.

ing not homosexuals generally but only heterosexual men and women who experimented with homosexuality. . . . But such a reading, however well-intentioned, seems strained and unhistorical. Nowhere does Paul or any other Jewish writer of this period imply the least acceptance of same-sex relations under any circumstances."[12]

New Testament scholar Bernadette Brooten also has this to say in her book *Love Between Women*:

> Paul could have believed that *tribades, kinaidoi*, and other sexually unorthodox persons were born that way and yet still condemn them as unnatural and shameful, this all the more so since he is speaking of groups of people rather than of individuals. . . . I believe that Paul used the word 'exchanged' to indicate that people knew the natural sexual order of the universe and left it behind. . . . Paul is condemning all forms of homoeroticism as the unnatural acts of people who had turned away from God.[13]

Some also try to argue that Paul was not condemning homosexual behavior within a committed relationship but only lustful homosexual behavior between people who did not love each other and did not have a committed relationship.[14] But such an interpretation is completely foreign to Paul's argument and ignores the wider witness of Scripture, which teaches that the only place where God approves of sexual behavior is within marriage between one man and one woman. In other words, homosexual behavior is always sinful and is not made into something that God calls "very good" simply because the people engaging in the behavior are consenting adults who have a committed relationship. Similarly, as incestuous behavior is always sinful between mother/son or father/daughter or brother/sister (or mother/daughter, father/son, brother/brother, sister/sister—to include homosexual behavior) and is not made into some-

> THERE IS FORGIVENESS AND NEW LIFE IN JESUS EVEN AS WE CONTINUE TO STRUGGLE WITH THE DESIRES OF OUR SINFUL NATURE.

12 See Louis Crompton, *Homosexuality and Civilization* (Cambridge, MA: The Belknap Press of Harvard University Press, 2003), 114.

13 See Bernadette Brooten, *Love Between Women*, (The University of Chicago Press, 1996), 244.

14 A good example of this argument is found in Vines, *God and the Gay Christian*, 95–116.

thing that God calls "very good" simply because the people engaging in the behavior are consenting adults within a committed relationship. Again, Louis Crompton comments on this: "The idea that homosexuals might be redeemed by mutual devotion would have been wholly foreign to Paul or any other Jew or early Christian."[15]

Others argue that in Romans 1, Paul was only condemning homosexual behavior when it took place within the context of idol worship.[16] Therefore, some argue, Paul is not condemning Christians who worship the triune God and who also engage in homosexual behavior within a committed relationship. The problem with this argument is that Paul's point is that all sin begins with the rejection of God and His Word, which then leads not only to worship of idols but to all other sins as well. In other words, the affirmation of homosexual behavior is the result of the rejection of God and His truth. In addition, those who argue that Paul condemns homosexual behavior only when it takes place within the context of idol worship have a hard time explaining all the other sins that Paul condemns within the immediate context (see 1:28–32). Would they argue that such sins as coveting, envy, murder, gossip, disobeying parents, etc., are not sinful as long as people don't engage in them within the context of idol worship? No one would make this argument.[17]

THE AFFIRMATION OF HOMOSEXUAL BEHAVIOR IS THE RESULT OF THE REJECTION OF GOD AND HIS TRUTH.

Paul also condemns homosexual behavior in 1 Corinthians 6:9, where he uses the Greek word *arsenokoitēs* (from the Greek word *arsen*, which means "male," and the Greek word *koitē*, which means "bed") to refer to men who have consensual sex with other men. The Greek word *arsenokoitai* is not found in any other Greek literature of Paul's day, so some scholars have been curious about this word's origin. But most scholars now agree that Paul likely coined this word based on the Septuagint (Greek) translation of Leviticus 18:22 and 20:13 in order to show that he was not offering his own opinion but simply confessing the teaching of Scripture regarding

15 See Crompton, *Homosexuality and Civilization*, 114.

16 For example, see Connonley and Miner, *The Children Are Free*, 14–16.

17 There are other arguments some use to attempt to reinterpret Paul's clear condemnation of all homosexual behavior in Romans 1. For a thorough treatment of these revisionist arguments, see Eckstein, *Bearing Their Burden*, 85–106. Also see Michael P. Middendorf, *Romans 1–8* (St. Louis: Concordia, 2013), 145–50.

this sinful behavior.[18] We also find the same Greek word used by Paul in 1 Timothy 1:8–11, where he clearly condemns homosexual behavior.

Finally, some Christians who wish to dismiss what Holy Scripture clearly teaches about homosexual behavior will resort to poor analogy arguments in order to suggest that we need not take Holy Scripture seriously regarding the issue of homosexuality.

For example, some wrongly suggest that the Bible condones slavery and that we no longer follow the Bible's teaching in that regard, so why should we submit to what it says about homosexuality? But nowhere does the Bible command or condone slavery. Instead, it merely regulates the practice. In fact, the kind of race-based slavery that existed in the American South did not exist in biblical times. In addition, the reason Paul did not insist that Christians free their slaves was that in the Roman Empire slaves had no rights; if simply released, they would have had no way to provide for themselves or may have been captured by non-Christians who may have treated them very badly.[19] In contrast, Paul commanded Christian masters to care for their slaves and treat them fairly. This was countercultural teaching! In fact, the teaching of Scripture and the influence of Christianity is what led to its abolition in various parts of the world. There are also other very poor analogy arguments that are used to suggest that we need not take Holy Scripture seriously on the issue of homosexuality.[20]

The fact is that Holy Scripture condemns all homosexual behavior as sin—even when it takes place between consenting adults within a committed relationship. Even many Bible scholars who affirm homosexual behavior within committed relationships admit that Holy Scripture condemns it—but they then simply deny the authority of Holy Scripture on this issue.[21]

However, the Good News for those who struggle with same-sex desire and behavior, as well as for those who struggle with various heterosexual or nonsexual sins, is that there is forgiveness and new life in Jesus even as we continue to struggle with the desires of our sinful nature. Being a Christian does not mean that we no longer struggle with sinful desires and behaviors.

18 Regarding the origin of the Greek term *arsenokoitai*, see Robert Gagnon, *The Bible and Homosexual Practice* (Abingdon, 2001), 326. Also see William Loader, *The New Testament on Sexuality* (Grand Rapids: Eerdmans, 2012), 329–31.

19 See Paul Copan, *Is God a Moral Monster?: Making Sense of the Old Testament God* (Grand Rapids: Baker Books, 2011), 150–57; Gagnon, *The Bible and Homosexual Practice*, 443–52; John Nordling, *Philemon*. Concordia Commentary (St. Louis: Concordia, 2004), 75.

20 See Eckstein, *Bearing Their Burden*, 119–22. Also see Gagnon, *The Bible and Homosexual Practice*, 381–484.

21 For examples of this, see Gary David Comstock, *Gay Theology without Apology* (Cleveland: The Pilgrim Press, 1993), 39; John Shelby Spong, *The Sins of Scripture: Exposing the Bible's Texts of Hate to Reveal the Love of God* (New York: HarperCollins Publishers, 2005), 11; Brooten, *Love Between Women*, 302.

Instead, being a Christian means daily confessing our sins to God, daily rejoicing in His forgiveness in Christ, and daily striving to say no to sin and yes to God's loving plan for our lives because we love Him and trust that His plan for our lives is what is best. God's plan for our *sexual* lives is (1) sex between one man and one woman within marriage or (2) celibacy.

Five Spiritual States

Finally, regarding ministry with those who struggle with same-sex desire and behavior, we must consider five examples of "spiritual states" such people may be living in at any given time in their lives. I will then give advice on how we should attempt to minister to a person in each of these five "spiritual states."

1. Some people are non-Christians who know nothing or very little about the Christian faith. If such a person is also a practicing homosexual, we should not begin our witness to such a person by dealing with the issue of his or her homosexual behavior. In fact, our ultimate goal with any people who engage in homosexual behavior is not merely to get them to stop this behavior. Instead, our ultimate goal is to proclaim the Gospel of Jesus Christ to them through which the Holy Spirit creates repentance and faith in our hearts so that we can receive and believe in the forgiveness and new life that the Father gives us in His Son, Jesus. Without faith in Christ, ceasing from any type of sinful behavior does nothing to save us from our sinful condition.

Therefore, if a person who is practicing homosexual behavior is a non-Christian, then after building a trusting relationship with him or her, you will want to begin your witness with basic information about God, creation, the rebellion of Adam and Eve, original sin, and our need for the person and work of Christ, God's Son. Help this person to see how God's plan of salvation unfolds throughout the history recorded in Holy Scripture—finding its fulfillment in the birth, life, death, resurrection, and ascension of Jesus Christ. Once this person understands the nature of original sin and the hope we have in Jesus, you will then be in a position to deal with particular sin issues in his or her life—including homosexual desire and behavior. The last impression we want to give to a non-Christian is that Christianity is just one more performance-based religion that requires us to obey certain rules and live a certain way in order to be worthy of God's love. Instead, we want to show people the true God, who reveals Himself to us in the cross, where He sacrificed Himself to save His enemies and make them His children.

2. Some people who were raised as Christians and once believed in Christ have fallen into unbelief and now are very skeptical about the teachings of the Christian faith. Some who have lost their faith in Christ and have fallen into unbelief are also engaged in homosexual behavior. Such people may be willing to admit that Holy Scripture condemns all forms of homosexual behavior, but they dismiss Scripture's teaching about homosexual behavior because they now believe that Holy Scripture need not be taken seriously. They have many objections about the doctrines of Christianity. They have many arguments that supposedly prove that the Bible is full of contradictions and should not be trusted.

> JESUS' LOVE FOR SINNERS DOES NOT MEAN THAT HE TOLERATED OR AFFIRMED THEIR SIN.

Before we attempt to speak God's truth in love to such people regarding their homosexual behavior, we must first deal honestly with their objections to the Christian faith and their arguments against the authority of Holy Scripture. We may not have to discuss the basic teachings of Christianity since such people may already be aware of such teachings due to being raised as Christians and having once believed in Christ. However, we must be willing to engage in some apologetics with such people and help them to recognize that their objections to and arguments against the Christian faith are unfounded.

However, we must also remember that apologetics can only take us so far. Apologetics is a useful tool to expose the falsehood of people's objections to the Christian faith and arguments against taking Holy Scripture seriously. But we can never bring people to faith in Christ through rational discussion alone. Therefore at some point in the apologetics process, we need to ask such people if we can simply share what we believe with them. If they give us permission, then we tell them God's story of salvation as recorded in Holy Scripture. We should not attempt to defend God's plan of salvation nor should we try to make God's plan of salvation sound rational—as though we could ever do that. Instead, we must simply proclaim the Gospel and allow the Holy Spirit to create faith in their hearts.

Once the Holy Spirit gives people new hearts of faith, their objections to and arguments against God's Word will begin to fall away as the skepticism of their sinful nature is gradually overcome by their trust in the authoritative Word of God. They will begin to live by faith and not by sight. Once we have gone through this process, we can then address particular sin issues in their lives— including their homosexual behavior. Remember: our ultimate goal is not to get such people to stop their homosexual behavior. Our ultimate goal is for them to trust in Jesus as their Lord and Savior.

3. Some people who are currently involved in homosexual behavior say that they believe in Christ and that they agree with every teaching of the Christian faith. They even stress that they submit to the authority of Holy Scripture. However, they justify their homosexual behavior because they believe that Christians have misinterpreted the Bible's prohibitions against homosexual behavior. They have been led to believe that God does not condemn homosexual behavior as long as it takes place within a loving, committed, consensual, monogamous relationship.

Once we build a trusting friendship with such people, we should ask if they would be willing to study Holy Scripture about this issue. We should say to such a person: "We both believe that salvation comes through faith in Christ alone. Also, we both agree that we should submit to the authority of Holy Scripture. Can we study Holy Scripture together so we can learn what God truly teaches about homosexual behavior within a loving, committed, consensual, monogamous relationship? If you can show me from Scripture that I am wrong about God condemning even such homosexual behavior as this, then I will repent of my error and affirm your homosexual behavior within a loving, committed, consensual, monogamous relationship. However, if I can convince you from Holy Scripture that God does condemn even your type of homosexual behavior, then will you be willing to acknowledge your error, repent of your sin, and rejoice in the forgiveness and healing that Jesus longs to give you?" If such a person is honest about his or her respect for the authority of Holy Scripture and his or her desire to live according to God's will, then such a person should be willing to study Holy Scripture and be willing to submit to what it says about homosexual behavior.

If such a person does study Holy Scripture with you and is convinced that his or her type of homosexual behavior is also condemned by God's Word, then you must assure this person that he or she is completely forgiven and holy in God's sight because of Jesus and His work on our behalf. You will need to surround such a person with Christian love and support as well as prayer, because it will be a difficult struggle for him or her to turn away from his or her homosexual behavior—especially if he or she has been in a long-term relationship with his or her partner.

4. Some people who practice homosexual behavior are involved in liberal Christianity. Unlike the former Christians described in number 2 above, these people still consider themselves to be Christians—but their liberal form of Christianity has led them to deny some or all of the basic teachings of the Christian faith. Very often such liberal Christians do not believe that Scripture is the inspired and inerrant Word of God. Instead, they believe the Bible *contains* "teachings from God." One example of these "teachings from God" is the unconditional love of Jesus, who, because He loves unconditionally, therefore supposedly affirms or at least tolerates many behaviors that the Bible clearly condemns as being sinful—and usually, according to liberal Christians, such behaviors that Jesus supposedly affirms or at least tolerates are of a *sexual* nature.

Of course, such liberal Christians are being selective about which sins Jesus supposedly affirms or tolerates because most liberal Christians would not be willing to assert that Jesus would affirm or tolerate murder, theft, and gossip. Therefore, their Jesus ends up affirming whatever sins they believe ought to be affirmed. In addition, such liberal Christians usually believe that the "Holy Spirit" (however they define "him, her, or it") does not only speak to us in Holy Scripture but also inspires us directly in our individual "hearts"—and if they believe the "Spirit" is leading them to affirm their homosexual behavior, then you must affirm their subjective experience of the "Holy Spirit."

HOLY SCRIPTURE CONDEMNS ALL HOMOSEXUAL BEHAVIOR AS SIN.

The fact is that some liberal Christians are willing to admit that Holy Scripture clearly condemns even homosexual behavior within loving, committed, consensual, monogamous relationships—they then simply deny that Scripture's teaching on this issue has any authority over us today. *Therefore, quoting them the Scripture's prohibitions against all forms of homosexual behavior usually does not make an impact on them.*

Many who are involved in liberal Christianity embrace "relativism," a philosophy that asserts that truth is subjective and that there are no moral absolutes that govern all people of all times and places. Ironically, such liberal Christian relativists, who deny moral absolutes, usually insist that those who believe all forms of homosexual behavior are sinful are *absolutely* wrong. The problem with liberal Christian relativists is that they are not able to have a logical, intelligent either/or discussion without deconstructing their own worldview.

Simply put, just like the former Christian described in number 2 above, we need to be willing to engage in some rational discussion and apologetics with liberal Christians in order to show them the inconsistency of their thinking and the errors that result from their liberal view of Holy Scripture. However, as with the former Christians in number 2 above, rational discussion and apologetics alone will not bring them back to the truth.

Once again, at some point in our discussions with such people, we must ask permission to share with them what we believe. If they agree, we simply speak the truth in love to them—without trying to defend it or make it sound rational—and allow God's Holy Spirit to lead them out of the bondage of liberal Christianity into the true liberty that flows from childlike faith in God's inspired and inerrant Word, which is fulfilled in the person and work of Christ for us. Once the Holy Spirit works through the Gospel to give such people faith in the authority of God's Word, we will then be in a position to discuss the issue of their homosexual behavior and their need to repent and trust in the forgiveness and new life that only Jesus can give them.

WE CAN NEVER BRING PEOPLE TO FAITH IN CHRIST THROUGH RATIONAL DISCUSSION ALONE.

5. Some people who are burdened by homosexual desire agree with Holy Scripture that all forms of homosexual behavior are sinful. However, some of these same people have never heard the true Gospel and so they are in despair under God's wrath. If we ever meet such a person, we must understand that the last thing he or she needs to hear is that homosexual behavior is sinful. God's Word has already convicted him or her of sin. God's Law has done its job and His Law has taken this person as far as it can. God's Law can only lead us sinners to despair under His wrath. God's Law can never comfort a despairing heart nor can God's Law move us to cease our sinful behavior for godly reasons.

Therefore, if we meet a person who is convicted of the sin of his or her homosexual behavior and knows that he or she deserves God's wrath, then we must proclaim the Gospel: "Your sins are forgiven for Christ's sake. You are holy and innocent in God's sight. God loves you here and now. He will help you to resist your homosexual desires and live a pure life. If you do fall back into homosexual behavior during a moment of weakness, then you will fall into Christ's loving arms. He will pick you up and help you to live as His dearly loved and forgiven child." We must remember whenever we meet someone who is in despair under God's wrath because he or she agrees with God's Word that his or her homosexual behavior is sinful, that such a person needs to hear the Gospel!

CHAPTER 9

TRANSGENDER IDENTITY IN LIGHT OF BIBLICAL IDENTITY

Robert W. Weise

On August 13, 2013, Governor Jerry Brown signed into California law Assembly Bill No. 1266. This bill took effect January 1, 2014, permitting transgender persons from K–12 to use the restroom of their sexual preferential choice.[1] The July 2015 issue of *Vanity Fair* published an extended article on the partial sex reassignment surgery of Bruce Jenner to Caitlyn Jenner.[2] More recently, two cases relating to the California law have made the press: one occurring in Hillsboro, Missouri,[3] and the other in Palatine, Illinois, District 211.[4] On March 23, 2016, North Carolina Governor Pat McCrory signed House Bill DRH40005-TC-1B, which restricts the use of bathrooms to the biological sex (birth sex) of a person.[5] The Ann and Robert H. Lurie Children's Hospital, Chicago, Illinois, received $5.7 million to study the effect of puberty blockers given to 280 14-year-old adolescents.[6] All of these events continue to bring further attention to the transgender lifestyle and its biblical implications for human existence and sexual identity. How should the Christian, as well as the Body of Christ, especially Christian parochial schools, respond and witness to those who struggle with a person's unwillingness to live within their Creator/creature framework as a male or a female, a man or a woman?

1 Assembly Bill No. 1266, CHAPTER 85, An act to amend section 221.5 of the Education Code, relating to pupil rights, http://leginfo.legislature.ca.gov/faces/billNavClient.x html?billid=201320140AB1266.

2 Buzz Bissinger, "He Says Goodbye, She Says Hello," *Vanity Fair* (July 2015): 50–69, 105–6.

3 Doug Moore, "Trans Issue Divides School: Transgender Student Wants to Use Girls' Bathrooms" *St. Louis Post-Dispatch*, September 1, 2015, 1A–2A.

4 Mitch Smith and Monica Davey, "Illinois District Violated Transgender Student's Rights, U.S. Says," *New York Times*, November 2, 2015, http://nytimes.com/2015/11/03/us/illinois-district-violated-transgender-students-rights-us-says.html?_r=0. According the *Wall Street Journal*, December 4, 2015, this case has been settled. The school district voted to allow a high school student who was designated male at birth but identifies as a girl to change in a curtained-off area in the girl's locker room. The district had previously offered the transgender male to girl a separate changing room, but his family denied this offer. Douglas Belkin, "Illinois, Transgender-Student Case Is Settled," *Wall Street Journal*, December 4, 2015, 5A.

5 General Assembly of North Carolina Second Extra Session 2016, House Bill DRH40005-TC-1B (3/22), A Bill to be Entitled an Act to Provide for Single-Sex Multiple Occupancy Bathroom and Changing Facilities in School and Public Agencies and to Crated Statewide Consistency in Regulation of Employment and Public Accommodations, H.B. 2, March 23, 2016, House Principal Clerk. (Signed by Governor Pat McCrory on the evening of March 23, 2016.)

6 Sara Reardon, "Transgender Youth Study Kicks Off," *Nature* 531 (2016): 560.

How this sociocultural shift occurred from the binary, biblical—male and female—to the new normal of "have sexual identity any way you want it" to same-sex marriage to transgender choices is well documented. Theological books such as *From Sin to Amazing Grace: Discovering the Queer Christ*[7] and *Omnigender: A Trans-religious Approach*[8] have generated a myopic-deconstructionist view of the Creator/creature biblical story centered around feminist influences of Gnosticism.

This chapter will provide a brief overview of recent transgender history and its terminology. It will also address current trends in transgender biblical interpretation, locating their origins in the New Gnosticism. This New Gnosticism focuses on the internal Self, a Oneness with the divine as our true identity. This idea denies our God-created human nature as a body and soul, an embodied male or female person. As Pastor Burfeind defines this aspect of the New Gnosticism: "We are spirits, or sparks of divinity, trapped in the prison cell of this material world."[9] The key to unlocking this prison cell or cage is formulated under the pretext of "the Other."[10] In addition, theological implications and pastoral care will be addressed as Christians approach those who struggle with their *sex identity from conception*[11] (conception-sex identity). Hence, the goal of this chapter is twofold: first, to provide resources for those who would like to learn more about transgender culture and its historical development; and second, and most important, to seek to increase the reader's background knowledge, both secular and theological, to enable the reader to actively proclaim the biblical witness of God's created order of male and female.

> DECEPTION LEADS TO MISUNDERSTANDING, MISUNDERSTANDING LEADS TO WRONG CONCLUSIONS, AND WRONG CONCLUSIONS MAY LEAD A CHRISTIAN TO COMPROMISE THEIR CHRISTIAN WITNESS.

7 Patrick S. Cheng, *From Sin to Amazing Grace: Discovering the Queer Christ* (New York: Seabury Books, 2012), 170

8 Virginia Ramey Mollenkott, *Omnigender: A Trans-Religious Approach* (Cleveland: The Pilgrim Press, 2007), 223.

9 Peter M. Burfeind, *Gnostic America: A Reading of Contemporary American Culture & Religion according to Christianity's Oldest Heresy* (Toledo: Pax Domini Press, 2015), 20, 43. Peter M. Burfeind is a called and ordained pastor of The Lutheran Church—Missouri Synod serving Holy Cross Lutheran Church and Student Ministry, the University of Toledo, Toledo, Ohio.

10 Burfeind, *Gnostic America*, 43. "The Other" is either the man or woman trapped in their current gender; therefore, the key to unlocking this imprisoned flesh is to become the Other, that is, man to woman or woman to man.

11 "Sex identity from conception" refers to the sex of the child that is determined by the union of sperm and egg in the one-cell embryo called a zygote. There is no such biological/embryological term such as biological birth sex. The use of biological birth sex is ill-advised. See *sex* under definitions for further explanation.

Historical Overview

TERMS DEFINED

Voluminous professional and technical literature on transgender topics has existed for many decades.[12] The complex historical development of transgender people is interwoven into the lesbian, gay, and bisexual movement. Christians need to have a basic understanding of the following terms, phrases, and concepts as they are used within their context so that they can be informed and engaged when conversations regarding the ongoing softening of biblical teachings on human anthropology and sexuality arise. In a society wherein political correctness and the "greatest happiness principle" continues to deconstruct terms and their meanings so that all things are permissible, but not beneficial or helpful, Christians must continue to be informed not only on the correct use of terminology but also on the biblical witness of what it means to be a created human creature in Christ.

Distinctions help us keep terminology and concepts understandable and usable within their context.[13] When distinctions are blurred or words or phrases are generated so that "the ends justify the means," a clear picture of the use of a word or phrase, its context, and what it is teaching is impossible. The result is deception. Deception leads to misunderstanding, misunderstanding leads to wrong conclusions, and wrong conclusions may lead a Christian to compromise their Christian witness. Galloy writes: "Those who govern the culture's language govern the culture. Why? Because words shape ideas and affect the way people think. Put simply, words teach. . . . The culture war is largely a war of words, and no one fights it better than the media. They know better than anyone that if you want to change the way people think, just change the words."[14]

Defining various transgender-related terms will assist the reader in understanding its historicity, as many of these terms are misunderstood and codified under the general umbrella term *sexual orientation*.

Sexual Orientation: Relates to someone's romantic and sexual attraction to another person. One may be attracted to a person of a different gender, the same gender, "both" or all genders, or to no one at all.[15]

Gender: The word relates to the terms *man* or *woman, boy* or *girl*. As a social construct, the biological, social, and psychological interact to define

12 Susan Stryker and Paisley Currah, "Introduction" in *Transgender Studies Quarterly* 1, no. 2 (2014): 3.

13 See Nigel M. de S. Cameron, "Democracy's Greatest Trial: Four Key Challenges for the Biotech Century," *Ethics and Medicine* 19, no. 3 (2003). 177.

14 R. Galloy, "A Prolife Semantics Guide," *New Oxford Review* 72 (2006): 17.

15 Nicholas M. Teich, *Transgender 101: A Simple Guide to a Complex Issue* (New York: Columbia University Press, 2012), 14.

gender in the public square.[16] "Gender" is a social/cultural construct. Susan Stryker writes: "Gender is simply what we call bodily sex when we see it in the mirror of representation."[17] Gender is awareness of being or becoming "man or woman." Hence, gender is not the same as sex. The words *man* and *woman* refer to gender. No one is born a woman or a man—rather, as the saying goes, "one becomes one" through a complex process of socialization.[18]

Sex: Sex is not the same as gender, although the terms are used interchangeably in everyday speech. Sex is biological. The words *male* and *female* refer to sex. Sex refers to reproductive capacity or potential—whether an individual body produces one or the other of two specialized cells (egg [oocyte] or sperm [spermatozoon]) necessary for our species to physically reproduce itself.[19]

Embryologists, those who specialize in the continual development of a human being from the union of the sperm and egg (fertilization) through the eighth week of development, define *sex* as follows: The embryo's chromosomal sex is determined at fertilization by the kind of sperm (X or Y) that fertilizes the oocyte (egg); hence, it is the father, rather than the mother, whose gamete determines the sex of the embryonic human being. Fertilization by an X-bearing sperm produces a 46,XX zygote, which normally develops into a female, whereas fertilization by a Y-bearing sperm produces a 46,XY zygote, which normally develops into a male.[20]

> THIS GREAT DISTURBANCE AND UNDERTOW WITHIN A SOCIETY THAT CONTINUES TO SINK ITS TEETH INTO "WHATEVER" AND "HAVE IT YOUR WAY" PHILOSOPHY REGARDING HUMAN SEXUALITY ESPOUSES THE NEW GNOSTICISM IN THE TWENTY-FIRST CENTURY.

Intersex: When there is normal sexual differentiation, the appearance of the external and internal genitalia is consistent with the sex chromosome complement (i.e., XX or XY). Because early embryos have the potential to develop as either males or females, errors in sex determination and differentiation result in various degrees of intermediate sex—*intersexuality*

16 For additional information, see the *Diagnostic and Statistical Manual of Mental Disorders*, 5th ed., (DMS-V), (Washington DC: American Psychiatric Publishing, 2013), 451.

17 Susan Stryker and Stephen Whittle, eds. *The Transgender Studies Reader* (New York: Routledge, 2006), 9.

18 Susan Stryker, *Transgender History* (Berkeley, CA: Seal Press, 2008), 11.

19 Stryker, *Transgender History*, 7–8.

20 Keith Moore and T. V. N. Persaud, *The Developing Human: Clinically Oriented Embryology*, 7th ed. (Philadelphia: Saunders, 2003), 35.

or *hermaphroditism*. Hermaphroditism implies a discrepancy between the morphology of the gonads (testes/ovaries) in the appearance of the external genitalia. A person with ambiguous external genitalia is an *intersex* or *hermaphrodite*.[21]

Transgender: Within LGBT (**L**esbian **G**ay **B**isexual **T**ransgender) literature, the most consistent definition of transgender is as an umbrella term with many different identities existing under it. A couple of those identities are *gender-variant* and *genderqueer*.[22] A nonclinical definition by Elizabeth Rets defines the transgender in a broad manner to "include a range of gender expressions."[23]

Clinically, *transgender* is defined as those persons who identify with a different gender than their birth gender; that is, a child born a male believes he is female and changes his outward appearance conforming to that transient gender.[24] *Trans* has become shorthand for transgender people. To use the term *transgender* as a noun rather than as an adjective is viewed by LGBT people as disrespectful.

Transsexual: A person who has transitioned to the opposite sex socially, often with the aid of hormone therapy and sexual reassignment surgery.[25] Hence, the use of the following abbreviations in literature relating to transsexualism: Female-to-Male (FTM) or Male-to-Female (MTF).[26]

Cis-gender: People who are not transgender; their gender identity matches up with the sex they were assigned at birth.[27]

Cross-dresser: This is intended as a nonjudgmental replacement for "transvestite." According to Stryker, "it is usually considered to be neutrally descriptive of the practice of wearing gender-atypical clothing rather than associating that practice with an erotic impulse. The practice of cross-dressing has many meanings and motivations: besides being a way to resist or move away from an assigned social gender, it could be a theatrical practice (either comic or dramatic), part of fashion or politics (such as the

21 Moore and Persaud, *The Developing Human*, 318.

22 Teich, *Transgender 101*, 2. While this is only one author's definition, my research presented *transgender* in a broad sweeping manner including whatever the author decided that it covered. Regardless, it was used routinely to make general references to persons who were either unhappy with their birth sex (male or female) or put more generally, "trapped in the wrong body" from birth.

23 Elizabeth Rets, "Teaching Transgender History, Identity, and Politics" *Radical History Review* 88 (2004): 166.

24 For more information, see DSM-V, 451.

25 For more information, see DSM-V, 451.

26 Kay Siebler, "Transgender Transitions: Sex/Gender Binaries in the Digital Age," *Journal of Gay & Lesbian Mental Health* 16 (2012): 77. The literature that covers "transgenderism" and "transsexualism" frequently uses the terms interchangeably or the latter, "transsexualism," is defined as a sub-category of transgenderism. Of course, this will depend on the author's bias and contextual use in his or her writings.

27 Teich, *Transgender 101*, 130. Simply put: When you are born as a male, you identify as male throughout the rest of your earthly life, and similarly, when you are born as a female, you identify as a female for the rest of your earthly life.

practice of women's wearing pants once was), part of religious ceremonies, or part of celebrating public festivals and holidays (such as Mardi Gras, Carnival, or Halloween)."[28] Some men and women dress in the opposite clothes, both outerwear and underwear, in the privacy of their home. These practices are not considered transgender.

Queer: This is a term that is used collectively by feminist authors of LGBTQ (Queer) communities. As Stryker writes: "I don't want to say 'gay, lesbian, bisexual, transgender, drag,' in which individuals, along with male and female prostitutes who might well be heterosexual every time I need to refer to a group collectively."[29]

A Brief Historical Overview

The history of transgender studies is complex and appears to be driven by third wave feminism.[30] Only a few of those persons involved in this third wave as well as the first and second waves of feminism[31] are referenced below, yet there are many, many more that could be listed.[32]

The intersection of transgenderism or transgender studies with the emergent New Gnosticism, as it relates to procreation, is summed up by feminist Anne Fausto-Sterling in her book, *Sexing the Body: Gender Politics and the Construction of Sexuality*. Herein she relates the importance of including diverse sexual beings as "normal" as well as questioning the need for the current culture having only two sexes.[33] She adds: "We inhabit a moment in history when we have the theoretical understanding and practical power to ask the question unheard of before in our culture: "should there be only two sexes?"[34] That God created male and female means nothing.

---

28 Stryker, *Transgender History*, 17–18.

29 Stryker, *Transgender History*, 24.

30 Stryker, *Transgender History*, 3. The first wave of feminism focused on dress reform, access to education, political equality, and, above all, suffrage in the nineteenth and early twentieth centuries; the second wave, also known as the women's movement of the 1960s and '70s, addressed a wide range of issues, including equal pay, sexual and reproductive freedom, recognition of women's unpaid work in the household. The third wave feminism has been, in part, a generational response to some of the perceived shortcomings of the second wave, particularly the tendency of second wave feminists to overlook differences among women in their eagerness to see "woman" as a unifying political category. Third wave feminism has been more attuned to the intersections of race, class, and sexuality within gender and more receptive to critical and theoretical work in gender studies that calls into question the usefulness of "woman" as the foundation of all feminist politics.

31 Stryker, *Transgender History*, 3.

32 Stryker and Whittle, *The Transgender Studies Reader*, 200, 752 [50 authors listed]; Susan Stryker and Aren Aizura, eds. *The Transgender Studies Reader 2* (New York: Routledge, 2013 [50 authors listed]; Katherine Johnson, "From Gender to Transgender: Thirty Years of Feminist Debates" *Social Alternatives* 24 (2005): 36–39.

33 More on this viewpoint can be located in Anne Fausto-Sterling, *Sexing the Body: Gender Politics and the Construction of Sexuality* (New York: Basic Books, 2000), 15.

34 Fausto-Sterling, *Sexing the Body*, 77.

Along with these authors and many others, the transgender phenomenon made one of its biggest strides when the "T" was added to the acronym LGBT in 1995. According to Stryker, the shift in nomenclature toward "LGBT" community, rather than a "queer" one, marks the beginning of a new phase in the social history of sexual and gender identity politics in the United States.[35] This brings a "focus" to the transgender movement, apart from its association with the LGB movement.

The origin and development of the term *transgender* is often given to Virginia (formerly Charles) Prince, a Southern California advocate for freedom of gender expression.[36] For a complete overview of the chronological history of the transgender phenomenon in its movement to deconstruct the biblical male-female binary and raise itself to the pinnacle of cultural and societal acceptance, see Mercedes Allen's contributions to the Bilerico Project website.[37]

The New Gnosticism and Transgender Ideology

With the current push for the transgender lifestyle by power-based third wave feminists, pro-transgender lobbyists, and the media with their constant use of "gender," the New Gnosticism has proven to be the dark horse in the Supreme Court's approval of same-sex marriage, and it lies behind the insurgence of the transgender movement that is seeking society's approval via gender-neutral bathrooms for everyone. This great disturbance and undertow within a society that continues to sink its teeth into "whatever" and "have it your way" philosophy regarding human sexuality espouses the New Gnosticism in the twenty-first century.

George Weigel believes (and I concur) that the New (Neo) Gnosticism finds its roots in the sexual revolution of the 1960s. This ancient heresy redressed itself when the sexual revolution found its basis in postmodern relativistic deconstruction, radical individualism, and the quest for an egalitarian society of "one-for-all and all-for-one." Hence, political correctness surfaced at all levels of the political and social environment. As George Weigel writes: "Contemporary Gnosticism, which is most powerfully embodied in the sexual revolution, has given all of this a new twist by masking its essential deprecation of The Way Things Are by what appears, at first blush, to be a hyper-materialism: a cult of sensitivity *über alles* in which

35 Fausto-Sterling, *Sexing the Body*, 136.

36 Stryker and Whittle, *The Transgender Studies Reader*, 4.

37 Mercedes Allen, The Bilerico Project, www.bilerico.com.

sexual gratification, in any form among consenting adults, is the highest of goods and the most inalienable of personal liberties."[38]

Gnosticism is an ancient heresy that has found new terrains to reclaim its way as the truth and the life. This revival and resurgence comes to our twenty-first century in the form of its heretical teaching: first, God, as we know the triune God according to the Scriptures, is replaced in this New Gnosticism by a superior "self-understanding, knowledge." Second, this New Gnosticism believes that we are caged in the wrong physical body (form), and so to remove ourselves from this encagement we must seek knowledge from within the "Self."[39] And the Self is god.[40] Therefore, since one's self-understanding is god, each person is in control of his body and its physical makeup. Knowledge, for the Gnostic, comes from within, not outside, the body. Therefore, gender is no longer a biological reality, but a construct of personal "self-identification." But to condone this main tenant of the New Gnosticism is to deny the actual God-created physical forms of the male and female bodies.[41]

As I mentioned earlier, this approach feeds into the current egalitarian push wherein the Gnostic heresy teaches that "only those who had attained *gnosis* (knowledge) about their true Source (the higher deity [in themselves—the *Self*]) understood the bodiless Self-ness of their existence. Its salvation program was one of escape, escape of Self from materiality and this oppressive world order."[42] Hence, within the context of the transgender movement, the New Gnosticism finds a "partner" in those who want to escape the cage of their conception-sex identity for a more comfortable "self" in the opposite gender, man to woman or woman to man.

This New Gnosticism, the old dressed in new clothes, therefore remains the proponent of "the Self" and metaphysical nihilism. As Weigel adds: "Gnosticism has sought the good *outside* of reality as we perceive it through the materials of this world . . . reality is to be rejected, and thereby overcome."[43] He adds: "In this respect, the most powerful expression of the ancient cultural toxin of Gnosticism in the 21st-century West is the ideology of gender—the body of thought that quite naturally occupied the cultural vacuum left when metaphysics and any sense of reality-grounded thinking

38 George Weigel, "Reality and Public Policy" *National Affairs* 15 (Spring 2013): 124–25.

39 Burfeind, *Gnostic America*, 35.

40 Burfeind, *Gnostic America*, 24.

41 Burfeind, *Gnostic America*, 41–42.

42 Burfeind, *Gnostic America*, 6.

43 Weigel, *Reality and Public Policy*, 124.

about the human condition collapsed, when technology made it possible to sunder sex from procreation readily and inexpensively, and when the law built a high wall of protection around sexual encounters between consenting adults."[44] As a result, "maleness and femaleness [are] not The Way Things Are. 'Male' and 'female' [have become] 'cultural constructs,' usually manipulated by those in power for purposes of domination (Gnosticism thus adding a *soupçon* of Marxism to its ideology of plasticity)."[45]

> THE TRANSGENDER COMMUNITY, TOGETHER WITH ITS ASSOCIATED COMMUNITIES, SEES GOD OUTSIDE THE BIBLICAL, AUTHORITATIVE TEXTS OF THE OLD AND NEW TESTAMENTS.

Since the body is malleable, plastic, "wishy-washy," and meaningless to the transgender's conception-sex identity, you can change "whatever" to be self-determined. This metaphysical nihilistic view of the body, in which nothing matters, is typified by the infamous phrase used by so many persons, especially teens: "whatever." To the New Gnostic, the body is a wet blanket; the sooner it is gone, the better.[46] This is how those who seek "to become" womanized or manized view the body—as a mass of mutable material.

As Simone de Beauvoir, the existentialist philosopher, writes: "One is not born, but rather becomes, woman. No biological, physical, or economic destiny defines the figure that the human female takes on in society; it is civilization as a whole that elaborates this intermediary product between the male and the eunuch that is called feminine."[47] De Beauvoir denies the very nature that man and woman are given as male and female: the basic element of our humanity. The denial of this biblical binary is at the heart of the New Gnosticism. It digs its heals into transgender philosophy and ideology. Therefore, the biblical account of the creation of man and woman, male and female—"Then God said, 'Let Us make man in Our image, after Our likeness' . . . so God created man in His own image, in the image of God He created him; male and female He created them" (Genesis 1:26–27)—is no longer part of the transgender identity. This biblical bina-

44 Weigel, *Reality and Public Policy*, 125.

45 Weigel, *Reality and Public Policy*, 125.

46 Weigel, *Reality and Public Policy*, 125.

47 Simone de Beauvoir, *The Second Sex*, ed. and trans. Constance Borde and Sheila Malovany-Chevallier (New York: Vintage Books, 2011), 283. This is the first line of her book under the subheading, *Part One, The Formative Years, Chapter 1, Childhood*. As you may recall, this is quoted by Judith Butler. This is one of the most quotable lines that I found in all of the transgender literature that I researched for this chapter to justify transgender transformations.

ry does not apply, for the Self rules. As Weigel concludes: "From now on he is merely spirit and will."[48]

The New Gnostic deconstruction of biblical human sexuality has a long history in the feminist movement for those who continue to seek sexual equality and normalization for transgender persons. In spite of the multitude of articles and books that I researched, I was hoping to find support and affirmation for human sexual identities of "male" and "female." But alas, this was not to be. The social construct—gender—always surfaced and continues to disrobe the biblical witness regarding human sexuality.

Robin Phillips affirms this in his *Salvo* article entitled, "Gender Benders: Is My Sexual Identity an Accident Just Waiting to Happen?"[49] He found no evidence in his research that male and female have any objective reality. He believes that under the current deconstructionist attitude toward human sexuality, society is heading for a "unisex utopia" that is resulting in the liquefying of the "sexist" distinctions between men and women.[50]

Judith Butler, a pioneer in transgender ideology and the disrobing of the binary "male and female" movement, reaffirms Phillips' and my conclusions that transgender ideologies are knowingly or unknowingly undergirded by the Gnostic view of the body.[51] Butler believes that gender is an act. It is not a stable identity; rather, gender is an identity tenuously constituted in time, instituted in an exterior space through a stylized repetition of acts. Hence, a person's bodily gestures, movements, and styles of various kinds constitute the illusion of an abiding gendered self. Gender is a constituted social temporality.[52] Katherine Johnson concurs, adding: "Thus, there is not 'real' male or female body, only an attainable ideal to aspire to become. Hence, 'male and female' are fiction."[53] Of course, this is precisely Butler's point: you can be whatever you want to be.

The use of the social construct—gender by those who support transgender—amplifies the liquefaction of the biblical binary of male and female, man and woman. Thus, the ongoing feminist-deconstruction of the body (male and female) and soul disrobes and dismantles the doctrine of creation as recorded in Genesis 1:26–27 and Genesis 2:4–25. The next section will give a brief overview of the New Gnosticism and its view of God

48 Weigel, *Reality and Public Policy*, 127.

49 Robin Phillips, "Gender Benders: Is My Sexual Identity an Accident Just Waiting to Happen?," *Salvo* 11 (2009).

50 Phillips, "Gender Benders," 39–40.

51 Judith Butler, *Bodies That Matter: On the Discursive Limits of Sex* (New York: Routledge, 1993), xviii.

52 Butler, *Gender Trouble*, 191.

53 Johnson, "From Gender to Transgender," 36.

and Jesus. As you will see, the deconstruction of the Trinity and Jesus, as true God and true man, fits the New Gnostic hermeneutic: "whatever" and "nothing matters."

The New Gnosticism: The Transgender God and Jesus

The most recent review of the New Gnosticism and its influence on theological thinking regarding LGBTQI (**L**esbian **G**ay **B**isexual **T**ransgender **Q**ueer **I**ntersex) perspectives is found in Peter M. Burfeind's 2015 book, *Gnostic America: A Reading of Contemporary American Culture & Religion according to Christianity's Oldest Heresy*. Another excellent resource for the Gnostic influence within twenty-first-century Christendom is Hans Jonas's book *The Gnostic Religion: The Message of the Alien God and the Beginnings of Christianity*.[54] In this section, you will see the New Gnosticism expressed both in its negation of the Lord God's biblical creation as well as God's incarnation.

A Transgender View of God

As we shall see in the next few authors, the transgender community, together with its associated communities, sees God outside the biblical, authoritative texts of the Old and New Testaments, hence the label "Queer God." This Queer God is radical love that is so extreme that it dissolves existing binaries such as gay/straight, masculine/feminine, and male/female.[55] Transgender persons say that the "traditional view" of the Bible is used politically and confirms the popular notion that God is a God who condemns.

From Marcella Althaus-Reid's perspective, the Queer God understood within the New Gnosticism is based on a libertine hermeneutic: "This libertine hermeneutical circle will help us to understand and unravel a Christian God who comes to us in drag."[56] The Queer God seeks to liberate God from the closet of traditional Christian thought.[57] Her god created Adam and Eve as bisexuals. This view is reflected in the work of Virginia Ramey Mollenkott, who argues that Adam was initially a hermaphrodite.[58]

Nancy Wilson's approach, as others in the third wave feminist deconstructionist venue, establishes a historical-critical reconstructionist view of

54 Hans Jonas, *The Gnostic Religion: The Message of the Alien God and the Beginnings of Christianity*, 3rd ed. (Boston: Beacon Press, 2001).

55 Cheng, *From Sin to Amazing Grace*, 93.

56 Marcella Althaus-Reid, *The Queer God* (New York: Routledge, 2003), 3.

57 Althaus-Reid, *The Queer God*, introductory note, 2.

58 Mollenkott, *Omnigender: A Trans-Religious Approach* (Cleveland: The Pilgrim Press, 2007), 98.

the Bible.[59] Wilson notes that "the feminist interpretation of Scripture will be upfront concerning being selective about which texts will be authoritative *for* women *about* women. Scripture passages that oppress women are not now, nor have they ever been, holy or authoritative for women. Because women did not have the resources or power to write or study the Bible, or to go on the canon of Scripture, we have to do that now, after the fact."[60]

Such views are applied to the Bible from within the LGBTQI movement. The standard is that LGBTQI persons read the Bible to fit their view of that community. They relate how God freed His people from oppression and slavery using the words of God: "Let My people go" as well as Jesus' words in Luke 4:18–21, especially verses 20 and 21. This interpretation of the Scriptures is a ubiquitous hermeneutic of transgender persons embodied in this New Gnosticism.

Like so many feminists who write on LGBTQI, or more specifically transgender persons, queer theorists draw from extrabiblical sources to justify their conclusions. Quoting from Tikva Frymer-Kensky's commentary on the Woman's Bible Commentary, Wilson says that "the monotheist is not sexually a male. . . . God is asexual, transsexual, or metrosexual period . . . but [He] is never sexed."[61] As you recall, the New Gnosticism posits a "whatever" hermeneutic.

God is the god of deconstruction. Vanessa Sheridan and Mollenkott add in their book titled *Transgender Journeys* that God loves gender-variant persons faithfully and unequivocally, accepting and welcoming them freely and fully into the family of believers just as all Christians.[62] Transgender proponents believe that the Church is edified, and God's liberating love is always made manifest whenever any of God's people are able to overcome oppression and achieve peace and joy despite the negative circumstances. This idea is expressed when a transgender person believes that their conception-sex identity is an artifice and needs to be modified to the other gender, from male to female or female to male.

Nancy Wilson writes, "We need to be free to experiment, try on new ideas, even make mistakes, change our minds, and say the outrageous, without being labeled 'heretical' or 'blasphemous.'"[63] Other feminist au-

---

59 Nancy Wilson, *Outing the Bible: Queer Folks, God, Jesus, and the Christian Scriptures* (Indianapolis: LifeJourney Press, 2013), 22.

60 Wilson, *Outing the Bible*, 23

61 Mollenkott, *Omnigender*, 106–7

62 Virginia Ramey Mollenkott and Vanessa Sheridan, *Transgender Journeys* (Resource Publications, 2003), 68.

63 Wilson, *Outing the Bible*, 21.

thors on this subject write that God's love and grace embrace all groups of people, regardless of race, creed, gender, and sex; therefore, God shows no partiality,[64] and this includes LBGTQI orientations. She concludes that since Adam and Eve have produced gay and lesbian children, we should not blame those who are LGBTQI for their lifestyles. Rather, we should blame Adam and Eve—or better yet, give God credit for our wonderful diversity.[65]

THE TRANSGENDER VIEW OF JESUS CHRIST

The New Gnosticism as expressed in the person of Jesus Christ covers a broad spectrum of interpretations. Within these references, one can see the negation of the incarnation. For example, Wilson, who writes on her relationship with men and women as recorded in the Bible, believes that the most obvious way to see Jesus as a sexual being is to see Him as bisexual in orientation, if not also in His actions.[66] Mollenkott says that we have already seen that Jesus of Nazareth is not exclusively a male Savior after all, judging from his/her parthenogenetic birth.[67] The denial that Jesus Christ is not truly man denies His existence and the reality that He is true God and true man. The implications for this are profound, especially as they relate to the incarnation, salvation, and the end times.

> THE MINISTRY OF PRESENCE IS THE KEY TO WORKING WITH PERSONS WHO STRUGGLE WITH THEIR SEXUAL IDENTITY, LEADING THEM TO TRUE HEALING THROUGH REPENTANCE, FAITH, AND FORGIVENESS.

Gender Dysphoria

A person struggling with their gender identity may exhibit emotional distress. Gender dysphoria is caused by a disjunction between one's birth gender and the gender that they experience. For example, a man may undergo a distressful struggle between the sex he was born with and the gender he prefers to experience; that is, a man may exhibit emotional distress over being born a man, and believe he feels more comfortable as a woman.[68]

64 Wilson, *Outing the Bible*, 80. Quoting Acts 10:34–35.

65 Wilson, *Outing the Bible*, 83.

66 Wilson, *Outing the Bible*, 111.

67 Mollenkott, *Omnigender*, 127.

68 For additional information, see DSM-V, *Gender Dysphoria*, 451.

The American Psychiatric Association introduced the term *gender dysphoria* as a replacement for *gender identity disorder* (GID) in order to address the emotional side of gender issues.[69] This change to *gender dysphoria* removed *transgender* from the category of "sexual disorders." Yet, it remains that those transgender persons who are diagnosed with gender dysphoria are classified as having a mental disorder. This classification is important, as, according to Teich, many transgender persons suffer from gender dysphoria.[70]

The editors of the DSM-V made this change because they believed that GID was a stigmatizing term.[71] Removing the stigma is the first step in social change; in this case, it focused on taking the transgender community out of the mental health field and moving toward an accepting society. Of course, this replacement definition becomes helpful when a transgender person seeks to modify their physical appearance from their conception-sex identity.

Transgender persons who struggle with their physical and emotional identities ask: "What or who am I?" A transgender person may ask: "What must I become to release myself from this current identity and be happy?" This is the reality of transgender persons, especially adolescents. A few characteristics of gender dysphoria in children may be summed up as follows, and should exist for approximately six months or longer to be classified as gender dysphoria:[72]

a. A determination to become a gender different than one's birth gender.
b. Children displaying a robust penchant to role-play or pretend in another gender.
c. A robust penchant for activities, toys, and games that are usually found in the daily activities of the opposite gender—that is, a boy playing with girl toys, games, or other activities and vice versa. This includes a very strong dismissal of male games, activities, and toys and the same for a female's strong dismissal of female games, activities, and toys.
d. A partiality toward playing with friends of the opposite gender.

69 See *Gender Identity Disorder*, in Diagnostic and Statistical Manual of Mental Disorders Fourth Edition, Text Revision, DSM-IV-TR (American Psychiatric Association, 2000), 576–82.

70 DSM-IV, 79.

71 Teich, *Transgender 101*, 84.

72 For additional information, see DSM-V, 452.

e. A very resilient displeasure of one's birth physical makeup. Hence, a very strong craving to have the physical primary (reproductive organs demonstrable at birth) and secondary (pubic hair, breasts, beards, etc.) characteristics of the preferred gender, other than the one they are born with.

Adolescents and adults struggling with gender dysphoria may exhibit a few of the following characteristics that must be demonstrable for six months or longer:[73]

a. A clear disconnection between a person's desired or expressed gender and their primary or secondary sex appearances (see *e* under children with gender dysphoria for definition of primary and secondary sex appearances). This includes a robust desire to rid one's self of their primary and secondary sex characteristics, and preference for the primary or secondary physical characteristics of the opposite gender.
b. A longing to be housed in the opposite gender. Likewise, this includes the longing to be treated as the preferred gender a person occupies.
c. A person struggling with their birth gender as man or woman demonstrates distinctive emotional feelings and reaction of the opposite sex.

This brief review of gender dysphoria needs to be approached from the view of the transgender literature in light of gender dysphoria's replacement of the label *gender identity disorder*. While the aforementioned summary of gender dysphoria is necessary, we need to be alerted to the struggle of all persons within the transgender lifestyle. We are not "shrinks"; we are churchmen and women who are concerned about those who battle with their sexual identity in light of the biblical creation witness. This appreciation may bring them to us and us to them for better listening, connection, and conversation as we care and bear their burden in Christ, yet not approving of their disassociation from their conception-sex identity.

Since gender dysphoria will be encountered by church workers and those whom they serve, we must be alerted to the complexities of this identity and be ready to provide basic Christian care and referral to those whose vocation will assist those suffering from gender dysphoria within the transgender community. There are no quick fixes to this struggle, yet there is Jesus, whose word doesn't return empty to Him but accomplishes the pur-

73 For additional information, see DSM-V, 452–53.

pose for which He sent it. The ministry of presence is the key to working with persons who struggle with their sexual identity, leading them to true healing through repentance, faith, and forgiveness.

God's Human Creatures and Pastoral Care

The disconnection of the biblical Word of God—that we are embodied persons, male and female—from the transgender definitions of man and woman continues to find its basis in New Gnosticism to the conclusion that "the end justifies the means." Are Adam and Eve AWOL (absent without leave) as male and female, man and woman? Yes, as Scott Stiegemeyer writes: "The Scriptures clearly teach that God created man as male and female. But for a number of complex and poorly understood reasons, there are people in the world as we presently experience it for whom a definite either/or answer is elusive."[74]

The Commission on Theology and Church Relations (CTCR) of The Lutheran Church—Missouri Synod finds:

> The entire Christian tradition and the majority of Christian churches today have opposed such changes in perspective. The basis for such opposition is precisely because our embodiment is understood as an aspect of our creation by God and therefore instructive regarding behavior that is good and pleasing to Him. Human embodiment indicates simply and eloquently God's intention for sexual activity—that male and female by becoming "one flesh" might end their aloneness in lifelong unity with one another and, according to God's blessing, in the procreation of children (Gen 1:26–28; Gen 2:18–24). Homosexual or bisexual desire and activity is therefore viewed as aberrant (see Gen 19:4–11; Lev 18:22; 20:13; Rom 1:24–27; 1 Cor 6:9; and 1 Tim 1:10), because it contradicts the meaning and purpose of one's embodiment as male or female.[75]

The male/female binary as proclaimed by the Lord Creator God in Genesis is what we are: male and female. To ignore biblical authority and the interpretation of the Scriptures to suit feminist views on transgender-

74 Scott E. Stiegemeyer, "How Do You Know Whether You Are a Man or a Woman?" *Concordia Theological Quarterly* 79 (2015): 22.

75 Commission on Theology and Church Relations, *Gender Identity Disorder or Gender Dysphoria in Christian Perspective*, (St. Louis: The Lutheran Church—Missouri Synod, 2014), 4.

ism allows these proponents to treat the biblical witness on human sexuality in service to "Self" rather than the Word of God. Their biblical witness becomes an "interpretation of convenience" and a "hermeneutics of having it your way." This approach allows transgender and queer theories to fit specific biblical passages into "self-justifying" their approval and normalization of the transgender lifestyle.

The male-female duality as the creative pattern of human fellowship requires our fidelity to our sexual identity, a willingness to be male *or* female.[76] David L. Adams writes:

> In order to promote its position, the pro-homosexual movement must disconnect personhood from sexuality. That is, it must argue that an individual's biological sex is not a central feature of one's existence as a person. This is essentially a neo-Gnostic position, in which the sexual identity of the person is distinct from the sexual identity of the body in which the person, understood to be essentially a spirit, soul, or consciousness, is imprisoned. Thus the sexual identity of the body may be ignored, denied, or altered to conform to the individual's higher self-understanding. This is a direct challenge to the biblical and historic Christian understanding of the human person as a unity in which body and soul are inextricably joined by the divine creative act, and inseparable both in time and eternity. . . . To attempt to escape the fact of our sexuality is to attempt exactly the "flight from creation" which the 1981 CTCR document[77] noted, "besets the contemporary world and contemporary Christendom," and which it reminds us, ". . . ought to be resisted in the name of the Redeemer who is also our Creator."[78]

As the explanation of the First Article of the Apostles' Creed reminds us: "I believe that God has created me together with all that exists. God has given me and still preserves my body and soul: eyes, ears, and all limbs and senses; reason and all mental faculties."[79]

---

76 CTCR, *Gender Identity Disorder*, 33.

77 CTCR, *Gender Identity Disorder*, 34.

78 David L. Adams, "The Challenge of Homosexuality: What Is at Stake?" *Concordia Journal* 31 (2005): 228.

79 Martin Luther, The Creed: The First Article: On Creation, the Handbook, The Small Catechism [of Dr. Martin Luther] for Ordinary Pastors and Preachers, *The Book of Concord*, ed. Robert Kolb and Timothy Wengert (Fortress Press, Minneapolis, MN, 2000), 354.

The transgender phenomenon is not going away. It will continue to surround us with its ongoing New Gnostic platitudes along with the political normalization that attempts to deconstruct and liquefy the biblical binary of male and female. Rebelling against God's created design for His human creatures brings suffering and the desire to "be what you want to be." This is part of our fallen world. This operative foundation is manifesting itself in books for prepubescent and adolescent children. One such book is entitled *Red: A Crayon's Story*.[80] Stephanie Brill and Rachel Pepper's book *The Transgender Child* maintains that children dealing with sexual identity issues need encouragement and help from family members. Their book offers practical suggestions on how to do this.[81] However, encouraging children or anyone to live another sexual identity is not the way to go. Parents need to be aware if their son believes that he has a boy's brain but a girl's body or vice versa. The use of puberty blockers, sex reassignment surgery, or hormones to change one's physical appearance to that of the other sex, as mentioned in the introduction of this chapter, is not the way to go.

REBELLING AGAINST GOD'S CREATED DESIGN FOR HIS HUMAN CREATURES . . . IS PART OF OUR FALLEN WORLD.

Dr. Mark Yarhouse, professor of psychology and Hughes Chair of Christian Thought in Mental Health Practice at Regent University, Virginia Beach, has written a book relating to the difficulties that persons who suffer from gender dysphoria encounter.[82] He presents the following suggestions for families and church professionals working with those struggling with gender dysphoria and transgender lifestyles. His main question that transgender persons are asking is this: "What does the church have to offer me?"[83] I will summarize those areas of Yarhouse's book that I believe are applicable to what Lutherans believe, teach, and confess regarding God's authoritative word on creation: (1) The church should leave its doors open to all, since many transgender persons have either been rejected by churches or believe that no one will want them to enter into the "sanctified halls" of the local church. The church is missional and should be focused on the relationship aspect of "getting to know them" as they are.

80 Michael Hall, *Red: A Crayon's Story* (New York: Greenwillow Books, 2015).

81 Stephanie Brill and Rachel Pepper, *The Transgender Child: A Handbook for Families and Professionals* (San Francisco: Cleis Press, 2008), 38.

82 Mark A. Yarhouse, *Understanding Gender Dysphoria: Navigating Transgender Issues in a Changing Culture* (Downers Grove, IL: InterVarsity Press, 2015).

83 Yarhouse, *Understanding Gender Dysphoria*, 147.

(2) Listen and learn as much as you can about gender dysphoria and the transgender person from our transgender neighbors—they are the experts. (3) Provide clarity and thoughtful teaching on human sexuality according to the Word of God, not compromising what you believe, teach, and confess. (4) Learn from those who are trained in these areas and who work with gender dysphoria and transgender persons in a professional capacity. Pastors and other professional church workers are excellent resources to a multidisciplinary treatment team. (5) Time is relative when working with transgender persons and the various clinical aspects of gender dysphoria. Therefore, the Church should provide sensitive pastoral care to those in the Body of Christ who are navigating this terrain.[84]

In conjunction with Yarhouse's suggestions, a few additional comments are necessary on pastoral care based on a biblical understanding of the natural law and on the fact that we are created in His image; male and female He created them. Christians, especially pastors, are grounded and remain faithful to the Confessions and Scriptures without being legalistic, but remain servants proclaiming the love of God in Christ in this fallen, corrupted world. Hence, the pastor must not compromise his call, yet he must listen and learn about the deepest struggle of the spirit and flesh from those who are battling gender dysphoria and transgender identity.

A pastoral heart of caring and compassion will establish a working relationship with a transgender person. My experience is that they know that you do not approve of their lifestyle, even if they have undergone sex reassignment surgery, yet their stepping forward tells you that they want you to listen, be honest, and be caring according to your vocation. As Pastor Luther said, "The church is the inn and the infirmary for those who are sick and in need of being made well,"[85] especially in healing from sin. And the Church's glory in large measure is that it may petition God for His help, on the basis of His Word and promise in Christ.

As the CTCR document *Gender Identity Disorder or Gender Dysphoria in Christian Perspective* states in relation to Luther's comment:

> Loving pastoral care for the individual seeks to provide a spiritually nurturing, encouraging, and accepting "safe place" to someone who may well have suffered from actual

84 Yarhouse, *Understanding Gender Dysphoria*, 146–60. There are aspects in the context of these pages that are more clinical than related to pastoral care. In addition, I have avoided those areas that are vague and do not appear to promote repentance and faith in the words and promises of Jesus.

85 AE 25:263.

> or perceived ostracism, mockery, and animosity. He or she may view the church with suspicion or share the common assumption that Christianity is more concerned with moral judgments, cultural battles, or political victories than about broken and suffering people. In accepting the struggling individual, a relationship of interpersonal trust develops. Within that relationship there will be natural opportunities to make Christ known, to call the person to trust in his promises and love, and to show that the purposes and commands of God for our lives are for our good.[86]

A pastor, family member, or friend must always be ready to seek guidance and assistance from mental health professionals, yet always remain with those whom they love and care for as they struggle with their sexual identity. Following up and not abandoning those with whom you work regarding their sexual identity struggles is paramount.

The current trends in the transgender movement—such as seeking approval of gender-neutral bathrooms through legislation and the ongoing deconstruction of the biblical binary of male and female under the umbrella of the New Gnosticism—must be met with open ears and a pastoral, Christian heart. Lutheran elementary schools, middle schools, high schools, and universities must be tuned in to this current trend and the proposed laws regarding the use of bathrooms and showers and other public facilities on their campuses. The ears and hearts of pastors and fellow Christians must never neglect Confession and Absolution. Rather, we must always seek out our transgender neighbors with the blessed intent of "winning a brother or sister" back to their Lord and Savior Jesus Christ for the salvation of their soul. As Pastor Stiegemeyer concludes: "Our churches are called to be sanctuaries of grace and mercy to all."[87]

---

86 CTCR, *Gender Identity Disorder*, 9.

87 Stiegemeyer, "How Do You Know Whether You Are a Man or a Woman?" 48.

CHAPTER 10

FROM TABOO TO DELIGHT: THE BODY, SEX, AND LOVE IN VIEW OF CREATION AND ESCHATOLOGY

Gifford A. Grobien

Sexual libertines and conservative Christians both want the same thing.

Can this claim be true after all that the essays in this book have presented? Gender identity at odds with sex? Variety in partnerships breaking the heterosexual monogamous mold? Training in sexual identity over against modesty? Without a doubt, libertines and conservatives pursue their goals in radically different ways. Yet, in the end, they generally pursue the same goal, at least in contemporary Western societies: to achieve the greatest possible sexual fulfillment. Or, we might say, to achieve the greatest sexual delight.

The difference in approaches clearly has to do with how each group understands fulfillment and delight. Indeed, it has been the task of the previous essays to consider what is delightful according to the Lord's hope for man created in His image. These efforts have set forth a constructive view of sex in particular areas to open up our understanding with respect to particular questions today. In so doing, they have also indicated behaviors that go against sexual fulfillment, behaviors that are forbidden or that ought normally to be avoided. In times past, these behaviors have been labeled "taboo." Yet, if *taboo* suggests anything especially mystical about sex or corrupting about its misuse, then this word is perhaps unhelpful. The unique character of sex has to do with its bodily intimacy and the modesty that surrounds it (1 Corinthians 6:18; Genesis 3:7). If sexual taboo makes us think that other sins do not offend holiness in a fundamental way, then we misunderstand holiness.

Better than taboo—a socioreligious designation—is the word *sin*. Although we seek what is fulfilling and delightful, this quest includes discerning what is not fulfilling and what is not delightful. Wherever there is truth, falsehood is excluded. Wherever goodness, wickedness is warned against. Whatever the Lord institutes and calls His people into, alternatives are unhealthy for life. They are not truly fulfilling. That is what the warnings and prohibitions in these essays have served to express: a call away from sin. A call away from the unfulfilling to the fulfilling in Christ.

So the argument proceeds over what is fulfilling and what is not. What is delightful? While the other essays have addressed this question in particularities, this final essay will address this question broadly. It attempts to present a theology of sex that, while not comprehensive due to space constraints, nevertheless engages biblical texts about sex to interpret core elements of human sexuality in view of its intended destiny in the divine life, reconciled to the Father, by the life and work of Jesus, abiding in the uniting presence of the Holy Spirit. Key insights into the delight of human sexuality will come from a consideration of its origins in creation and its eschatological destiny. Interspersed throughout, core doctrines of secular sexuality, particularly sexual fulfillment and sexual identity, will be considered comparatively to provide insight into what is truly delightful and how the Church cares for all people in the area of sex.

Eroticism as Fulfillment

Michel Foucault notes that sexual fulfillment among non-Christians generally is uncovered in the practice of the erotic arts. Their "truth" of sex is revealed through the practice of various kinds of sexual activity, in which experiences a person comes to know what is truly fulfilling. Such experience informs the practice of sex itself, refining and enhancing it for even greater pleasure.[1] Initiation and formation in the erotic arts ideally occurs under a master, who reveals the truth of sex. Because of the bodily, experiential nature of sex, knowledge of it cannot simply be passed on in words. Rather, it requires an intimate discipleship with the master. But the reward is unparalleled. Growth in the discipleship of sex leads to a life of ecstasy and fulfillment, which Foucault compares implicitly to a heaven-like state. It "transfigures the one fortunate enough to receive its privileges: an absolute mastery of the body, a singular bliss, obliviousness to time and limits, the elixir of life, the exile of death and its threats."[2] The erotic arts, for the unbeliever, are a path to salvation.

More simply, even for those who do not become enraptured by the pseudo-mysticism of sex, the clear purpose of sex in this understanding is that of sexual arousal and expression. The physical pleasure of sex is the

---

1 Michel Foucault, *The History of Sexuality* (New York: Pantheon Books, 1978), 1:57.

2 Foucault, *The History of Sexuality*, 1:57.

ultimate goal of sexual activity. It is through the physical experience that other benefits may be increased. Sex is pleasurable; ergo the sexual practice that results in the greatest pleasure ought to be my aim in my sexual activity. In this view, fulfillment is bodily pleasure.

This way of thinking further feeds an attitude that each person should follow his sexual desire. If the highest end of sex is sexual pleasure, then a person ought to pursue in his sexual activity that which he sexually desires, that which arouses him sexually. This desire becomes an identity, as that which informs a person's sexual life. And to the extent that sexual life encompasses life purpose in general, as it does for those who see sexual pleasure as the ultimate fulfillment, then sexual desires determine identity—whether heterosexual, homosexual, bisexual, queer, etc.

THE FULFILLMENT OF SEXUAL PLEASURE DOES NOT DETERMINE HOW FULFILLING LIFE IS.

It is this identification of sexual desire with personal identity that the Bible challenges. While sex is an element of identity, identity is not caught up in sex, and the fulfillment of sexual pleasure does not determine how fulfilling life is. This argument will be laid out in the following sections. However, if sex is not simply about maximizing sexual pleasure, what is the role of pleasure in sex? Should Christians resist pleasure outside of marriage, but within marriage embrace an attitude that "anything goes"? Is pleasure one of several goals in sex? Or is true sexual delight found also in other elements of a sexual relationship? To answer these questions, we must review the theology of sex, especially as laid out in creation and eschatology.

Sex and Human Nature

> The Lord God formed the man (*'adam*) of dust from the ground and breathed into his nostrils the breath of life, and the man (*'adam*) became a living creature. . . . The Lord God took the man (*'adam*) and put him in the garden of Eden to work it and keep it. . . . But for Adam there was not found a helper fit for him. (Genesis 2:7, 15, 20)

In the brief account of the creation of man in Genesis 1:27, Moses mentions that man is made in the image of God, that man is created male and female. The Hebrew word *'adam* is used here for man, meaning man in general, or mankind. This does not mean that Adam is not an individual, but that man as such is created from the beginning with a nature that is common to all men. Further, man is made male and female from the beginning. Both male and female have the same human nature. Nature is more fundamental than sex, and sex does not change one's nature as human.[3]

The character of this creation as male and female is given a greater account in Genesis 2. Here the creation of man does not jump so quickly to the creation of man as male and female. Man, indeed, undergoes a significant, if brief, experience to impress upon him his nature in the world—how he exists in relation to the rest of creation. Here he is, having a body like the animals, yet being made in the image of God, unlike the animals. What is this bodily vocation in the image of God to which *'adam* is called? What is the work of mankind vis-à-vis the rest of creation? In addition to uncovering answers to these questions, *'adam* is to discover that it is not good for him to be alone. Although fully human, although truly and completely of human nature, it is not good for this nature to be alone. Nothing is missing from his nature, but something else is missing: the opportunity to relate by having someone fit for him. Nothing of his nature is missing, but the opportunity for personal relationships with other creatures is missing.[4]

Although *'adam* is put through the motions of considering the animals, it is implicit from the outset that none of these will be a helper fit for him. The animals pass before him as objects to be named, not partners for doing equal work in the image of God. The Lord Himself says that He *will* make him a helper fit for him. The future tense is not insignificant here. Not only does the Lord know that none of the animals will be a helper fit for the man and that such a helper still needs to be created, but it is significant that the man's helper is created after him, not before him as the rest of the animals and the world are. The world is created, after which mankind is created to exercise dominion over the rest of creation (1:26, 28). The helper fit for the man is not part of this creation to be dominated. Rather, the helper will be fit, complementary, and partnered with him. This helper will be a person with whom he relates, not an animal to dominate.

> So the LORD God caused a deep sleep to fall upon the man, and while he slept took one of his ribs and closed up its place with flesh. And the rib that the LORD God had taken from

3 John Paul II, *Man and Woman He Created Them: A Theology of the Body*, trans. Michael Waldstein (Boston: Pauline Books and Media, 2006), 134–39, 156–61.

4 John Paul II, *Man and Woman He Created Them*, 146–53.

> the man He made into a woman and brought her to the man. Then the man said, "This at last is bone of my bones and flesh of my flesh; she shall be called Woman, because she was taken out of Man (*'ish*)." (Genesis 2:21–23)

'Adam recognizes in the woman his very nature. She is bone of his bones and flesh of his flesh. That she is a woman does not make her a different nature. She is a fit helper to the man, part of mankind, remaining in the image of God. Her complementary nature suggests, rather, that they will relate to each other in a special way, in a personal way that dispels loneliness.[5]

Sex differentiation presents the deep capacity for personal relationship given to humankind. When Adam sees Eve, he sees someone who complements him sexually. It is also at this point that the Hebrew *'ish*, meaning a male human person, not mankind in general like *'adam*, is used. Marriage and sexual relations follows immediately in verse 24. Adam and Eve become one flesh almost as though returning for a moment to the state of general humanity held by *'adam* prior to the creation of the woman. Yet, this time they unite freely, personally, as a gift of self to the other. Joining together, they remember their creation and anticipate the procreation of children that would come forth as the fruit of their union. They are gifts for each other, subjects to communicate themselves, communication through knowing and sharing. Through this communication, they come to know each other intimately; they come to know each other as persons, not as objects. One is not to dominate the other, as they do to objects, that is, to the world and to the animals.[6]

> Therefore a man shall leave his father and his mother and hold fast to his wife, and they shall become one flesh. . . . Now Adam knew Eve his wife, and she conceived and bore Cain. (Genesis 2:24, 4:1)

Sexual relations communicate intimate knowledge between partners. Sexual relations are not the only way to know a person, but they are presented as the most intimate way in our natural experience of knowing someone. As the man and the woman see each other as complementary and relatable, their relation occurs most intimately through their complementarity, through their sex. The woman comes before the man not as an

5 John Paul II, *Man and Woman He Created Them*, 161–65.

6 John Paul II, *Man and Woman He Created Them*, 177–91, 210–16.

animal to be dominated—and he sees this very clearly from the beginning. She is of his nature, bone and flesh; she is woman, the complement of man, just as he is the complement of the woman. Thus she is not something to be dominated or ruled over, but she is his companion.

Although she is in one sense a gift from God, her complementary nature to the man means she as a person and subject also wills to give herself to the man. As a true, free person in the image of God, she is no one's object. Yet as a person, she desires to relate to the man, and she does so not only through talking, but through complete communication of her person. She gives of herself. It is the same for the man. They are persons, complementary persons capable of full communication with and knowledge of each other. This communication and knowledge of a person includes the free, willing gift of self. If the gift of the self is not free, then it is not truly communication of the whole self. It is not truly love.

Loving sexual relations from the beginning are the free gift of the woman to the man and the man to the woman, that they might know each other as their own flesh. Thus while sex does not constitute nature or the divine image in man (as a human person is in God's image regardless of whether the person is male or female), sex becomes the personal way in which a person can most deeply communicate himself or herself to another in the natural order of creation. While philosophy can speak of the one-flesh union as a union of bodies,[7] theology speaks of this union as a union of persons, the communication and knowing of each other. It is the gift of the self, hearkening to the unity of humanity in creation. Through sexual relations, a husband and wife come together in remembrance that they are of one nature, just as the woman was taken out of man in creation. Yet by choosing to come together in union, they affirm their distinctive persons: they are not simply alike, but they are complementary; so complementary that they can unite as persons, as one flesh. As if in remembrance of this complementary unity that is from the beginning, the union of flesh is designed to bear fruit in procreation. As the personality of the man and

SEXUAL RELATIONS ARE NOT THE ONLY WAY TO KNOW A PERSON, BUT THEY ARE PRESENTED AS THE MOST INTIMATE WAY IN OUR NATURAL EXPERIENCE OF KNOWING SOMEONE.

7 Sherif Girgis, Robert P. George, and Ryan T. Anderson, "What Is Marriage?" *Harvard Journal of Law & Public Policy* 34 (2011): 251–55.

woman were shown forth in them being made male and female from the beginning, personality is affirmed again in their coming together by the creation of a new human being.

Three notable points should be emphasized here. First, marriage is analogous to the trinitarian life. As Father, Son, and Holy Spirit are one nature yet three persons, so the man and the woman are one nature, yet distinct persons. Personal communication in both contexts is not merely through language, but through the communication of the self: Father, Son, and Holy Spirit through perichoresis—that is, the interpenetration of one another's persons without the mixing of persons—and husband and wife through sexual relations. As such, marriage, as the union of persons, reflects a truth about God.

ALL HUMAN BEINGS, REGARDLESS OF SEX, ARE MADE HEIRS OF THE KINGDOM ON ACCOUNT OF CHRIST'S LOVE FOR US RECEIVED THROUGH FAITH.

Second, as noted, sex does not constitute nature, nor is it inherent of nature. A human being is human in the most fundamental sense, regardless of whether he is male, female, or a eunuch who has "been so from birth" (Matthew 19:12). If one is a man, he is not less human than others; if one is a woman, she is not less human than others; if one is intersex, he is not less human than others. One's sex is not determinative of one's nature as a human being, and therefore does not qualify a person any more or less for the kingdom of heaven. All human beings, regardless of sex, are made heirs of the kingdom on account of Christ's love for us received through faith.

Third, however, each human being is characterized to some extent by sex. A person is not a person without some genetic, hormonal, and physical attributes of sex. Because of the character of genes, hormones, and physical features, a person's sex is closely integrated with his personal identity. While usually these attributes present a person as male or female, rarely these attributes present a person's sex much less definitively. Perhaps some attributes, such as the hormonal, may seem to be at odds with other attributes, such as the physical.

Our consideration so far also suggests the purpose of sexual activity. Rather than finding its purpose in sexual pleasure, sexual relations reflect the communion of Father, Son, and Holy Spirit, pointing to the ultimate relation of this communion. This relation, in fact, is one into which we are invited—a participation in the divine nature (2 Peter 1:4), a point that will be developed further below. Further, sexual activity has its fulfillment in personal communication. This personal communication is the intimate sharing of oneself with another in a kind of paradigmatic relation between those for whom it is not good to be alone. Such personal communication includes physical pleasure. Yet, pleasure is in service of this personal communication, not the other way around.

Pleasure, Communication of Self, and Bonding

Through sexual relations, spouses receive intimate knowledge of each other. Such knowledge is communicated not through words (although words may certainly accompany this communication), but through the bodily relationship itself. One's bodily character, one's sex, communicates with the other in the act of becoming one flesh.[8] This bodily language is perhaps best given voice in the poetry of the Song of Songs. Throughout this book, the lovers express their delight in each other with reference to each other's bodies and sexual intimacy, primarily through the language of metaphor. Such indirect language does serve modesty—not the modesty of the lovers but of the reader. The lovers have no need for modesty in their conjugal act, in which they take full and proper delight. The modesty, rather, is for the hearer. Such modesty suggests that the conjugal act is not something to be described in its intimacy. It is not an act for observation. Observation inevitably is adulterous, the interjection into the conjugal act by a third party. The metaphorical language of the Song furthermore upholds the conjugal relationship because it cannot be encompassed in verbal language. To describe the sex act does not do justice to the personal communication and intimacy that is occurring.[9] Only the language of the body, only the sharing of each other's bodies in sexual union, is the proper expression of the conjugal act.[10]

In this relationship, the lovers in the Song of Songs come to a full and intimate knowledge of each other: "You are altogether beautiful, my love; there is no flaw in you" (4:7) and "he is altogether desirable" (5:16). In both cases, the word *altogether* uses the Hebrew *kol*, meaning "wholly" or "all." The language of the body communicated in sexual relations gives full knowledge of one spouse to the other.

8 John Paul II, *Man and Woman He Created Them*, 536.

9 This is also one reason that pornography—and, frankly, less graphic but nevertheless clearly implied depictions of sexual relations—is sin. Besides its lascivious nature, it also diminishes the meaning of sexual relations, and thereby degrades it.

10 John Paul II, *Man and Woman He Created Them*, 552–58.

Such intimate communication occurs in a context of trust and strengthens trust. With this in mind, the prohibition against adultery does not aim to limit sexual pleasure, but to protect the trust and intimacy that is shared between two, one male and one female, corresponding to each other for unity in one flesh according to the institution from the beginning. The prohibition against adultery buttresses the true fulfillment of sexual intimacy and directs the man and the woman toward this true fulfillment. The trust is to be so great that no shame is felt between a husband and wife. It is the fullest expression of personal communication freely as a gift, without concern that this gift will be rejected in exchange for another. Without concerns of adultery, such intimacy is not only physical, but emotional, passionate, and of one mind. The Song of Songs, then, gives extended and poetic voice to the brief comment in Genesis 2:24, that the two become one flesh.

The Song of Songs makes it readily apparent that delight is not merely in sexual arousal and expression, but in emotional intimacy, trust, and comfort. Throughout chapter 3, the woman speaks of her beloved as "him whom my soul loves." When she hears his voice, she pines, "My soul failed me when he spoke" (5:6). This is not the excitement of mere sexual arousal, but the ecstatic emotional connection of one person for another person. Such emotion binds their lives together, so much so that they are in pain when they are separated or their relationship is otherwise disrupted. This unparalleled love, comfort, and trust of marriage is summed up at the end of the song, when the bond of love is proclaimed to have no rival: "Set me as a seal upon your heart, as a seal upon your arm, for love is strong as death, jealousy is fierce as the grave" (8:6). Love, comparable to personal communication and relation, is the ultimate fulfillment and delight of their sexual relations.

DELIGHT IS NOT MERELY IN SEXUAL AROUSAL AND EXPRESSION, BUT IN EMOTIONAL INTIMACY, TRUST, AND COMFORT.

That such an emotional bond is not the same as sexual arousal or attraction is further confirmed by the man's exclamation: "You have captivated my heart, my sister, my bride" (4:9). Although he is clearly sexually attracted to and involved with the woman, his excitement here has to do with the feeling of his heart. Furthermore, the love he feels is compared to the deep familial love he might have for his sister. This is not to say that his feelings for his bride and for his sister are the same. Rather, they are comparable. True love exists not only between those who are sexually related, but in various relational bonds. Besides familial love, we may also include love within the Church.[11] Love between married couples builds upon sexual relations, but it is not the same as sexual relations. Conversely, love does not depend on sexual relations, although it may be served by sexual relations. While there is emotional intimacy connected to sexual attraction and relations, this deeper bond and attachment of love itself is not distinctively sexual.

Physiology of Love

While this might sound like an odd claim at first, such an understanding is in harmony with current sociopsychological, physiological, and neurological research. Love, even simply defined as a "deep affective connection," differs from erotic attraction, even though they are interconnected in romantic relationships.[12] Sexual desire is directly mediated by steroidal hormones, such as estrogen and testosterone, while these hormones' roles in emotional attachment appear to be nil to minimal, subordinate to other hormones, and indirect at best.[13] Steroids do appear to play a role in early phases of romantic relationships, likely in stimulating sexual attraction rather than emotional attachment.[14] Emotional attachment appears to be mediated by other neurochemicals, such as oxytocin and vasopressin, influencing broader feelings of reward, trust, emotional pleasure, and attachment, which are also factors in nonromantic relationships and bonds.[15] Likewise, brain imaging suggests that brain regions stimulated by association with a romantic partner have more in common with nonromantic love and nurturing than with sexual desire, other than early in a relationship, when sexual attraction serves as the primary bond while emotional attach-

THE EMOTIONAL ATTACHMENT OF LOVE AND THE ATTRACTION OF SEXUAL DESIRE ARE DISTINCT FACTORS IN A RELATIONSHIP.

11 For example, as Paul exhorts the Colossians to put on "love, which binds everything together in perfect harmony" (Colossians 3:14).

12 Sari M. van Anders, "Beyond Sexual Orientation," *Archives of Sexual Behavior* 44, no. 5 (July 2015): 1183.

13 Lisa Diamond, "Emerging Perspectives on Distinctions between Romantic Love and Sexual Desire," *Current Directions in Psychological Science* 13, no. 3 (June 2004): 117; Sari M. van Anders and Peter Gray, "Hormones and Human Partnering," *Annual Review of Sex Research* 18 (2007): 61–62, 74–77.

14 A. de Boer, E. M. van Buel, and G. J. ter Horst, "Love Is More Than Just a Kiss: A Neurobiological Perspective on Love and Affection," *Neuroscience* 201, no. 2 (2012): 118, 120.

15 Diamond, "Romantic Love and Sexual Desire," 117–18; M. Numan and L. J. Young, "Neural Mechanisms of Mother-Infant Bonding and Pair-Bonding: Similarities, Differences, and Broader Implications," *Hormones and Behavior* 77 (2016): 108–9; Van Anders and Gray, "Hormones and Human Partnering," 77–79.

ment grows.[16] All of this is to say that the emotional attachment of love and the attraction of sexual desire are distinct factors in a relationship.

At the same time, although sexual desire and emotional attachment are physiologically distinct, sexual partners often develop emotional attachment because such bonding is more likely to form with prolonged social contact, and sexual relations are an intimate kind of social contact.[17] Furthermore, sexual stimulation triggers the release of oxytocin and vasopressin, clearly linking the bodily activity of sexual relations with emotional attachment. During and for a brief time after sexual activity, oxytocin levels are high, encouraging attachment between sexual partners.[18]

The physiology of love, then, suggests that romantic relationships may be triggered by sex steroids and related hormones, but that these hormonal changes are short-lived, about six to twelve months. Long-term, loving relationships rely on oxytocin, vasopressin, and other attachment hormones to develop committed, emotional attachment. The love of such relationships is quite similar, physiologically speaking, to deep friendships.[19]

This broad dynamic of the interrelationship between sexual desire and attachment harmonizes with the theological argument made so far: sexual fulfillment does not have as a simple end the enjoyment of sexual pleasure. Rather, sexual activity aims at care for and attachment with another person through the personal communication of oneself. Quite simply, sexual relations find fulfillment in true love.

Self-Sacrificing Love

Ephesians 5 gives further expression to the personal communication of conjugal relations and the character of marital love, which symbolizes the communication of Christ to His Church. St. Paul quotes Genesis 2:24, that a husband and wife become one body (Ephesians 5:31). The husband's communication of himself to his wife and his coming to know her are aspects of this becoming one flesh. As one body, the husband cannot but love his wife, just as he would care for his own body (5:28–29). Yet Paul expands on this love. It is not just intimacy, but also self-sacrificing, sanctifying love (5:25–27). Such communication is a redemptive communication, by which

16 Diamond, "Romantic Love and Sexual Desire," 117; De Boer, van Buel, and ter Horst, "Love Is More Than Just a Kiss," 117–19.

17 Diamond, "Romantic Love and Sexual Desire," 118.

18 Jacek Debiec, "From Affiliative Behaviors to Romantic Feelings: A Role of Nanopeptides," *Federation of European Biochemical Societies* 581, no. 14 (2007): 2582; S. Zeki, "The Neurobiology of Love," *Federation of European Biochemical Societies* 581, no. 14 (2007): 2575–76; Diamond, "Romantic Love and Sexual Desire," 118.

19 De Boer, van Buel, and ter Horst, "Love Is More Than Just a Kiss," 120–21.

Christ not only shares Himself, but in so doing restores the people who make up the Church from sin to holiness, from Satan to the Father, from death to life.[20]

Marital love, therefore, includes sexual relations, emotional bonding, and the sacrificial love of the husband to serve and strengthen his wife. To this we might include the submission of the wife, which, in the context of Ephesians 5 seems to be the joyful reception of the husband's sacrificial love. That is, the wife does not despise, manipulate, or take advantage of the husband's love, but receives it with thanksgiving, delight, and her love for him.[21]

The picture that this sacrificial, marital love sets forth for us, however, sets before us a vision beyond the marriage relationship. In Ephesians 5, marriage is explained as a metaphor of the divine love of Christ for His Church. While such love includes the mystical unity of being one with Christ, this union with Christ is not a sexual union. The natural, bodily union of sexual relations pictures for us the spiritual, bodily union of Christ with His Church. Personal, communicated love, so deeply exemplified in the natural world by marriage, is actually expressed in a greater way by Christ's redemptive love for the Church. Marriage is not an end in itself, but it points us to God's communication of Himself to us in Christ. In the kingdom of heaven, sexual relations and marriage itself will pass away, and the communication of personal love will occur eternally in the bond of the Church, in the Body of Christ. Personal self-giving finds expression fundamentally in communion with Christ. The personal communication of God to His people takes the place of the conjugal communication between the husband and wife, which was a sign of the divine communication in the kingdom.

Thus the picture of love accompanying sexual relations is greater than sexual relations: it is true personal love, exemplified by Christ and carried out by every Christian for other members in the Body of Christ. Marital sexual relations present a picture of this intimate, personal love within the Body of the Church, yet, finally, marriage and sexual relations are surpassed by this bonding together in the Body of Christ, by this participation in the divine life.

20 John Paul II, *Man and Woman He Created Them*, 507–10.

21 John Paul II, *Man and Woman He Created Them*, 485.

> In the resurrection they neither marry nor are given in marriage, but are like angels in heaven. (Matthew 22:30)

As significantly as sex characterizes our natural life and pictures for us the love of personal communication, sex recedes to the background after the resurrection of the dead. This does not mean that we will be asexual—and there is no reason to think that we will be—but simply that sexual relations themselves no longer have a place. In the resurrection, there is one Bride, the Church, and one Bridegroom, Jesus Christ, and they are bound together in a love not of sexual relations, but of personal communication of the divine life in the Holy Spirit. The symbolism of sexual relations will be obsolete in the face of the direct experience of the divine life.

> HOMOSEXUAL ACTS ARE NOT THE PERSONAL COMMUNICATION OF THE SELF WITH A COMPLEMENTARY PERSON TO BECOME ONE FLESH, MALE AND FEMALE, AS IT WAS IN THE BEGINNING.

This penultimate character of sex has profound pastoral implications already for us in this life. Most fundamentally, engaging in sexual relations is not definitive of a person's identity, existence, or ability to love and be loved. The divine life that we will experience in fullness in the resurrection we already share in our life in the Church. Christ is already our Bridegroom by His ministry, Passion, crucifixion, resurrection, and ascension. We are already one body with Him, not through sexual relations, but by being united to His death and resurrection in the seal of Holy Baptism (Romans 6:3–5). We continue to be nourished and cherished, not through sexual relations, but by the partaking of His body and blood in the Holy Communion. We stand purified and sanctified in Christ, not through sexual relations but through His tender "wooing" of words of forgiveness, mercy, peace, and grace.

> There are eunuchs who have been so from birth, and there are eunuchs who have been made eunuchs by men, and there are eunuchs who have made themselves eunuchs for the sake of the kingdom of heaven. Let the one who is able to receive this receive it. (Matthew 19:12)

The overall point of Jesus' argument in Matthew 19 is that marriage and sexual relations are for one man and one woman, as so instituted "from the beginning." While adultery in particular is rejected, it is rejected on the basis of the foundational reasoning: a man leaves his parents and becomes one flesh with his one wife. This foundational reasoning, in turn, not only excludes adultery, but also defines sexual relations for all. Simply put, those who are not one man and one woman do not marry and do not become one flesh in sexual relations. Who are these eunuchs? Strictly speaking, those who are eunuchs from birth are those whose sexual development leaves them unable to have sexual relations. This may include some intersex. More broadly, those with ambiguous or conflicting sexual development and inclinations, those with same-sex attraction, or those with transsexual inclinations might relate to this designation of "eunuch from birth." Again, strictly speaking, this seems only to apply to those who are unable to have sexual relations (and thus unable to marry—the point of discussion for Jesus), but those who do not desire sexual relations in accordance with their physical sex may also resonate with this designation. Those made eunuchs by men include those who have undergone sex reassignment surgery. Those who engage in sexual stimulation with those of the same sex, likewise, are not truly engaged in sexual relations or marriage, for this is not sexual relations between a man and a woman, as instituted from the beginning. Homosexual acts are not the personal communication of the self with a complementary person to become one flesh, male and female, as it was in the beginning.

But the counterpoint is that Jesus' comments about eunuchs indicate that true personal fulfillment does not require sexual activity. Any of the eunuchs mentioned—whether from birth, made so by men, or for the sake of the kingdom—are not sexually active in Jesus' understanding. Yet their capacity to love is by no means relegated to a secondary level. In the resurrection, our love will not be second best. Likewise, the one who makes himself a eunuch for the kingdom is not settling for a love that is second best, but is putting into action now the eternal love in the kingdom that is symbolized by marital love and sexual relations.

> The unmarried man is anxious about the things of the Lord, how to please the Lord. But the married man is anxious about worldly things, how to please his wife, and his interests are divided. And the unmarried or betrothed woman is anxious about the things of the Lord, how to be holy in body and spirit. But the married woman is anxious about world-

> ly things, how to please her husband. . . . So then he who marries his betrothed does well, and he who refrains from marriage will do even better. (1 Corinthians 7:32–34, 38)

For the sake of the kingdom of heaven, which is already among us in the Church, some may give of themselves nonsexually. The eunuch for the kingdom of God is concerned for the affairs of the Lord. Far from being secondary, this life is also concerned with true love, is commendable, and is "better" even, in the absolute sense, than marriage.

Consequently, while sex is deeply bound up with a person's identity and relation, fulfillment of this identity and love do not depend on sexual relations themselves. Sexual relations are deeply significant because they symbolize the love of Christ for the Church, and they do indeed bind together spouses in a unique, natural love. Yet, deep love can also be practiced as a Christian apart from sexual relations, with attention to the Lord's concerns, for the sake of His kingdom.

Sexual Fluidity and Reconciliation with the Church

The created nature of marriage and its symbolic meaning show that conjugal relations are structured in a certain way: the personal gift of the self of complementary partners—one man and one woman—who unite as one flesh in view of their shared nature and complementary relationship given in creation, in order to bind their lives together in love, with the hope of procreation as a fruit of this union. That some sexual activity is aberrant and prohibited is due not to an arbitrary command but in view of the created order and, most important, because marriage symbolizes Christ's sacrificial love enjoyed by the Church in union with Him.

Sexual fulfillment is not merely or ultimately about achieving sexual pleasure and higher levels of it. To approach sex in this way is highly reductionist—not only of sexual fulfillment itself, but of those who participate in such sexual activity. It is to reduce the body—whether of oneself or of others—to an object of sexual desire. Far is this from the cry of Adam, who saw in Eve his fit helper, bone of his bone and flesh of his flesh, to share with him in the exercise of the image of God over creation.

Yet in our efforts to extol the virtues of sex, to raise it out from the unbelieving stance that it serves mere physical pleasure, and to present it as the intimate communication of self, have we not in fact ostracized further the fornicator, the swinger, the one inclined toward same-sex or transsexual acts, the sex addict, and others who do not find themselves inclined toward marriage as we have set it forth?

This is where we come to the heart of the question of identity and how a person is to see himself in relation to the world and as reconciled to God in Christ. In relation to the world, conventional wisdom has all but abandoned the view that one is not defined by his sexuality. The current claim of Western conventional wisdom is that we are oriented a certain way due to complex, interconnected factors of genetics, development, and nurture, and that we cannot depart from this orientation. And if we cannot depart from our sexual orientation, which is so much a part of our identity, then those not oriented toward the theology of sex explained above are excluded.

We have already noted to some degree the way this conventional wisdom diverges from biblical theology. To reiterate, it is not that some sexual activity is arbitrarily excluded, but that sexual activity has an inherent institution and cannot rightly be departed from without itself failing to fulfill what is expected of it. More than this, we have noted that to engage in sexual activity does not make one more or less of a human person. As powerful as sexual activity communicates personhood and love, it is finally only a metaphor for the ultimate expression of love and personhood, love among those who share in the divine life. To share in this divine life and to love as God loves does not depend on sex. No matter one's sexual condition—in fact, regardless of it—one is brought into the divine life by the Holy Spirit, and one participates in this divine life and its love by the Holy Spirit. Theologically, therefore, appropriate sexual activity or the abstaining from it may not match a person's sexual desire or orientation. Can such a conflict be overcome? In today's sociopolitical environment, can such a conflict even be set forth for consideration anymore?

Recent psychological studies in the area of sexual fluidity may offer a means of rapprochement between the theology of sex and secular notions of sexual identity and fulfillment. Lisa Diamond, professor of psychology at the University of Utah, has observed for more than a decade that sexual orientation does not appear to be fixed, but has some fluidity. Most of her research has focused on women, but her recent research also includes men.

One important premise for this work is the distinction between sexual desire and love or attachment, which we have already considered to some extent. Sexual desire seeks sexual stimulation and pleasure, and the kind of sexual pleasure sought by a person is labeled conventionally as sexual orientation.[22] Love and attachment, on the other hand, refers to the emotional bonding between people—that is, their desire for proximity, emotional and intellectual intimacy, resistance to separation, pleasure in mutual activities, and desire to care for each other. At a fundamental level, sexual desire and love operate distinctly from each other. On the other hand, each does appear to contribute to the other in some way. We already noted above how sexual stimulation stimulates attachment hormones and increases feelings of bonding between sexual partners. Reciprocally, Diamond argues that sexual desire can be aroused between close friends. Sexual desire between friends can be stimulated where there was not previously attraction to the sex of the friend. The close emotional bond, in some cases, triggers a sexual attraction. Her early research indicated that this was more likely with women, due to the responsive character of female sexual desire.[23]

In a later lecture, Diamond argues that sexual fluidity is also prevalent in men.[24] The pattern of change differs, in that men tend to be more exclusive than women (men identify more strongly as heterosexual or homosexual compared with women, who are more likely to identify as bisexual), but the propensity to change is similar; that is, both men and women tend to change in their sexual orientation at similar rates.[25]

Diamond suggests a dynamic systems model for understanding sexual orientation. In this model, various personal factors interact and contribute to psychological self-understanding. These factors include genes, hormones, family history and dynamics, cultural expectations, relationships, significant events and experiences, thoughts, feelings, and inclinations. How these factors interact gives structure to a person, but more important, the changing significance of factors can cause a restructuring of a person's self-understanding.[26] Early in one's existence, genes and developmental

22 Van Anders, "Beyond Sexual Orientation," 1178.

23 Diamond, "Romantic Love and Sexual Desire," 118; Lisa Diamond, "The Desire Disorder in Research on Sexual Orientation in Women: Contributions of Dynamical Systems Theory" *Archives of Sexual Behavior* 41, no. 1 (2012): 77.

24 For example, in her research, 31 percent of self-identified exclusively gay (not bisexual) men reported being romantically attracted to a woman or women in the previous year, and 20 percent reported wanting to have sexual relations with a woman, while 12 percent actually did have sexual relations with at least one woman. Fifty-six percent of self-identified bisexual men previously identified as exclusively gay, and 18 percent of exclusively gay-identifying men previously identified as bisexual. Furthermore, this is not unique to LGBT groups. Twenty-five percent of heterosexual men reported a same-sex attraction, and 13 percent reported a "propensity" toward such an attraction. Actual same-sex contact for heterosexuals was reported at 9 percent for men versus 2 percent for women. See Lisa Diamond, "Just How Different Are Male and Female Sexual Orientation?" Lecture, Cornell University, Ithaca, New York, October 17, 2013. Diamond argues that sexual fluidity has not been well-identified by researchers because of the problem of sampling and because researchers simply are not looking for it. Samples for this kind of research were typically small, non-random, and self-selected. If a subject identifies as gay, he will be assumed to be gay, unless specific questions about behavior are asked and analyzed, as Diamond does in her research.

25 Diamond, "Just How Different Are Male and Female Sexual Orientation?"

26 Diamond, "The Desire Disorder," 78.

hormones typically contribute to one's sexual inclinations. As one is raised in a family, nurturing relationships and experiences will grow in influence. A significant, unusual, or traumatic experience may contribute to a shift in one's thought and behavior. As a person matures, his own reflection, emotions, and friendships may also influence his understanding of his sexual inclinations and desires. Diamond warns researchers to be "careful about presuming that [labels of orientation] represent natural phenomenon."[27]

THEOLOGICALLY, THE CHURCH HAS NEVER DENIED OR ABANDONED THAT SIN OUGHT TO BE TURNED AWAY FROM.

Even from a psychological perspective, we also must include specifically one's spiritual life, religious practices, and catechesis as factors in such a dynamic model. Diamond would certainly include these as experiences, cultural norms, etc. Yet theologically, we must emphasize the work of the Holy Spirit in strengthening a person in a sexually upright life, in calling a person to repentance from sexual sin, and even, in other cases, in giving "them up in the lusts of their hearts to impurity" (Romans 1:24).

Diamond sees that, among the many factors that contribute to sexuality, the interplay between sexual desire and attachment are potential triggers for shifts in each other. That is to say, a person may develop bonds of affection for a person to whom he is sexually attracted, especially if they engage in sexual activity together. Conversely, a person with whom one has a close bond of emotional attachment may become the object of sexual attraction. This relationship may not seem unusual, until we recall that Diamond is referring primarily to sexual orientation and not limiting attraction to those of the opposite sex.[28] Notably, a close friendship with someone of the same sex may lead to sexual attraction for that person.

However, the converse is also true. If a person experiences primarily same-sex attraction, a close friendship with someone of the opposite sex could trigger sexual attraction for that person. Similarly, by distancing oneself from a same-sex relationship, this could play a small role in moving away from same-sex attraction. In other words, while Diamond in no way suggests that sexual orientation is a simple choice that a person makes

27 Diamond, "Just How Different Are Male and Female Sexual Orientation?" A recent important systematic review of sexual orientation and identity concludes similarly that scientific evidence does not support the claim that people are born with a fixed sexual orientation or gender identity (apart from physical sex). See Lawrence S. Mayer and Paul R. McHugh, "Sexuality and Gender: Findings from the Biological, Psychological, and Social Sciences," *The New Atlantis* 50 (Fall 2016): 7–143.

28 Diamond, "Romantic Love and Sexual Desire," 118.

from one day to the next, her research does suggest that behavioral habits and notable experiences will influence sexual inclinations and desires. This opens up possibilities for the Church to serve those who will hear her call to sexual fulfillment by inviting them into habits, lifestyles, and relationships that will serve true sexual fulfillment and thwart sexual behavior based on desire and physical pleasure.

> Or do you not know that the unrighteous will not inherit the kingdom of God? Do not be deceived: neither the sexually immoral, nor idolaters, nor adulterers, nor men who practice homosexuality, nor thieves, nor the greedy, nor drunkards, nor revilers, nor swindlers will inherit the kingdom of God. And such were some of you. But you were washed, you were sanctified, you were justified in the name of the Lord Jesus Christ and by the Spirit of our God. (1 Corinthians 6:9–11)

Theologically, the Church has never denied or abandoned that sin ought to be turned away from. Sexual sin, of course, as St. Paul's list indicates, includes fornication, adultery, etc., besides same-sex acts, but it has been the question of same-sex attraction that has perhaps put the Church at its greatest impasse with the popular culture in recent years, with the latter's assumption that sexual orientation is fixed and simply needs to be accepted. Yet, of whatever kind the sexually immoral acts are, St. Paul clearly expects repentance from the Corinthians, that they no longer engage in sexually immoral acts (1 Corinthians 6:13–20). To whatever extent sexual immorality may be instantiated in a person's psychology, St. Paul nevertheless expects the pursuit of sexual morality.

The research on sexual fluidity offers a way of considering the psychology of sexual repentance, which can work in service to the Church's resources of Confession and Absolution, pastoral care, and spiritual direction. Such consideration goes beyond just the question of sexual orientation. The temptations of sexual sin of any sort are certainly influenced by the factors of dynamic systems psychology: past experiences, habits, relationships, sociocultural expectations, etc. The question and opportunity for the Church, then, is to identify ways in which the Church can walk alongside her members to support them in embracing behaviors and experiences that will contribute to repentance from sexual sin and the embrace of a sexual morality that reflects the love of Christ for His Church. What relationships does a person have that accommodate or encourage sexual misbehavior? What behaviors lead into a sequence of actions ending with sexually immoral acts? What events and expectations of a person's upbringing contributed to his attitudes about sexuality and his own inclinations and desires, and can the Church help a person repent of these and move forward from them? Did the person suffer abnormal fetal development, which may contribute to conflicting inclinations, and how can the Church help the person to be restored to a life of love and/or sexual fulfillment?

On the positive side, what forgiving, supporting, and strengthening practices has the Church to offer her people? The Church can provide a context for healthy, appropriate relationships with people of both sexes. She can intentionally set up mentoring, friendships, and caring relationships as resources to call a person back from tempting behaviors and situations. She provides a context for learning the theology of marriage and family, and for putting this into practice in the home. And most important, she offers the gifts of Christ Himself: His Baptism, His Word, His forgiveness, His body and blood as the regular care for the person's soul to strengthen him against temptation and to continue to free him from the work of the devil, the bondage of sin, and the judgment of death.

Sexual Delight and Fulfillment

Sex according to the Scriptures is not constituted in prohibitions, but in the positive expression of sexual relations with one's spouse. Yet, such relations are penultimate to the divine love that marriage and sexual relations point to. The greatest love, the greatest delight and fulfillment of love, is to participate in this divine love as a member of Christ's Body in the Church. In the resurrection, such love will not be symbolized by sexual relations, but practiced directly in the fellowship of Jesus by the Holy Spirit. Indeed, this fellowship already exists in the Church, and this love is already practiced in this life, albeit in an imperfect and hidden way. Nevertheless, our Lord's commendation of celibacy for the kingdom of heaven already in this life is a key to understanding the true delight and fulfillment to which sexual relations direct us. Both sexual relations in marriage and the practice of celibacy are congruent with and symbolize the divine personal communication of the kingdom of heaven. Sexual morality, whether in marriage or in the single life, is to give positive expression to this personal communication of divine love, and to enjoy it in its fullness.

CONTRIBUTORS

Rev. Tom Eckstein is pastor of Concordia Lutheran Church in Jamestown, North Dakota, and also the second vice-president of the North Dakota District of the LCMS. During his twenty-five years as an LCMS pastor, he has ministered to people who struggle with unwanted same-sex attraction. He is the author of *Bearing Their Burden: Speaking the Truth in Love to People Burdened by Homosexuality* (Lulu, 2010). He served on the LCMS's "God's Gift of Sexuality" task force from 2013 to 2015. He has given presentations throughout the United States on Scripture's teaching regarding homosexuality and how to do ministry with people who have same-sex attraction.

Rev. Dr. Gifford A. Grobien (PhD, University of Notre Dame) is an assistant professor of systematic theology at Concordia Theological Seminary in Fort Wayne, where he has served since 2012. He teaches and researches in the area of Christian ethics. Recent publications include "Marriage, Divorce, and Remarriage: The Triumph of Culture?" *Concordia Theological Quarterly* 79, nos. 3–4, and "The Christian Voice in the Civil Realm," *Concordia Theological Quarterly* 78, nos. 3–4. Prior to his call to the seminary, he was assistant pastor at Emmaus Lutheran Church in South Bend, Indiana, from 2006 to 2012.

Dr. Donna J. Harrison is a board-certified obstetrician and gynecologist and serves as executive director of the American Association of Pro-Life Obstetricians and Gynecologists. She has authored many articles on beginning of life issues from a scientific and medical perspective. She also teaches continuing education courses to physicians and testifies in the public policy arena.

Rev. David A. Kind is pastor of University Lutheran Chapel in Minneapolis, Minnesota. He is the author of *Oremus: A Lutheran Breviary* (2015) and *About Our Liturgy: Meaning, History, and Practice* (2003). Kind holds a bachelor's degree in history from the University of Minnesota and a master of divinity degree from Concordia Theological Seminary.

Dr. Cynthia E. Lumley is principal of Westfield House, the house of theological studies of the Evangelical Lutheran Church of England , a partner synod of the LCMS. She was commissioned as an LCMS deaconess in 2010 after receiving her MA from Concordia Theological Seminary, where she was associate director of deaconess studies from 2009 to 2013. She began her formal theological education after a twenty-five-year career in the pharmaceutical industry. Lumley received her PhD in radiation biology from the University of London in 1983 and is pursuing an MA in Christianity and the arts.

Rev. Dr. Benjamin T. G. Mayes is assistant professor of historical theology at Concordia Theological Seminary in Fort Wayne. He serves as co-general editor of Luther's Works: American Edition and general editor of Johann Gerhard's Theological Commonplaces (Concordia Publishing House). His PhD dissertation in historical theology (Calvin Theological Seminary, 2009) focused on the development of Lutheran casuistry literature in the sixteenth and seventeenth centuries, and its instruction on divorce and remarriage.

Rev. Dr. Christopher Wright Mitchell has a BS, MA, and PhD (1983, Hebrew and Semitic Studies) from the University of Wisconsin—Madison and an MDiv (1987) from Concordia Seminary. He served as a pastor in Minnesota and has been at Concordia Publishing House since 1989. He edits the Concordia Commentary series and authored the volume *The Song of Songs*. He and Carol have enjoyed thirty-nine years of wedded bliss and are the proud parents of three adult children.

Rev. Dr. Matthew Rueger is pastor of St. John Lutheran Church in Hubbard, Iowa. He and his wife were blessed with seven children. Rueger earned his bachelor's degree at Concordia College in Mequon, Wisconsin, majoring in theological languages. He received an MDiv at Concordia Theological Seminary, Fort Wayne (1990), and a PhD in Christology at the University of Durham, England (2004). Rueger is the author of *Sexual Morality in a Christless World* (2016).

Rev. Dr. D. Richard Stuckwisch is pastor of Emmaus Lutheran Church in South Bend, Indiana, where he has served since his ordination in May 1996. He and his wife are blessed with ten children and now enjoy welcoming grandchildren. Stuckwisch earned his MDiv (1993) and STM (2003) from Concordia Theological Seminary in Fort Wayne, and his PhD in liturgical studies from the University of Notre Dame, South Bend, Indiana (2003). Stuckwisch served on the *Lutheran Service Book* project as a member of the lectionary committee from beginning to completion.

Rev. Dr. Robert W. Weise is a professor emeritus of practical theology at Concordia Seminary in St. Louis. He is also The Lutheran Foundation of St. Louis Chair in Pastoral Ministry and the Life Sciences. Weise has an MS and PhD in zoology and an MDiv from Concordia Seminary. He and his wife, Janice, are blessed with five daughters and eight grandchildren. He served ten years as senior pastor at parishes in Bunker Hill and Springfield, Illinois. Dr. Weise has been on the faculty of Concordia Seminary since 1992.